Preventing Child Maltreatment in the U.S.

The Latinx Community Perspective

T0385956

Violence against Women and Children

Series editor, Judy L. Postmus

Millions of women and children are affected by violence across the globe. Gender-based violence affects individuals, families, communities, and policies. Our new series includes books written by experts from a wide range of disciplines including social work, sociology, health, criminal justice, education, history, and women's studies. A unique feature of the series is the collaboration between academics and community practitioners. The primary author of each book in most cases is a scholar, but at least one chapter is written by a practitioner, who draws out the practical implications of the academic research. Topics will include physical and sexual violence; psychological, emotional, and economic abuse; stalking; trafficking; and childhood maltreatment, and will incorporate a gendered, feminist, or womanist analysis. Books in the series are addressed to an audience of academics and students, as well as to practitioners and policymakers.

Hilary Botein and Andrea Hetling, *Home Safe Home: Housing Solutions for Survivors of Intimate Partner Violence*

Preventing Child Maltreatment miniseries:

Milton A. Fuentes, Rachel R. Singer, and Renee L. DeBoard-Lucas, *Preventing Child Maltreatment in the U.S.: Multicultural Considerations*

Esther J. Calzada, Monica Faulkner, Catherine A. LaBrenz, and Milton A. Fuentes, *Preventing Child Maltreatment in the U.S.: The Latinx Community Perspective*

Melissa Phillips, Shavonne Moore-Lobban, and Milton A. Fuentes, *Preventing Child Maltreatment in the U.S.: The Black Community Perspective*

Royleen J. Ross, Julii M. Green, and Milton A. Fuentes, *Preventing Child Maltreatment in the U.S.: American Indian and Alaska Native Perspectives*

Preventing Child Maltreatment in the U.S.

The Latinx Community Perspective

ESTHER J. CALZADA, MONICA FAULKNER,
CATHERINE A. LABRENZ, AND MILTON A. FUENTES

Rutgers University Press

New Brunswick, Camden, and Newark, New Jersey, and London

Library of Congress Cataloging-in-Publication Data

Names: Calzada, Esther J., author. | Faulkner, Monica, author. | LaBrenz,
Catherine, author. | Fuentes, Milton A., author.
Title: Preventing child maltreatment in the U.S. : the Latinx community
perspective / Esther J. Calzada, Monica Faulkner, Catherine LaBrenz,
Milton A. Fuentes.
Description: New Brunswick, NJ : Rutgers University Press, [2022] |
Series: Violence against women and children | Includes bibliographical
references and index.
Identifiers: LCCN 2021055690 | ISBN 9781978822887 (paperback) |
ISBN 9781978822894 (hardback) | ISBN 9781978822900 (epub) |
ISBN 9781978822917 (mobi) | ISBN 9781978822924 (pdf)
Subjects: LCSH: Child abuse—United States. | Child abuse—United States—
Prevention. | Child welfare—United States. | Hispanic American children—
Social conditions. | Hispanic American families—Social conditions.
Classification: LCC HV6626.52 .C35 2022 | DDC 362.760973—dc23/eng/20220215
LC record available at https://lccn.loc.gov/2021055690

A British Cataloging-in-Publication record for this book is available from the
British Library.

References to internet websites (URLs) were accurate at the time of writing.
Neither the author nor Rutgers University Press is responsible for URLs that may
have expired or changed since the manuscript was prepared.

♾ The paper used in this publication meets the requirements of the American
National Standard for Information Sciences—Permanence of Paper for Printed
Library Materials, ANSI Z39.48-1992.

www.rutgersuniversitypress.org

Manufactured in the United States of America

Para nuestros hijos/as y parejas que han caminado juntos a nosotras y para nuestros clientes que nos han permitido caminar junto a ellos.

Esther, Mónica, Catherine, y Milton

Contents

Preventing Child Maltreatment in the U.S.

The Latinx Community Perspective

Introduction

> The prosperity of the United States
> and the prosperity of the Hispanic
> community, as the fastest-growing
> community, are one and the same.
> The destinies are one and the same.
>
> —Julian Castro

Children who experience maltreatment are at high risk for physical, cognitive, social, emotional, and behavioral problems (Gilbert et al., 2009). In the United States, more than seven million allegations of child maltreatment are made to child protective services every year, a rate that has been increasing modestly but steadily for several years (U.S. Department of Health & Human Services, 2019). Reports of child maltreatment represent a wide range of circumstances, from unsubstantiated cases to cases of severe abuse or neglect that lead to child fatalities.

The response to child maltreatment in the United States is rooted in child-saving efforts from the early nineteenth century that largely focused on removing children from parents who were deemed unable to provide appropriate care for their children (Popple & Vecchiolla, 2007). These early efforts to protect children were largely, if not exclusively, focused on White children who were placed in urban orphanages or sent to new families via orphan trains. As more comprehensive child protection systems developed in the United States, two major trends emerged that created a disparate impact for families and children of color, especially those with limited socioeconomic resources. First, a traditional law enforcement perspective was applied such that the priority was investigating families instead of helping them. This perspective, which persists, criminalizes behaviors that are outside of the standard White middle-class norms and disproportionally harms those parents who cannot access support services for substance use and mental health issues. Second, placement of children into foster care became the standard intervention to address child maltreatment, ignoring more collectivist and family-centered responses that preserve the family unit and honor the cultural values and strengths of Latinx populations.

Supporting Latinx children and families is a complicated endeavor that calls for a deep understanding of cultural and contextual issues and how those issues have been underexplored and, we contend, undervalued by child protection systems. At the population level, the experience of Latinx families in the child welfare system, as in other systems in the United States, is driven by macro forces that are rooted in sociopolitical and historical realities that reproduce social inequalities. In this book, we tackle the vast and complex issues of child welfare and maltreatment in the Latinx population.

Overview of Book

The goal of this book is to provide an in-depth, nuanced, and practical resource for mental health providers (e.g., counselors, social workers, psychologists), policy makers, advocates, educators, and researchers/academicians committed to serving Latinx children and families. In the first chapter of this book, we provide contextual and cultural considerations for understanding Latinx families in the United States. The Latinx population is large, growing, and tremendously diverse. As we write this book, one out of every four children in the United States is Latinx; 95 percent of these Latinx children are U.S.-born citizens (Mather, 2016). We begin this chapter with a discussion of the diversity of the Latinx population. We then review critical cultural and contextual concepts, including oppression, *familismo*, interdependence, spirituality, acculturation, and intersectionality, and consider their influence on family functioning and parenting in the Latinx community.

In chapter 2, we discuss child maltreatment within the Latinx population. We present an overview of child maltreatment definitions and research findings regarding prevalence of child maltreatment in the Latinx population. Because child maltreatment is linked to various risk factors, we discuss macro-, family-, and child-level factors that might increase the likelihood of child maltreatment. Finally, we use the public health model for childhood essentials, along with other theories, to understand safety, stability, and nurturing in Latinx families.

In chapter 3, we explore the broader topic of trauma and its impact on children, families, and future generations. The impact of child maltreatment on Latinx populations is not well documented in current research. However, our understanding of the impact of trauma on development, functioning, and healing is continuously growing. Drawing from neuroscience and theories of trauma-informed care, we explore how Latinx populations, depending on their specific identities, may experience trauma that both compounds the impact of child maltreatment and creates cycles for perpetrating child maltreatment.

Chapter 4 provides an in-depth examination of the empirical literature on parenting, including discipline practices such as spanking, in Latinx families. The use of spanking and other forms of physical discipline has been debated for several decades, and scholars remain polarized in two schools of thought: those who consider spanking and physical punishment to negatively influence child development, and those who consider spanking to be an acceptable form of discipline, with no clear negative or only minimal impact on child development. Amid this debate, the question of culture has repeatedly emerged, as scholars have questioned the generalizability of past study findings and practitioners have struggled to apply best practices to the needs of diverse families. Diverse cultural beliefs regarding discipline and child-rearing more generally lead to differences in parenting, which in turn influence child development.

In chapters 5, 6, and 7, we explore practices and interventions for reducing risk factors and leveraging protective factors for families in which there is a risk for child maltreatment or in which abuse or neglect has already occurred. Chapter 5 provides an overview of child maltreatment prevention approaches, including various home visiting and parent education programs, that are widely used in prevention efforts. We discuss the cultural relevancy of these programs and evidence of their effectiveness with Latinx families. In chapter 6, we delve into more targeted interventions for families who have already experienced a referral for alleged maltreatment. We discuss family preservation services and alternative response programs used by child protection services and how those can best meet the needs of Latinx families. Finally, chapter 7 explores resilience and healing among Latinx children and families who have experienced maltreatment. We discuss system-level interventions such as foster care, kinship care/guardianship, reunification, and adoption. We also address the court system as a decision maker in child maltreatment cases and inherent biases that exist within that system for Latinx populations. Finally, we discuss interventions that address trauma and healing for children and families.

The final chapter, chapter 8, focuses on future directions in child maltreatment research and practice with Latinx populations. Specifically, we discuss how the content covered throughout the book can guide next steps for professionals (e.g., scholars and practitioners). Implications for policy and advocacy are explored.

In each chapter, we have embedded content to help the reader apply research and theory to practice. We start with the presentation of three practice cases, found in the case studies at the end of this introduction. We then draw on these case studies in each chapter to illustrate the application of the scholarship to child maltreatment in the real world. Each case is fictional, but developed based on common trends seen in practice. We encourage the reader to refer to the case studies in broader and deeper ways in relation to the themes and issues presented in this book.

Positionality: Our Reflexive Narratives

The ways in which we, as authors, approach the issue of child welfare is driven by our identities—who we are and what we have experienced. We recognize that objectivity in science is relative, and that we are called to engage in reflexivity, or understanding the ways in which our unique perspectives influence our interpretation of the research, especially in multicultural scholarly pursuit (Cumming-Potvin, 2013). In the section below, we offer each author's positionality so that the reader may hold in mind the potential biases that our identities introduce in our thinking and writing.

Esther J. Calzada is a light-skinned heterosexual and cisgender woman and the daughter of Dominican immigrants. Spanish was her first language, but her dominant language as an adult is English. Her father is a medical doctor, which granted her considerable socio-economic privilege throughout her childhood and young adult life. She holds a doctoral degree in clinical child psychology and is a professor in the University of Texas at Austin's Steve Hicks School of Social Work. Her research and teaching are heavily informed by her personal experiences growing up in an immigrant family, where she was immersed in Dominican culture at home and U.S. Americanized culture outside the home. She is married and has three children, ages twelve, seventeen, and eighteen. One of her children has a history of major depressive disorder, and Esther's experiences parenting a child with a mental health disorder have also deeply shaped her thinking about families and children. She holds great respect and admiration for all parents engaged in the herculean task of raising children.

Monica Faulkner is a light-skinned, mixed ethnicity, heterosexual, cisgender woman. Her mother is a second-generation Mexican American and her father is White. Monica spent her early childhood on the California/Mexico border and later lived in San Antonio, Texas. She is deeply proud of her Mexican roots and is continuously improving her Spanish-speaking skills. She was raised in a two-parent, middle-class family and had the privilege of having what she needed as a child. As a social worker, she worked with survivors of family violence, sexual violence, and child maltreatment—many of whom were Latinx immigrants. She is a research associate professor and director of the Texas Institute for Child & Family Wellbeing at the Steve Hicks School of Social Work at The University of Texas at Austin. She is married and has two children.

Catherine A. LaBrenz is a White, cisgender woman who was raised in a single-parent household in Ann Arbor, Michigan. She is bilingual (English and Spanish) and worked as a child welfare practitioner in Santiago, Chile, for seven years prior to entering academia. As a *gringa* who worked with child-welfare-involved families in Latin America, she has paid special attention to her own privilege and positionality, as well as to the structural barriers families face in accessing services and opportunities. Her experiences as the spouse of a recent Chilean immigrant to the United States and the mother of a mixed-ethnicity four-year-old daughter have led her to recognize the role of intersectionality and diversity within Latinx families and communities and how factors such as national origin, educational status, language, race, and class may exacerbate exclusion and discrimination. She is currently an assistant professor at the University of Texas at Arlington School of Social Work.

Milton A. Fuentes is a light-skinned Puerto Rican male who was a first-generation college student. While his sociocultural profile is nuanced and informed by many factors, including his race, ethnicity, gender, sexual orientation, and class, he is a firm believer in intersectionality, recognizing that these factors are interconnected, informing, enhancing, and compromising each other in a very dynamic manner. His appreciation for collectivism colors his understanding for most, if not all, social concerns, requiring a systemic approach to their resolution. Additionally, the ethnic oppression he experienced as a child and witnesses as an adult leads him to frame this concern through a *mujersimo* lens. Moreover, the resiliency he observes in his Latinx community inspires him to embrace perspectives that promote prevention, wellness, strengths, and liberation.

Collectively, we as authors share many privileged identities (e.g., light skin), experiences (e.g., education), and values. Namely, we are each personally and professionally dedicated to the active promotion and engagement of diversity, equity, advocacy, and social justice. Because our guiding values, cultural contexts, and lived experiences unquestionably shape our perspectives on child maltreatment, we encourage the reader to hold our social positionality and identities in mind while reading this book and considering its content. We also invite the reader to consider their own positionality and how their cultural background and life experiences shape how they receive the information contained in this book and in the broader scholarship on child maltreatment.

Positionality: Our Beliefs and Assumptions Guiding This Book

In addition to our personal identities, we discuss the beliefs and assumptions that guided the writing of this book. Each of us brings a unique professional perspective to this work with the intention of making a positive contribution to understanding child maltreatment within Latinx families. First and foremost, the content of this book is intended to expand the understanding of child maltreatment by examining the broader societal factors that impact families. Based on our work in the child welfare field, we have not encountered a parent who did not love their child and rarely have we encountered a child who did not want love from their parent. Thus, we reject any attempts to broadly characterize parents involved in child protective services as bad people. Pathologizing parents rather than helping them has led to the forced separation of over 400,000 children in the United States who are in foster care each year (U.S. Department of Health & Human Services, 2020). Thus, we think about parents in the context of their lived experiences, opportunities, and choices.

Additionally, we recognize that safety is culturally situated and defined. While certain acts, such as sexual abuse, are taboo across cultures, there is variation in how communities view physical abuse, emotional abuse, and neglect. In the United States, "safe" child-rearing standards have been defined by White middle-class standards that themselves have changed over time. Thus, any non-White group may have their own conceptualizations of safe that are less stringent, but do not amount to child maltreatment. Unfortunately, oversurveillance of non-White families often leads to their involvement in child protective services because their conceptualizations of safety are different.

Finally, we do not believe that the constructs of ethnicity or race make any parent more or less likely to perpetuate child maltreatment. In writing a book about child maltreatment in the Latinx community, we do not imply that Latinx families are at a higher risk of harming their children. However, we recognize the risk for maltreatment, as in any population, as well as the unique structural barriers and discrimination that Latinx families may face within the child welfare system and other intersecting systems. As such, we believe there are unique considerations that professionals need to understand in working with Latinx families to fairly and equitably assess safety concerns.

Case Studies

Throughout the book, we have embedded content to help the reader apply research and theory to practice. We start with the presentation of three practice cases, below. We then draw on these case studies in each chapter to illustrate the application of the scholarship to child maltreatment in the real world. Each case is fictional but developed based on common trends seen in practice. We encourage the reader to refer to the case studies in broader and deeper ways in relation to the themes and issues presented in this book.

Case 1: Bianca

Bianca is an eight-year-old Mexican girl born in a rural town near the Arizona and Mexico border. Her parents were never officially married but considered themselves husband and wife. Her mother was seventeen years old when she gave birth to Bianca, and Bianca's father, age twenty-five, had left for the United States prior to her birth. The plan was for him to find work and bring Bianca and her mother to live with him in the United States. He crossed into the United States without authorization and found work in construction. He eventually settled in Phoenix, Arizona, and sent money to Bianca's mother to support them.

In Mexico, Bianca and her mother lived with her maternal grandparents and two maternal uncles who were teenagers. The family lived in poverty in a two-room home where one room served as the sleeping quarters and the other room functioned as a living room and kitchen. The home was modest, with packed-down dirt floors and indoor plumbing, but no heat. Bianca's grandfather and uncles worked in the fields, and her mother sold trinkets from their home to generate extra income. Bianca is very attached to her grandmother, who served as her daily caregiver while the other adults worked. Her grandmother was incredibly warm and responsive. On the rare occasions when Bianca would misbehave, her grandmother would threaten to spank her with her *chancla* (sandal), but really only spanked her once for not sitting still during Mass. Bianca's mother was also attentive; even though she was tired at the end of the day, she would make time to play with Bianca and teach her letters, numbers, and colors. On the weekends, Bianca would spend all day helping her mother garden and sew.

After four years, Bianca's father felt stable enough to have Bianca and her mother join him. Bianca and her mother entered the United States with the help of a coyote (a smuggler who helps people cross the border for pay). After they crossed into the United States from Mexico, the coyote separated Bianca from her mother by placing them in separate vehicles. When Bianca's father reached their meeting spot three hours later, the coyotes demanded additional money before they would release Bianca. Bianca witnessed her father shoot one of the coyotes before grabbing her from the vehicle.

Bianca and her parents, who had never lived together, settled into their apartment in Phoenix. Bianca had not known her father except for phone calls. Even though they now lived together, he left for work before she was awake and often missed dinner to work extra hours. Because her first new memory of him was when he shot the coyote, Bianca was scared of him and did not show affection for him. She preferred to address all her requests to her mother. Bianca's father was unsure how to bond with her and the emotional distance between them grew.

Bianca qualified for a Head Start program. Although Bianca's mother cleaned houses while Bianca was at school, she always made sure to pick up and drop off Bianca because she felt it was important to interact with the teachers. After school, they would walk home together, stopping at a park to play. Through the Head Start program, Bianca's mother learned about new discipline strategies and began to use time-outs. Bianca's father, on the other hand, felt that time-outs coddled children. Bianca's mother utilized threats to spank with the chancla just as her own mother had with her and Bianca, but she never spanked Bianca and instead would simply raise her voice. Bianca's father would also yell when Bianca misbehaved.

Stress in the family grew when Bianca's father broke his arm at a construction site and lost his job. Without access to health care, her father's injury never healed properly. Bianca's father began drinking and verbally abusing her mother. Over a six-month period, her father's aggression became physical. Bianca witnessed her father hit her mother on multiple occasions.

Around this time, Bianca began to misbehave. She would cry and hit her mother and teachers during drop-off. Her mother would leave with the teacher's encouragement, but Bianca would not engage with other children and would bang her head against the floor and sit in a corner crying until she fell asleep from exhaustion. When her mother would return, she would cry and cling to her mother. Even at home, she would not leave her mother's side. Bianca's mother missed cleaning appointments while dealing with Bianca's behavioral problems.

One evening, Bianca's father's physical aggression resulted in a neighbor calling the police. The police arrived at the home to find Bianca's mother had multiple bruises on her body. Her mother was taken to the hospital and her father was arrested. Child protective services was called to care for Bianca because her mother was deemed unable to protect her. Bianca was taken into custody and placed with a foster family.

Case 2: Dominic

Dominic is a six-year-old Puerto Rican boy who lives in New York City, where his mother, Daniela, was born and raised. Daniela was sixteen years old when she had Dominic and now, at the age of twenty-two, has a second child, an infant girl. Dominic's biological father is not a part of his life, but Dominic developed a positive relationship with his half sister's father. However, Daniela left her daughter's father when he began using drugs in the home. She found drug paraphernalia in the home and confronted him. Dominic was present during the confrontation, which became physical when Daniela tried to leave the home. Daniela is currently living with a different partner, a thirty-five-year-old man named Rodrigo, who has become a stable father figure to Dominic and the baby.

Daniela works as a teacher's aide in a local day care, and her partner is on disability. Dominic's maternal grandparents live in the same apartment building and enjoy spending time with the children, but have a strained relationship with Daniela. Daniela feels that her parents criticize and undermine her parenting and are unsupportive of her relationship with Rodrigo. Their visits together often end with Daniela grabbing her children and leaving her parents' screaming and crying.

Daniela's parents left Puerto Rico when they were first married. They struggled financially as they worked to eventually own their own small restaurant. Daniela's parents were strict and they had high expectations for all five of their children. Discipline in their household involved a great deal of yelling and the use of guilt to get children to behave. All four of Daniela's older siblings went to college and have professional careers in accordance with their parents' wishes. Daniela's parents express frequently that they failed her. Daniela's many nieces and nephews are well mannered and adored by her parents. However, Daniela's parents feel she is too lax with Dominic because she tends to rely on the techniques she has learned in her day care job to redirect him and reinforce good behavior.

When Dominic was three years old, he was kicked out of the day care center where Daniela worked. His teacher complained that he was loud, disruptive, hyperactive, and aggressive with his peers. When Dominic was expelled from another day care center less than a year later, Daniela spoke with his pediatrician, who diagnosed him with attention deficit hyperactivity disorder (ADHD). Despite the recommendation by the pediatrician, Daniela chose not to medicate Dominic and he spent the next year at home with a host of family members when they were available to take care of him. Earlier this year, Dominic started kindergarten and is struggling to follow directions, sit still, and make friends. His teacher is patient and understanding and works closely with Daniela and Rodrigo to help Dominic do better in school.

Over the past month, Daniela began experiencing fatigue, feelings of sadness she couldn't shake, difficulty sleeping, and difficulty motivating herself to socialize with her friends or even do basic household tasks like cooking. She found that she was too tired to play with Dominic and take care of his sister after work. She could see how sad this made Dominic, and she would often cry and feel guilty. They would spend a great deal of time watching television together until Daniela would eventually fall asleep.

Recently, Daniela made an evening appointment to go see a doctor recommended to her by a co-worker. Daniela asked her parents to watch the children, but they said they were busy at home. Rodrigo was away visiting his daughter. Daniela turned a movie on for Dominic, gave him chips and a drink for a snack, and told him to stay in bed until she returned. She was taking the baby with her, the health clinic was nearby, and she expected to be back before the movie was over. While she was gone, Dominic left the house to go upstairs to his grandparents' apartment, as he had done on his own many times before. No one answered, so he went back home. But the door was locked. A neighbor saw him alone, pounding on the door, and called the police. That night, child protective services took custody of Dominic, later placing him in kinship care with his grandparents.

Case 3: Audriana

Audriana is a fifteen-year-old girl living in Los Angeles with her mother, older sister, stepfather, and three younger half brothers. They live in a home owned by her step-uncle, who lives in the home as well.

Audriana's biological father was killed in Honduras by a local gang when her mother was pregnant with her. Audriana's mother witnessed the murder and received death threats against her and Audriana's sister if she went to the police. Gang members harassed Audriana's mother at work and she lost her job at a local clothing store. Fearing for their lives, Audriana's mother took her sister and fled to the United States. They traveled with a group who walked and rode on buses. At one point during the journey, Audriana's mother was forced to perform sexual acts on a man who threatened to rob her if she did not. She became hypervigilant and had trouble sleeping after that incident. Audriana's mother and sister sought asylum at the border and were granted permission to remain in the United States pending the outcome of their case. Audriana's mother settled in Los Angeles with an aunt, who had previously migrated to the United States. Audriana was born three months later.

Audriana's mother met her stepfather at a local Pentecostal church her aunt attended. The church community was very supportive and helped her mother find work. Audriana's mother married her stepfather when Audriana was two years old. Her stepfather was also from Honduras. Although he had overstayed a work visa, he had also witnessed violence in Honduras and had no intention of returning. Audriana's half siblings were each born two years apart. Due to the high cost of living in Los Angeles, the family lives with her step-uncle, who owns a three-bedroom home. Audriana and her sister share a converted room in the garage, her parents have a room, her uncle uses the primary bedroom, and her brothers share the third bedroom.

Audriana has a distant relationship with her mother. Following her migration and resettlement, Audriana's mother became depressed and distant. When Audriana was little, her mother struggled to care for her and her sister. Audriana's aunt stepped in and served as the primary caregiver. When Audriana was older, her half brothers consumed much of her mother's time. When Audriana did interact with her mother, it was to help her take care of the house, make meals, and care for the younger siblings. From a young age, Audriana took on a lot of adult responsibilities. Her mother believed it was the least Audriana and her sister could do given all the sacrifices she made to bring them to the United States.

Audriana's parents are strict and the family remains engaged in their church, which is conservative, is patriarchal, and promotes modesty for women. Audriana and her sister are not permitted to wear pants or makeup or to cut their hair above a certain length. Both girls participate in choir at school. They are not permitted to spend the night at friends' homes or attend events with boys.

When any of the children in the home misbehave, they are spanked. Audriana's mother will typically use a kitchen spoon to hit her children on their bottom. Audriana's stepfather will use his hand to hit them on their bottoms; for severe punishments, he will use a belt. For example, Audriana's half brothers were severely whipped when they were caught shoplifting candy from a local convenience store and a police officer brought them home. Her mother rationalizes that a whipping in America is better than being murdered in Honduras.

Audriana's behavior changed when she turned fifteen. She began doing poorly in school and claimed she had no energy for any activities. When a pastor at church talked with her, Audriana disclosed that her step-uncle had been coming into her room at night and "touching her." She stated that she was afraid to tell her mother. The pastor reported the abuse to her parents. Audriana recanted her story, but her sister disclosed that her uncle had begun having sex with her when she was thirteen. Audriana's parents believed the girls were lying. Their stepfather called them whores, slapped both girls across the face, and whipped them with a belt. The following day, a counselor at school called child protective services. Following an investigation, the girls' mother was given the choice of (1) having the daughters removed, (2) having the uncle leave the home, or (3) leaving the home with the girls to live elsewhere. Audriana's uncle refused to leave his home. Audriana's parents could not afford to live elsewhere and they maintained that the girls had fabricated the entire story. Audriana and her sister were removed from the home and placed in an emergency shelter.

Closing Summary

Child maltreatment is prevalent and costly to individual children, families, and society, making it a significant public health and human rights concern. Understanding child maltreatment allows all stakeholders—parents and families, child welfare workers and advocates, and others invested in healthy communities—to better address the underlying causes, prevent incidences, and intervene effectively when maltreatment occurs. This requires careful consideration of the culture and context of children and families served through child welfare efforts. Our goal is to center the cultural context of Latinx families to better inform and ultimately enhance supports for Latinx children in the United States. In the next chapter, we provide contextual and cultural considerations for better understanding Latinx families and child maltreatment in Latinx populations in the United States.

1

Contextual and Cultural Considerations for Understanding Latinx Families in the United States

> We need to . . . cherish and preserve the ethnic and cultural diversity that nourishes and strengthens this community, and this nation.
> —César Chávez

The Latinx population in the United States, especially the child population, is large and growing. In this chapter, we summarize the demographic profile of the Latinx population and then review various issues that impact Latinx family functioning. Like all minoritized groups in the United States, Latinx communities face structural barriers rooted in oppression and cultural differences in values, beliefs, and behavior patterns that influence the everyday experiences of parents and children (Coll et al., 1996). We consider a nuanced understanding of these contextual and cultural considerations, specifically as a basis for exploring issues of child maltreatment in the Latinx population.

The Latinx Population in the United States

Being Hispanic or Latino is a designation conferred by the U.S. Census Bureau to the category of persons who trace their origins to any one of twenty or so Spanish-speaking countries. Nationally, 58.9 million persons (roughly 17%) identify as "Hispanic or Latino" and the population is expected to nearly double to 111 million by 2060, making it the largest racial/ethnic group in the country. Given the sheer size of the population, there is considerable diversity across demographic characteristics including race, ethnicity/country of origin, immigrant status, language use, and socioeconomic status. On the whole, though, the Latinx population is predominantly Mexican origin (63%), U.S.-born and English-speaking (66%), and disproportionately impacted by poverty (24%) (Flores, 2017).

Over time, the U.S. Census Bureau has used a number of different terms for the category of persons that it designates as Latinx. The 1930 census counted "Mexicans," replaced by the terms "Hispanic" in the 1970s, "Spanish/Hispanic origin" in the 1980s and 1990s, "Spanish/Hispanic/Latino" in the 2000s, and "Hispanic, Latino, or Spanish origin" in 2010 (Cohn, 2010). Public use of ethnic labels, both within and outside of the population, has shifted accordingly. The term "Latinx" emerged as an evolution of the term "Latino," which is inclusive of people from the Caribbean, Mexico, Central America, and South America regardless of Spanish language use, to be inclusive of persons regardless of gender and gender identity (Salinas Jr. & Lozano, 2019). In 2018, the National Latina/o Psychological Association changed its name to the National Latinx Psychological Association (NLPA) and its journal name to *Journal of Latinx Psychology*, providing some indication of the salience and permanence of the term in academe. We join with the National Latinx Psychological Association in using the label Latinx to affirm our commitment to inclusion across diverse ethnicities, language groups, gender identities, and sexual orientations.

Ethnicity

Latinx is a pan-ethnic designation, comprised of numerous ethnic subgroups. Ethnicity refers to social grouping based on shared country of origin, language, values, and customs. Because ethnicity is typically defined based on country of origin, the most common Latinx subgroups in the United States are Mexican, Puerto Rican, Dominican, Salvadoran, and Guatemalan, with the vast majority being of Mexican origin (63.3%) (Flores, 2017). There may also be distinct ethnic groups within a given country of origin. For example, there are more than sixty Indigenous groups in Mexico, each with their own culture and language. Thus, while there are certain characteristics common to the Latinx culture that pervade across subgroups, we caution against assumptions of a monolithic and unidimensional Latinx culture.

Race

Latinx persons are of any race (as defined by the Census Bureau): White, Black, American Indian/Alaska Native, Asian, Native Hawaiian/Pacific Islander, or any combination of these. In the 2010 Census, more than half of the Latinx population described themselves as White and 37 percent described themselves as "other"; only 3 percent, or 1.2 million, selected Black. In a 2014 nationally representative study of Latinx adults, 24 percent identified as "Afro-Latino" (Lopez & Gonzalez-Barrera, 2016). Importantly, though, because race is socially constructed, it is often disavowed by Latinx populations who do not necessarily identify with a racial category. Moreover, because the racial hierarchy within the United States favors Whites, Latinx communities are stratified based on phenotype, with the greatest advantages for those who are White-passing (Dixon & Telles, 2017).

Immigrant Status

As of 2021, U.S. national discourse on the Latinx population was driven almost exclusively by debates over immigration. The political focus on immigration has in many ways distorted the size and nature of the foreign-born Latinx population, which in reality represents just one in three persons and has been steadily declining since 2007. The largest immigrant group in the United States is from Mexico (11.6 million, accounting for 26% of all U.S. immigrants) (Lopez et al., 2018), and approximately 52 percent of Mexican-origin children have at least one foreign-born parent (Gonzalez-Barrera & Lopez, 2013) even though the vast majority of the children themselves are U.S.-born.

Immigrants from any country of origin enter the United States in different ways. The immigrant population in the United States is classified under four general legal categories that determine individuals' access to opportunities: undocumented, discretionary, temporary, and permanent.

Permanent status, also known as lawful permanent resident (LPR) or "having a green card," affords the most protections and benefits of the four legal categories. Still, LPRs are not allowed to vote, do not have access to certain public benefits, and do not have the right to remain in the United States indefinitely given that Congress can place any contingency on permanent status it deems appropriate (National Academies of Sciences, Engineering, and Medicine, 2015).

Temporary status is held by temporary visa holders who are entitled to limited periods of presence in the United States. Some of these visas are granted for particular employment or education purposes, such as seasonal agricultural jobs or academic positions. Non-employment-based temporary status, such as temporary protected status (TPS), provides temporary protection to individuals who are not able to return to their home countries because of environmental disasters or armed conflict. Individuals with temporary status are allowed to legally work in the United States. However, TPS does not offer a pathway to permanent residence or citizenship.

Finally, *discretionary status* is lawful status conferred through executive discretion that is not intended to result in permanent presence. As of 2021, Deferred Action for Childhood Arrivals (DACA) falls under this category, but advocacy efforts are calling for a path to legal permanent residence.

Undocumented status is the result of the development of legal statuses over the last century (National Academies of Sciences, Engineering, and Medicine, 2015). Almost half (45%) of all immigrants in the United States with this status entered the country legally and then fell "out of status" by either overstaying their visas or having their legal status revoked. Undocumented status, also called "unauthorized" or "illegal" status, affords few legal protections and is inherently unstable because of the constant risk of detention and deportation (Fernández-Esquer et al., 2017).

Given the access to political, labor market, health, and social opportunities legality affords in the United States, legal status shapes the everyday experiences of immigrant families, especially in mixed-status homes (i.e., citizen children of undocumented parents). Immigrants make up approximately 13 percent of the U.S. population. As of 2012,

42 percent of immigrants in the United States were naturalized citizens, 27 percent were legal permanent residents, 5 percent had TPS status, and 26 percent were undocumented (National Academies of Sciences, Engineering, and Medicine, 2015). Approximately one-quarter of Latinx children in the United States have at least one parent who is undocumented (Clarke et al., 2017). Of the 26 percent of the entire immigrant population in the United States that is undocumented, 77 percent is Latinx (Rosenblum & Soto, 2015). The undocumented population, while relatively modest in size, has been exaggerated and vilified (e.g., "illegals" and "aliens") in support of strict immigration policy and border control.

The Immigrant Paradox. Research with immigrant populations distinguishes between the foreign-born (i.e., first generation), their children (i.e., the second generation), and their grandchildren (i.e., the third generation). The first generation may be further distinguished based on age of arrival (i.e., the 1.75 generation arriving before age six; the 1.5 generation arriving between ages six and twelve; and the 1.25 generation arriving during the teen years). According to epidemiological research, U.S.-born individuals *and* those who immigrate as children or youth are more likely to experience health problems than foreign-born Latinxs who immigrate as adults, in spite of their relatively better socioeconomic circumstances (Alegría et al., 2006; Alegría et al., 2008; Breslau et al., 2005, 2009). These findings, referred to as the "immigrant paradox," are highly significant since they suggest higher risk for the two-thirds of the Latinx population that is U.S.-born. Notably, later-generation Latinx individuals who retain core cultural characteristics may be protected against negative outcomes, even in the face of adverse circumstances stemming from poverty and discrimination (Bornstein, 2017).

Language Use

The majority of Latinxs (69.0%) are English-proficient, and U.S.-born Latinxs (89.7%) are much more likely to be proficient in English than their foreign-born counterparts (34.6%) (Flores, 2017). Latinxs have varying levels of proficiency in Spanish; an estimated 38 percent predominantly or exclusively speak Spanish, and 36 percent are Spanish/English bilingual (Krogstad & Gonzalez-Barrera, 2015). Because of a history of colonization, many of the thousands of Indigenous languages once spoken throughout Latin America have died. Still, Latinxs in the United States with Indigenous backgrounds may speak an Amerindian language (e.g., Quechua, Nahuatl) as their first language.

Socioeconomic Status

On the whole, the Latinx population is disproportionately impacted by poverty. Latinx households are twice as likely as the general population to be poor. The rate of poverty, estimated at nearly 25 percent, reflects limited educational and occupational opportunities and inequities in pay and benefits, especially for Latinxs with limited English proficiency (U.S. Congress Joint Economic Committee, 2015). Importantly, families with young children are the most likely to live in poverty; nearly six million Latinx children grow up poor. In our view, these statistics reflect the nearly insurmountable structural and systemic barriers to economic success that face populations of color (Edelman, 2019).

Cultural and Contextual Considerations

The vast diversity within the Latinx population in the United States naturally results in a wide range of cultural and contextual considerations based on race, ethnicity, language, nativity, and immigration status. Although Latinx individuals are often assumed to have homogenous customs and beliefs, each individual and family has a unique set of experiences and history that shapes their reality. Thus, we present cultural and contextual considerations in this section that are common threads across many Latinx communities with the caveat that these may manifest to varying degrees for any given child, parent, or family.

Oppression

Oppression is an act of exploitation, suppression, and/or disempowerment of an individual, group, or community by those who hold power (Prilleltensky & Gonick, 1996). Oppression results in the dehumanization of groups who do not hold power and serves to further justify exploitation (Freire, 2014). Although oppression is often discussed in terms of race, Latinx individuals experience oppression related to multiple components of their identities including nativity, language, race, ethnicity, and gender (Kiehne, 2016).

Latinx individuals in the United States report that discrimination is a major problem (Molina et al., 2019). For example, Latinx individuals are less likely than White individuals to be shown housing units available for rent and are less likely to have landlords respond to their inquiries (U.S. Department of Housing and Urban Development, 2013). In the workplace, Latinx individuals report experiencing discrimination from supervisors and a decreased sense of safety (Guerrero & Posthuma, 2014; Hosoda et al., 2012). Additionally, although education is often thought of as the cornerstone of the American Dream, the schools that serve Latinx students tend to be segregated and underresourced. Moreover, Latinx families, particularly those headed by immigrant parents, face barriers to engaging with the traditional school system. Parents may work hours that prevent them from attending school events, or they may feel isolated due to language barriers. Schools then may perceive parents as unreliable and unconcerned with their children's education (Quiocho & Daoud, 2006).

Health Impacts. Social determinants of health are those factors that shape everyday experiences and environments that, in turn, influence health. Oppression and discrimination serve as social determinants. The "immigrant paradox" literature documents that the longer Latinx immigrants live in the United States, the more discrimination they face and the more likely they are to lose some of the protective behaviors that kept them healthy despite the stress of migration and resettlement. Discrimination results in reduced access to housing, employment and education, which undermines physical and mental health. Health issues are exacerbated for Latinx immigrants who are excluded from access to services. This exclusion is rooted in American ideals about who is worthy of public assistance. Latinx immigrants are generally viewed as unworthy of public assistance unless they were victims of crimes, trafficked into the United States, or pregnant women who will give birth to a U.S. citizen (Ayón, 2015). In these cases, policies generally allow access to public health programs such as Medicaid or Children's Health Insurance Program (CHIP).

In addition to immigration status, cultural, language, and racial differences between individuals and providers impact access to quality physical and mental health care (Floríndez et al., 2020). Differences in access to care and quality of care result in disparate health outcomes for Latinxs. For example, darker-skinned Latinxs have poorer health outcomes (Cuevas et al., 2016), and in young Latinx children, skin color is associated with poorer mental health (Calzada et al., 2019). Language proficiency may also impact health and mental health outcomes among Latinx individuals. For example, Sentell et al. (2007) found that 51 percent of English-speaking immigrants who reported needing mental health services received them, compared with only 8 percent of non-English-speaking immigrants. Accessing health care may be even more challenging for Latinx immigrants who speak a language other than Spanish (Feldman et al., 2009).

Family Functioning Impacts. As with physical and mental health, oppression and discrimination impact parenting. Parenting is a universally challenging experience. However, parenting stress, the psychological and physical burden of parenting responsibilities, is experienced differently across groups (Abidin, 1992; Belsky, 1984). Contextual factors such as social support and access to resources impact parenting stress. For example, Latinx parents without documentation report an overwhelming fear of being separated from their children that affects their daily work and childcare routines (Cardoso et al., 2018). Even for Latinx families who have migrated to the United States with legal protection, there is a fear of separation and law enforcement (Dreby, 2012). Calzada et al. (2020) found that in the context of an adverse immigration environment, positive parenting (i.e., parental behavioral control, parental support) was significant for protecting youth from engaging in externalizing behaviors, but positive parenting is more challenging when stress is high.

Latinx parents are also charged with helping their children navigate a discriminatory environment. To counter discrimination, parents may respond by comforting their child, educating them about immigration and the documentation status of their family, teaching them to prepare for and cope with discrimination, instilling in them ethnic pride, and teaching them to value diversity (Ayón, 2016). Parents may also respond to discrimination by reinforcing negative stereotypes of other ethnic groups or even reinforce stereotypes within the Latinx community, particularly those that favor lighter skin color (Ayón, 2016). Regardless of the strategies used, this aspect of socialization is an added demand put on Latinx parents.

Familismo

Familismo is a Latinx cultural value that refers to the interdependence, loyalty, closeness, and harmony that characterize the family unit (Falicov, 1998; Guilamo-Ramos et al., 2007; Yasui & Dishion, 2007). Familismo may manifest in different ways for each family unit, but common examples include young adults consulting parents and other elders on career decisions; extended family living in proximity to each other; real or perceived obligations to attend family gatherings; shared responsibility to care for young children and elders; and/or protection of sensitive information from those outside the family. Familismo aligns with a collectivist worldview and an emphasis on interdependence over independence.

Health Impacts. Familismo impacts the mental health of Latinx individuals, which may affect the likelihood of child maltreatment. Strong familismo is associated with increased parental monitoring and involvement in education, which in turn promote positive behavior and academic achievement (Calzada et al., 2014). Familismo also enhances the development of adaptive behavior through parental modeling of positive prosocial behaviors and reduces risk for child externalizing behaviors that can lead to substance abuse and other risky behaviors (Bailey et al., 2015; Calzada et al., 2014). However, if family obligations are too strenuous, it may increase stress and burden on the family system (Calzada et al., 2013; Calzada et al., 2014).

Family Functioning Impacts. Familismo influences family functioning by centering all activity on the well-being of the family unit rather than any one individual. The needs of the family are given priority over individual needs (Coohey, 2001). This unity within the family creates social support and fosters communication that results in increased resilience (Bailey et al., 2015).

Familismo can be both a protective and risk factor for child maltreatment. Among Latina mothers, those who report strong, positive family ties are less likely to be abusive toward children (Coohey, 2001). Latino fathers who report highly valuing familismo are less likely to use physical punishment as a form of discipline (Ferrari, 2002). Healthy and nurturing attachment to caregivers promoted by familismo serves as a protective factor against child abuse for both parents (Bailey et al., 2015). However, as noted above, if the demands of familismo overwhelm the family system, parenting stress may increase and contribute to negative and harsh parenting.

Gender Roles

In Latinx culture, as in most cultures and communities, responsibilities are often delineated by gender (Terrazas-Carrillo & Sabina, 2019). Latinx males are often socialized to embody the ideal of machismo. Machismo calls for men to lead their families by providing and protecting each member (Falicov, 2010). In contrast, *marianismo*, a term that references the Virgin Mary, calls for women to serve their families while being virtuous, humble, and subordinate (Castillo et al., 2010). Machismo and marianismo are rooted in upholding the honor of families. However, both values can manifest as harmful to individuals and families. For example, dominant machismo has been linked to perpetrating gender-based violence (Terrazas-Carrillo & Sabina, 2019). Machismo may contribute to increased rates of child maltreatment and domestic violence when men in the household rigidly adhere to gender norms and the reliance on physical punishment (Ferrari, 2002). At the same time, marianismo has been linked to the normalization of experiencing violent behaviors (Fuchsel et al., 2012).

Acculturation

The United States has often been described as a melting pot in which people from different countries and cultures blend into one "American" community. This idea of a melting pot embodies the ideal of assimilation, where a minority culture is absorbed into the majority culture. In reality, the process of cultural change as a function of continual contact between two groups, referred to as acculturation, is more nuanced (Padilla & Perez, 2003). Typically, the minority group acquires at least some elements of the dominant society like language, food, dress, music, and sports (Lara et al., 2005). Acculturation may also involve shifts in behaviors, values, and norms (Altschul & Lee, 2011). Importantly, though, most groups retain elements of their culture of origin, referred to as enculturation, even while adopting to the dominant culture. In general, the more time Latinx individuals live in the United States, the more they acculturate. Second and subsequent generations may not endorse or follow the values, traditions, and lifestyles from their culture of origin.

Health Impacts. The erosion of traditional culture across generations appears to have implications for physical and mental health outcomes (Calzada et al., 2020). In fact, many scholars understand the immigrant paradox, in which Latinx immigrants have better health outcomes than might be predicted based on their socioeconomic status (Abraído-Lanza et al., 2006; Camacho-Rivera et al., 2015), to reflect acculturation to the dominant American culture. Acculturation has been linked to poor diet, increased substance use, and, among women, poor pregnancy outcomes due to these negative health behaviors (Lara et al., 2005). More acculturated Latinx women are more likely to have low-weight births and premature births, and their infants have a higher mortality rate. The higher rates of substance use observed among more acculturated Latinx (Myers et al., 2009) can compromise healthy family functioning. Indeed, substance use is a primary risk factor for child maltreatment and placement into the foster care system.

The impact of acculturation on mental health is also nuanced. Immigrants experience acculturative stress as they adapt to the demands (e.g., linguistic, behavioral) of a new environment. Acculturative stress is associated with the loss of traditional support networks, lack of knowledge of community norms, and social isolation and discrimination in a new community (Miranda et al., 2000). Recent immigrants also may experience greater levels of stress related to the migration journey or stressful experiences in their home countries (Santisteban et al., 2012). Despite the acculturative stress experienced by Latinx immigrants, less acculturated Latinx individuals have fewer mental health problems (Miranda et al., 2000). In fact, Latinx individuals in the United States have fewer mental health issues than non-Latinx White populations in the United States (Calzada et al., 2020).

On the other hand, acculturation is associated with increased use of health care, particularly preventative care (Lara et al., 2005). Given that child maltreatment is commonly reported by medical professionals, the increased use of preventative care, especially for well-child checks, is likely a protective factor for families. Preventative care also can offer opportunities to educate and support parents.

Family Functioning Impacts. Latinx youth tend to acculturate more quickly than adults (Miranda et al., 2006), creating a parent-child acculturation gap that changes family functioning, cohesion, and conflict levels (Kwak, 2003). One manifestation of this acculturation gap relates to language. In Spanish-speaking families with children who have learned English, children often serve as "language brokers" to translate and convey information between their family and those who do not speak their language, such as educators, public safety officials, and health providers (Tse, 1995). Language brokering transfers power and control to children, who de facto become the arbiters of essential and sensitive information (Miranda et al., 2000). Latinx youth report positive feelings about translating nonsensitive issues as a way to contribute to the family (Anguiano, 2018), but language brokering in sensitive situations causes significant stress and negatively impacts mental health and academic achievement (Anguiano, 2018; Kim et al., 2020). High-stakes translations might occur in medical or legal settings, schools, or anywhere finances are being discussed. When translating in these situations, youth experience a confusing sense of parentification whereby they must assume some of the burden and responsibility for the family that is beyond their developmental age. Beyond the stressors of brokering, acculturation appears to increase youths' exposure to discrimination and other types of acculturative stress, leading to negative self-esteem, more internalizing problems, and higher risk of suicidal behavior (Gomez et al., 2011; Portes & Zady, 2002; Smokowski & Bacallao, 2007).

More generally, parent-child acculturation gaps may strain parent-child relationships, especially during adolescence when youth are most likely to engage in risky behaviors. Latinx adolescents tend to acculturate to American lifestyles more quickly than their parents and to adopt cultural elements that conflict with their parents' beliefs, particularly as related to peer relationships. A primary example is when mainstream American values of autonomy and individualism encourage youth to challenge authority and prioritize peer networks, which can be at odds with familismo (Smokowski et al., 2008). Research shows that parent-adolescent acculturation gaps generally decrease family cohesion, adaptability, and familismo (Smokowski et al., 2008). Since communication is valued highly in Latinx families (Sabogal et al., 1987), barriers to parent-child communication will likely cause disruptions in family functioning. In contrast, female adolescents who adhere to Latinx cultural norms report higher levels of family functioning (Ramirez & Hosch, 1991).

Religiosity and Spirituality

Spirituality refers to an individual's sense of meaning, peace, and purpose in the world, while religion refers to organized practices and beliefs (Oxhandler & Parrish, 2017). Religion in Latinx populations must be viewed within the historical context of colonialization that forced Indigenous populations to convert to Christian religions, primarily Catholicism, even as components of Indigenous spiritual beliefs were incorporated into Catholic traditions (Martínez, 2014). Today, most Latinx individuals in the United States identify as Catholic (55%), but that number is declining (Funk & Martinez, 2014). Roughly 16 percent identify as Protestant Evangelical, 5 percent as Protestant, 3 percent as other Christian denominations, 1 percent as other, and 18 percent do not identify with a religion (Funk & Martinez, 2014).

Spirituality represents a relationship with a higher power (Campesino & Schwartz, 2006). A core aspect of Latinx spirituality is a commitment not just to one's own relationship with God but also to family and community (Campesino & Schwartz, 2006). As such, Latinx spirituality may be understood as collectivistic rather than individualistic (Campesino et al., 2009). Latinx parents report that spirituality is beneficial both in terms of their connections to their families and as a positive coping strategy (Koerner et al., 2013). Attendance at religious services is associated with positive mental health outcomes and creates a support network for parents that helps to promote positive parenting practices (Altschul & Lee, 2011). Latinxs who have experienced trauma and/or have issues with substance use report using spirituality as a coping mechanism (Ai et al., 2016). On the other hand, strict interpretations of biblical texts may increase the likelihood of physical abuse (Rodriguez & Henderson, 2010), though other studies contradict this (Lee et al., 2014). Religion appears to have a negative impact on the acceptance of diverse genders and sexual orientations, as religious beliefs may lead families to reject members who do not conform to traditional gender norms (Przeworski & Piedra, 2020).

Case Illustrations

To further explore the lived experiences of Latinx families in the United States, we return to the cases of Bianca, Dominic, and Audriana presented in the introduction. As we discuss the relevance of cultural and contextual considerations, we encourage readers to reflect on the extent to which the child welfare system (i.e., its workers) considered the lived experiences of each family, as well as the role that the child welfare system played in further shaping their lived experiences. We further challenge practitioners to consider whether and to what extent each child was a victim of maltreatment and whether they needed to be removed from their homes.

Bianca

Oppression. Bianca and her parents are immigrants from Mexico who are living in the United States without legal authority to do so. Although her parents work hard, they do not have access to resources that other immigrants may have. They are unable to secure employment that pays enough for them to survive. They also lack access to health and unemployment insurance. When Bianca's father is injured, there is no alternate source of income for the family through disability benefits, and there is no support to even temporarily provide income for the family. Rather than assist in reducing these sources of stress in the family, the child welfare system ultimately removes Bianca. An alternative strategy would be to help the family re-establish stability through financial support, education, and treatment for alcoholism, along with helping Bianca's mother establish a separate household with Bianca to ensure her safety.

Familismo. Familismo provides strength for the family. Bianca's family, both immediate and extended, is close. Her extended family in Mexico has learned about what happened, and her mother's sister is trying to find enough funds to come to the United States to help Bianca's mother. Her paternal grandparents have been in contact with her father and are encouraging him to get support from his pastor and attend Alcoholics Anonymous groups, since they are offered at the church for free. These familial supports and strengths are not considered in the case planning.

Acculturation. Bianca's family is acculturating to mainstream American society. Since her father lived in the United States for four years prior to Bianca and her mother arriving, there is differential acculturation within the family. Bianca's father has already learned conversational English and adapted some aspects of his lifestyle. For example, since he was living alone, he primarily ate fast food in front of the television, whereas Bianca and her mother want to eat food prepared at home together as a family. Bianca's dad is the family's primary language broker, which means her mother depends on him and has little privacy. Neither parent is familiar with the child welfare system in the United States and are now faced with the hurdle of understanding and navigating a system that has the right to take their child.

Dominic

Oppression. Child welfare systems narrowly focus on the facts of the case as they relate to the protection of the child. In the case of Dominic, they saw a child who was unsupervised and removed him due to neglectful supervision. Ironically, Daniela's decision to take care of herself, which will support her in her parenting role, resulted in her losing her son. Our understanding of oppression guides us to examine this situation in the broader context of our societal policies and practices, rather than based on the actions of one individual. For example, why wasn't childcare more accessible and affordable to Daniela? Why couldn't Daniela leave work to attend a medical appointment while Dominic was at school? And finally, why didn't the child welfare system respond to their situation by assisting Daniela in finding childcare and mental health treatment so the family could remain together?

Familismo. Daniela's parents are clearly upset with her life choices and have expressed their disapproval. In the context of strong familismo, that disapproval is likely impacting her mental health. Still, while their disapproval is openly expressed and considered a strain on the entire family unit, they have not abandoned Daniela or the grandchildren. When child welfare services removed Dominic, Daniela's parents step in to care for the children because they consider grandparental care to be the optimal alternative to having Dominic with his mother.

Acculturation. Daniela's parents moved to New York City as young adults and raised their children in a Spanish-speaking home and according to their Puerto Rican values. Daniela, who is second generation, is much more acculturated to mainstream society. While she is proud to be Puerto Rican, she is likely much more individualistic than her parents and sees their rejection of her life choices as archaic. While she is bilingual, she is raising Dominic in an English-speaking home, limiting the communication between Dominic and his grandparents. The differential acculturation across generations is likely creating conflict and may be contributing to Daniela's mental health issues.

Audriana

Oppression. Audriana's family is a mixed-status family: her mother, stepfather, and older sister are undocumented immigrants, while Audriana and her half brothers are U.S. citizens. Because of the parents' undocumented status, they have limited ability to find work that pays a living wage so that they can afford their own home. When Audriana and her sister disclose sexual abuse, their mother is faced with the choice of losing her two older daughters or losing their home. Critical race theory would have us question why parents were given a constrained choice rather than real options to keep their family together and safe.

Familismo. Familismo, spirituality, and religion are intertwined for this family. The family unit is expected to participate in and follow religious guidelines. Audriana's disclosure of abuse to her pastor may have upset the family because it was a disclosure to someone outside of their family, especially someone in authority whom they respect. Her disclosure also likely brought shame upon the family and may have contributed to the physical violence perpetuated by her stepfather. Familismo also influenced the family's decision to move in with and remain with extended family.

Acculturation. Because Audriana's family has mixed statuses, we can assume that their acculturation processes into the United States have varied substantially. For example, Audriana's sister spent time in Honduras as a young child, but Audriana never did. Her mother and stepfather were raised in Honduras and view American teenagers as too independent and rebellious. Instead of listening to the girls when they make a disclosure, they accuse them of being typical American teenagers who fight against rules.

Closing Summary

The cases of Bianca, Dominic, and Audriana are complex, and although we strive to avoid stereotypes or oversimplifications of their cases, there are some illustrations that provide examples of how cultural considerations overlap with child maltreatment cases. To fully understand child maltreatment in Latinx families, it is imperative to look beyond the case facts and consider the experiences of the family in relation to oppression, familismo, acculturation, and religiosity. Using a lens of critical race theory, we can "flip the script" on our interpretation of cases and focus more on the societal elements that create impossible situations for families who most need support. In the next chapter, we present an overview of child maltreatment definitions and research findings regarding prevalence of child maltreatment in the Latinx population.

2

Understanding Child Maltreatment in the Latinx Population

A child who does not play is not a child, but the man who does not play has lost forever the child who lived in him and who he will miss terribly.
—Pablo Neruda

In this chapter, we discuss child maltreatment within the Latinx population. We begin with an overview of child maltreatment definitions and research findings regarding prevalence rates in the Latinx population. Next, we discuss macro, family, and individual risk factors, as they present in Latinx populations, that increase the likelihood of child maltreatment. Finally, we explore child maltreatment in the context of safety, stability, and nurturing (i.e., the public health model) utilizing various theoretical frameworks to explain unique experiences of Latinx families.

Prevalence of Child Maltreatment and Latinx Populations

The exact prevalence of child maltreatment is difficult to establish. Some children who are maltreated are never officially identified, while others who are not maltreated may enter the child welfare system for a host of other reasons. Moreover, determinations of harm, potential for harm, and threat of harm require the use of judgment, introducing subjectivity and bias in reporting and investigative processes. This may be especially true with children of color due to structural, institutional, and interpersonal racism (Dettlaff & Boyd, 2020; Dettlaff et al., 2011; Rivaux et al., 2008). With these caveats in mind, we review national statistics and retrospective reports on the prevalence (i.e., the proportion of children who experience) of child maltreatment in the Latinx population.

National Estimates

Child maltreatment is defined as abuse or neglect that occurs to individuals under eighteen years of age. Although definitions vary slightly across states, federal legislation defines child maltreatment as "any recent act or failure to act on the part of a parent or caregiver that results in death, serious physical or emotional harm, sexual abuse, or exploitation, or an act or failure to act that presents an imminent risk of serious harm" (Child Abuse Prevention and Treatment Act of 2010, P.L. 111–320). According to substantiated cases of child maltreatment at the national level, 8 per 1,000 Latinx children in the United States are abused or neglected, and patterns across type of maltreatment are consistent with those observed in the general population (U.S. Department of Health & Human Services, 2019). Specifically, national survey data from the early 2000s (i.e., the National Survey of Child and Adolescent Well-being) shows that among Latinx children referred to the child welfare system, the most common maltreatment experienced is neglect (34%), followed by physical abuse (20%), sexual abuse (6%), and emotional abuse (5%) (Garcia et al., 2017). Further analysis of this sample shows that neglect is most often characterized by a lack of supervision (Johnson-Motoyama, et al., 2012).

National survey data has also been used to examine prevalence rates of injurious spanking (spanking that resulted in bruises, cuts, and welts) and other forms of abuse among adolescents (Oscea Hawkins et al., 2010). These results revealed higher rates of injurious spanking in Latinx youth than in non-Latinx White youth. Of Latinx adolescents, 11 percent experienced spanking that resulted in bad bruises, cuts, or welts compared with only 7 percent of non-Latinx White youth; 6 percent had been thrown across the room or against a wall, floor, or other hard surface and hurt badly by a parent or other adult compared with 4 percent of non-Latinx White youth; and 6 percent reported that a parent or other adult in charge of them had beaten them up, hit them with their fist, or kicked them hard compared with 5 percent of non-Latinx White youth. Overall, 16 percent of Latinx youth reported experiencing physical abuse compared with 11 percent of non-Latinx White youth.

Regarding sexual abuse, national statistics of substantiated cases indicate a prevalence rate of 1.8 in 1,000 Latinx children (Seldak et al., 2010). However, other data sources suggest higher rates of sexual abuse. For example, Graham et al. (2016; 2018) found that of cases involving Latinx children reported to child protective services, 9.4 percent involved allegations of sexual abuse. They further found that cases of sexual abuse were more common but less likely to be substantiated when compared with non-Latinx White and Black children. Similarly, 8 percent of Latinx high school students report having experienced forced sex (Centers for Disease Control and Prevention, 2019). In contrast, only 7.1 percent of White students and 7.2 percent of Black students reported experiencing forced sex.

Retrospective Reports

Because national statistics only represent children who come into contact with formal systems, it is important to utilize other sources of information to understand prevalence rates. Maker et al. (2005) examined retrospective reports of child physical abuse in a high socioeconomic and ethnically diverse sample of 251 women and found that 78 percent of Latinxs reported experiencing at least one type of physical abuse as a child, a striking rate for any population and especially one with socioeconomic privilege. Ullman and Filipas (2005) asked 461 female college students about their childhoods and found that 33 percent of the Latinx sample reported having experienced sexual abuse as a child. Ulibarri et al. (2009) interviewed a community sample of Latinx women ($N = 204$) via telephone and found that 35 percent had experienced some form of sexual abuse; 31 percent of the abuse was perpetrated by a family member; and 52 percent was perpetrated by boyfriends, friends, or acquaintances.

Gonzalez et al. (2020) conducted a systematic review to synthesize the literature on Latinx women's experiences of interpersonal violence, including child maltreatment. According to their results, between 12 and 79 percent of Latinx children experience childhood physical abuse, between 2 and 47 percent experience sexual abuse, and approximately 50 percent experience some form of neglect. The wide range of estimates found in their study, which mirrors inconsistencies in the results reviewed above, underscores the difficulty of establishing true prevalence rates. Child maltreatment is challenging to define and measure, and research methods vary across studies. Prevalence rates appear highest when adults are asked to provide retrospective reports of their childhood experiences, perhaps as a function of time (i.e., retrospective reports capture all childhood experiences from 0 to 18) and cognitive capacity (i.e., adults have greater understanding of what constitutes abusive or neglectful behavior). Also, true cases of maltreatment may go undetected, underreported and/or unsubstantiated at the time of their occurrence.

Subgroup Differences in Latinx Child Maltreatment Rates

The Latinx population is incredibly diverse and subgroup differences may impact child maltreatment rates. In fact, estimates for the pan-Latinx population may obscure important differences based on the more specific and intersectional identities of Latinx children. In this section, we examine issues of diversity by presenting existing literature for three distinct subgroups based on immigrant status, ethnicity, and gender.

Immigrant Status

The immigrant paradox, a pattern of findings showing favorable outcomes on health and well-being for immigrant relative to U.S.-born Latinxs, may apply to child maltreatment. In a systematic review of the literature, Millett (2016) found higher rates of general maltreatment, physical, emotional, and sexual abuse, but not of neglect, in U.S.-born populations relative to foreign-born populations. Indeed, of the Latinx children who come to the attention of the child welfare system, 92 percent are U.S.-born and less than 8 percent are immigrant children (Dettlaff & Johnson, 2011). Moreover, an analysis of Latinx fathers found that foreign-born fathers were significantly less likely to be physically aggressive toward their children than U.S.-born fathers, even after controlling for child behavior (Lee et al., 2011). Still, the literature remains inconclusive, with some studies documenting lower rates of child abuse in foreign-born Latinx populations (Lee & Altschul, 2015; Lee et al., 2011), and others finding no differences (Bridges et al., 2010).

A more nuanced examination shows subgroup differences on some types of maltreatment but not others. Rates of physical abuse appear to be similar across generations of Latinxs (Dettlaff et al., 2009; Johnson-Motoyama et al., 2012; Cardoso et al., 2014), but risks for varying types of neglect are higher in foreign-born Latinx populations (Hussey et al., 2006; Johnson-Motoyama, 2015; Kimber et al., 2015). Dettlaff and Johnson (2011) found that immigrant Latinx children were more likely to experience physical abuse, whereas U.S.-born Latinx children were significantly more likely to experience emotional abuse. They also found that despite lower rates of involvement in the child welfare system, immigrant Latinx children were as likely to have their cases substantiated as their U.S.-born peers. Johnson-Motoyama et al. (2015) also documented differences depending on type of maltreatment with a national sample; according to their findings with Latinx children ages zero to three years in the child welfare system, physical and sexual abuse were higher, and neglect was lower, in cases with immigrant (relative to later-generation) Latinx children. Consistent with Dettlaff and Johnson (2011), case disposition (i.e., substantiation) was the same for the two groups.

Even within the immigrant subgroup of the Latinx population, considerable heterogeneity exists, driven at least in part by documentation status. Documentation status is posited to influence children's involvement in child welfare in a number of ways due to factors such as the limited access to resources available to undocumented children and parents and fear of authority and deportation (Gonzalez et al., 2020; Scott et al., 2014). A study with the Latinx child welfare population in Texas ($N = 9,398$) compared citizen/legal resident children with undocumented children and found substantially higher rates of sexual abuse (18% compared with 4%), but comparable rates of physical abuse (13% compared with 16%), and lower rates of neglect (47% compared with 57%), in cases involving undocumented children (Scott et al., 2014). Similar analysis using national data showed no significant differences between Latinx families based on nativity, citizenship, or documentation status (Cardoso et al., 2014).

Ethnicity

Less research has examined whether rates of maltreatment differ across ethnic subgroups in the Latinx population. Warner et al. (2012) asked a diverse group of Latinx women about their childhood experiences and found higher overall rates of childhood abuse among U.S.-born (38%) than foreign-born (28%) Latinx women—though foreign-born women reported more physical abuse. They also found the lowest rates of maltreatment among Cuban Americans (19%), and substantially higher rates among Puerto Ricans (32%) and Mexican Americans (33%). Race, per se, was not considered, but according to critical race theory/LATCrit, Afro-Latinxs (i.e., those who are phenotypically Black) are more likely to be involved in the child welfare system due to systemic racism (Dettlaff & Boyd, 2020). On the other hand, Cuban Americans in the United States are more socioeconomically advantaged than other Latinx groups (Motel & Patten, 2012), which may offset risk of maltreatment by providing families with social and health supports and resources. These mechanisms have not been explored in the extant literature.

Gender

Using an intersectional feminist/mujerismo perspective, vulnerability to different circumstances depends on the intersection of sex/gender and race/ethnicity. Much of the literature on child maltreatment among Latinx children does not fully explore intersectional identities. Nonetheless, we summarize the literature with regard to gender and race/ethnicity separately to encourage the field to consider issues of intersectionality and experiences of child maltreatment.

Gender differences are observed in rates of child maltreatment but only in risk of sexual abuse, which is higher among girls (Seldak et al., 2010). Because of the shame associated with reporting sexual abuse, there is, however, a likelihood that sexual abuse amongst boys is underreported. In a meta-analytic review of the literature on neglect, Stoltenborgh et al. (2013) analyzed prevalence rates from thirteen independent samples with a total of 59,406 participants. Consistent with past findings (Seldak et al., 2010), their results did not show any gender differences in rates of physical or emotional neglect. In a separate meta-analysis with 168 independent samples and 9,689,801 participants from around the world, Stoltenborgh et al. (2013) found that physical abuse occurs at approximately the same rate for boys and girls.

Children with Disabilities

Children with disabilities are at greater risk of becoming victims of child abuse and neglect (Legano et al., 2021). Children with disabilities have higher-level needs and require additional financial resources that increase parenting and family stress (Peer & Hillman, 2014). Lack of supports for the family and child compounds the risk of potential abuse or neglect. The prevalence of disabilities among different racial and ethnic groups appears to be related to definitions, health-care access, and school processes. For example, Latinx children have lower prevalence of disabilities compared with White or Black children, but these disparities appear to reflect a lack of access to health care and social services where children are screened and diagnosed (Boyle et al., 2011).

Ethnic/Racial Disparities in Child Maltreatment

Ethnic/racial disparities in child maltreatment have been documented for decades (Dettlaff, 2015), driven largely by differences in neglect and physical abuse referrals at the national level (Putnam, 2003). Child maltreatment investigations, which occur following a referral that is deemed credible, are highest in the Black population (53%) and second highest in the Latinx population (28%) (Kim et al., 2017). However, research focused on Latinx children (relative to Black children) is limited, precluding firm conclusions regarding disparities specific to the Latinx population.

Moreover, scholars question whether disparities observed in the literature reflect true ethnic/racial differences rather than socioeconomic differences. To address this, Mersky and Janczewski (2018) looked at rates of maltreatment in a sample ($N = 1,523$) of women who qualified for home visiting services for low-income families in Wisconsin. Based on their retrospective reports, 57 percent of women had experienced maltreatment as children, with differences based on racial/ethnic background. Rates were highest for non-Latinx White women across types of maltreatment and overall. For example, 62 percent of non-Latinx White women, but 55 percent of Latinx women, reported being maltreated as children. Rates of sexual abuse, emotional abuse, physical neglect, and emotional neglect were also lower in Latinx women compared with non-Latinx White women, whereas rates of physical abuse were the same across the two groups (43%). In parallel, the racial disproportionality index (RDI), which measures the extent to which racial/ethnic groups are over- or under-represented on a given outcome, shows disproportionality in child abuse reports among American Indian and Black, but not Latinx, children across the United States (Fluke et al., 2003). In other words, the percentage of Latinx children involved in child welfare is proportional to the size of the Latinx population. Non-Latinx White and Asian American children, in contrast, are *under*represented.

Thus, while we caution against firm conclusions regarding disparities involving Latinx children, we emphasize a number of issues related to disproportionality. First, risk factors stemming from poverty, social and economic marginalization, and lack of resources to support families are robust predictors of child maltreatment and are high in the Latinx population (Fluke et al., 2010). Second, institutional bias, rationing (i.e., of resources and services), visibility, and surveillance negatively impact *all* populations of color in the child welfare system, contributing to inequities (Bywaters et al., 2019). Third, implicit bias among child welfare professionals may impact decision-making, including substantiation (Cross & Casanueva, 2009; Dettlaff et al., 2011). And fourth, regardless of its relative prevalence, child maltreatment in the Latinx population, as in any population, is a significant public health and human rights priority. Approximately one-quarter of Latinx children are believed to be victims of child maltreatment, with the majority of those cases resulting from neglect.

Theoretical Considerations

Next, to ground our discussion of child welfare and maltreatment in Latinx communities, we draw on a number of relevant theoretical frameworks and concepts from various disciplines. At the broadest level, we apply the public health model for child maltreatment prevention, which presents safety, stability, and nurturing relationships as the foundation of a healthy childhood (Fortson et al., 2016). We then situate the experiences of Latinx children and families using theories to explore the unique context of child maltreatment in the Latinx community. In other words, we consider the implications of various theories for the safety, stability, and nurturing of Latinx children.

The Public Health Model of Child Maltreatment

The public health model advocates for universal prevention to promote public health at a population scale. In the case of child maltreatment, this model considers how infrastructure across systems (e.g., health, education) can reduce risk and enhance resilience for the sake of preventing abuse and neglect. The model identifies three basic needs of children. Safety refers to physical and psychological well-being of a child within their social and physical environment (Fortson et al., 2016). Stability refers to the extent that children have consistent and reliable social and physical environments for their optimal development (Fortson et al., 2016). Nurturing refers to the extent to which developmental needs of a child are met (Centers for Disease Control and Prevention, 2016). At its core, nurturing requires healthy attachments between children and their caregivers. This attachment sets the foundation for the child's growth and development (Music, 2016).

Each of these domains is influenced by the social positions of Latinx families in the United States. For example, shifting immigration policies impact the ability of parents and children to feel safe and secure and to provide stable home environments. Discrimination and access to resources may also lead to instability and increased stress, which can reduce the level of nurturing in the family unit. We consider a number of theoretical frameworks as foundational in understanding how safety, stability, and nurturing are uniquely challenging in Latinx populations because they can create uncertain, inequitable, and unsafe conditions for families. Collectively, these frameworks shed light on the myriad ways in which society supports, or fails to support, families and children.

The Developmental-Ecological Model of Child Maltreatment

According to the developmental-ecological model of child maltreatment, factors at all ecological levels, including child, parent, parent-child interactions, social, and cultural factors, interact to contribute to the likelihood of child abuse and neglect perpetration (Belsky, 1993). At the macro-level, poverty is arguably the most robust predictor of reported child maltreatment. We view poverty as a systemic and not an individual issue because of compelling evidence that poverty is created and maintained through structural and systemic inequities that impact non-White communities. Poverty and its correlates, including neighborhood condition (impoverished), educational status (low), employment status (unemployed or underemployed), marital status (single), and age (young parental age), are strongly related to parents' potential for being reported for abuse or neglect (Berger & Waldfogel, 2011; Li et al., 2011; Maguire-Jack & Font, 2017). Empirical evidence documents the high levels of parenting stress and the low levels of social support experienced by parents living in poverty. In turn, high stress and low support may contribute to maladaptive parenting practices.

In addition to stress and parenting practices, poverty relates to reported child maltreatment for three reasons. First, families living in poverty are under more surveillance from formal systems. These families are more likely to have a network of social service providers working with them who may identify child maltreatment. In contrast, families with more resources may only interact with medical and education professionals. Second, professionals may view poverty as incidences of neglect when children do not have similar resources compared to their children in financially secure homes. This bias stems from middle-class standards and is socially constructed. Finally, families in poverty are likely overrepresented in reports of maltreatment because they lack the resources to seek help to mitigate risk factors or impacts of abuse. Families with resources, in contrast, can access private therapists, parent education, substance use treatment, and other help as needed.

At the family level, parent characteristics, most notably parent psychopathology and negative or ineffective parenting, also increase the risk of maltreatment. Child maltreatment reports are more likely to be substantiated when caregivers have a history of drug and alcohol abuse, mental illness, or a recent arrest, and reports are more likely to be substantiated when caregivers have three or more of these risk factors (Walsh & Mattingly, 2012). Parents with current substance abuse problems are at especially high risk for perpetrating child maltreatment (Dunn et al., 2002; Kepple, 2017), with some research showing that two-thirds of child maltreatment cases involve parents with substance abuse problems (Wells, 2009). In fact, the Child Abuse Prevention and Treatment Act (CAPTA) requires health providers to report any infant identified as being affected by substance use. Maternal depression also plays a role (Conron et al., 2009); children of depressed mothers have a significantly higher risk (three to four times) of being referred for maltreatment (Weissman et al., 2004; Windham et al., 2004), and between a quarter and a half of child maltreatment cases involve a mother with depression (Chemtob et al., 2013; Conron et al., 2009; Smith et al., 2014).

The intergenerational transmission of violence, in which the perpetration of childhood maltreatment stems from the mother's own childhood abuse history, has been well documented in empirical studies (Dilillo et al., 2000; Taylor et al., 2009). Parents who were abused as children are not only more likely to abuse substances and experience depression as adults, but also more likely to view physical discipline as acceptable and appropriate (Crouch & Behl, 2001; Rodriguez & Richardson, 2007), especially if they are younger and less acculturated (Maker et al., 2005). In cases of child maltreatment, parenting practices have been described as harsh, impulsive, aversive, and ineffective, and parent-child relationships are challenging and conflictual (Scannapieco & Connell-Carrick, 2005; Stith et al., 2009). As noted above, these practices are often a reflection of stress and limited support.

Finally, at the individual level, children with difficult temperaments, with internalizing (e.g., anxious, sad, withdrawn) or externalizing (e.g., defiant, hyperactive, aggressive, impulsive) behaviors, with poor social skills, with a disability and/or who are generally viewed as problematic by their parents, are much more likely to be victims of child maltreatment (Stith et al., 2009). Parents of children with behavior problems experience higher levels of parenting stress and are more likely to use negative parenting practices (Morgan et al., 2002). Specifically, children's challenging behaviors increase stress and elicit negative or ineffective parenting responses from caregivers, which exacerbate child misbehaviors and lead to more negative parenting. These coercive processes have been linked with child mental health problems, and especially disruptive behavior disorders like oppositional defiant disorder and conduct disorder (Dishion et al., 1992), which further increases risk of maltreatment.

Integrative Model of Development

According to the integrative model of child development (Coll et al., 1996)—arguably the most widely applied developmental model for diverse populations—race and ethnicity serve as social position factors that "interact in ways to magnify or diminish the importance of [other developmental] factors" to ultimately "influence or create alternative developmental pathways" (p. 1895). In other words, this model applies the concept of intersectionality to the study of developmental trajectories of health and well-being by suggesting that social position factors collectively determine the context within which child development occurs. This integrative model of developmental competencies for children of color includes aspects of traditional developmental theory in concert with theory specific to minority children. The model argues that a child's social position results in social stratification (e.g., segregation), which interacts with other variables to influence developmental competencies. In other words, a child's race, ethnicity, social class, and gender set the stage for their social experiences within their schools and neighborhoods because of discrimination and segregation. In turn, children and families adapt to these experiences, and this "adaptive culture" (i.e., culturally derived coping strategies), along with individual and family characteristics, influence developmental outcomes. Indeed, disparities in wealth and health among adults are believed to stem from racialized experiences that begin in the first years of life (Cheng et al., 2015; Priest et al., 2013).

Critical Race (LATCrit) Theory

Critical race theory argues that racism is widespread, systemic, and perpetuated through societal ideologies, values, policies, and practices that favor Whites over people of color. From this perspective, race is a social construct based on phenotype (i.e., an observable set of physical characteristics like hair texture) and the meanings and implications of phenotypic characteristics for an individual in relation to others (Garcia, 2017). Put simply, race is "a proxy for shared biology and environment" (Kittles et al., 2007, p. 10). Like ethnicity, race is rooted in long-standing, complex historical and political contexts (Garcia et al., 2017; Roberts & Rizzo, 2021; Valdez & Golash-Boza, 2017). Thus, Latinxs are often viewed by society in terms of race (i.e., *ascribed race*), even as they themselves disavow racial categorization (Darity Jr. et al., 2005).

Structural racism is a pervasive and self-perpetuating system that creates and reinforces racial and ethnic inequities, and arguably influences populations of color more so than individual-level factors (Gee & Ford, 2011). Since colonization, U.S. social ideologies, policies, and processes have favored Whites categorically, with relative advantages also extended to people of color with European features and light skin tones (phenotyping/colorism) (Dixon & Telles, 2017; Reece, 2019). Zambrana (2011) argues that colorism is a key stratification variable for understanding the racialization—and thus the unequal distribution of power—in the racially heterogenous Latinx population in the United States. In other words, the structures that uphold inequities may be understood through an *intersectional* lens that implicates racialized institutional practices in some Latinx communities/subgroups more than in others.

Intersectionality Theory

Intersectionality theory emerged from Black feminist scholarship to emphasize the interconnected nature of social categories and argues that social position is best understood by considering the intersection of categories of difference such as race, ethnicity, immigrant status, gender, and age (Bauer, 2014; Crenshaw, 1989; Viruell-Fuentes et al., 2012). Ethnic designation alone (i.e., Latinx) is considered overly simplistic, since experiences are determined by the totality of the social groups to which a person belongs or is assigned. Specifically, individual experiences are situated at the crux of various systems of oppression (e.g., education, health, housing) that work in concert to create inequities (e.g., in maltreatment).

Social Control Theory

According to social control theory, the child welfare system, like other social systems, serves—intentionally and unintentionally—to civilize and regulate working-class families and thus perpetuate inequities (Van Kreiken, 1986). In this system, health professionals and educators replace parents and families as the arbiters of child health, safety, and well-being, leading to the prioritization of professional norms and practices over those of individual parents and families. That is, welfare policies and programs tell people how they should act and what they should believe, based on interests and values of mainstream society (i.e., White, middle class). In this way, the surveillance, monitoring, and intervening with family life become acceptable forms of social control over low-income communities, where parental autonomy is undermined, ostensibly for the welfare of children.

Acculturative Stress

Acculturation, or the process of adapting to the language, behavior, norms, and values of mainstream culture while simultaneously maintaining those of its culture of origin (Berry, 1997), has increasingly been identified as a risk factor for Latinxs, even as it is necessary, inevitable, and in some ways beneficial. Acculturation exposes immigrants to acculturative stress (Berry, 1997; Torres, 2010), a negative psychological response (termed *distress*, *stress*, or *strain* across studies) to the experience of immigration and acculturation. Consistent with theoretical models of stress, individuals appraise acculturative stressors in light of their ability to cope. In the absence of resources, stressors lead to negative emotional reactions.

Traditionally conceived as an immigrant phenomenon, acculturative stress is currently recognized as relevant to English-speaking later generations as well. For immigrant or unacculturated Latinxs, stress may most likely emerge from pressures *to* acculturate (i.e., to learn English, to adopt Americanized behaviors and values), and for later-generation or highly acculturated Latinxs, stress may most likely emerge from pressures *against* acculturation (i.e., to learn or maintain Spanish, to learn or maintain culture-of-origin behaviors and values) (Rodriguez et al., 2002). Empirical studies bear out that, across generations, Latinxs are exposed to a wide range of stressors in instrumental, interpersonal, and societal domains. Specific examples include linguistic isolation, limited economic opportunities, social exclusion, difficult intercultural exchanges, discrimination, and cultural conflict (Bekteshi & Kang, 2018; Cervantes et al., 2013; Finch & Vega, 2003; Hovey, 2000).

Feminist/Mujerismo Theory

Feminist theory also speaks to social stratification and inequity. Feminist theory emerged as a framework for transforming the patriarchal system that promotes and maintains sexism, sexual exploitation, and oppression (hooks, 2015). While feminist theory is often used in the understanding of violence against women, several scholars have started to consider how this theory can be used to understand child maltreatment (Featherstone & Fawcett, 1994; Lancaster & Lumb, 1999; Namy et al., 2017). Specifically, the use of a feminist lens reveals how women and children are disenfranchised by forces that promote and maintain male privilege, dominance, and power. Walker et al. (1999) provided a comprehensive historical perspective on the rights of children in the United States, highlighting how a paternalistic orientation has been applied toward children, deeming them as property, denying them basic human rights, and offering them differential legal protections. This paternalistic stance challenges their status as people, contributing to their maltreatment.

Several academic disciplines have considered how the core concepts of feminist theory intersect with their own particular epistemologies, related principles, and methods of inquiry. For example, Goodman et al. (2004) examined how the general spirit and major tenets of feminist theory could inform the social justice efforts of counseling psychologists and identified six key principles: engaging in self-examination, sharing power, giving voice to the oppressed, raising consciousness, focusing on strengths, and leaving clients with tools. Additionally, as feminist theory has evolved, so has an appreciation for the intersection of gender, race, and class, now a distinguishing feature of feminist theory (hooks, 2015). Intersectionality represents the synergy that is produced by the "vast array of cultural, structural, sociobiological, economic, and social contexts" (Howard & Renfrow, 2014, p. 95) that are salient to individuals and that shape their identities. In the same vein, Bryant-Davis and Comas-Díaz (2016), two psychologists of color, argue that traditional feminism fails to recognize the multiple identities of Black, Indigenous and People of Color (BIPOC) women and the marginalization associated with these identities. Within the Latinx community, they advocate for mujerismo (womanism), noting that it broadens traditional feminism "by focusing on the centrality of community, mutual caring, and global solidarity; while aiming towards collective liberation and transformation" (p. 10). Concentrating on the lived experiences of women of color, mujerismo aims to challenge oppression, promote empowerment, and foster liberation. Through unique tools such as storytelling, mixed-method research approaches, photovoice, and "artivism" (art that promotes activism), mujerismo broadens critical consciousness and advances social change. Given the role of religion and spirituality in the Latinx community, when appropriate and relevant, spirituality is leveraged within mujerismo to promote the optimal well-being of the community.

Case Illustrations

Our case studies illustrate several of the issues relevant to the occurrence of child maltreatment. In each case, family circumstances align with the theories outlined above, and the incidence of maltreatment can be understood as a function of specific risk factors. As we revisit each case, we encourage you to reflect on other risk factors you identify and how you might ground the conceptualization of these cases from a theoretical perspective. While resiliency will be discussed in chapter 7, we also encourage you to consider protective factors and strengths that might mitigate the maltreatment. Again, we challenge you to consider whether the children should have been removed from their homes and the ethical considerations in that decision.

Bianca

Risk Factors. Bianca has experienced multiple events that have impacted her safety and stability. Before her migration to the United States, her family had few financial resources, resulting in her family being separated across borders. The migration process also introduced a new trauma when Bianca's father shot the coyote for demanding additional pay. In the United States, the family is struggling financially since Bianca's father can no longer work in construction. Her father's alcohol use and domestic violence have added extreme stress to the family, and while Bianca was never physically abused, her safety and stability were compromised and she was ultimately separated from her family.

Theoretical Explanations. While many theories can be used to explain the family's stress, social control theory and mujerismo theory speak directly to the instability. Mujerismo theory attests to the patriarchal society that has continued to perpetuate violence against women, such as the physical and verbal abuse experienced by Bianca's mother. Social control theory extends this explanation by explaining how Bianca's mother, a victim of domestic violence in need of assistance, could be viewed and designated as a perpetrator of neglectful supervision, resulting in Bianca's removal. Social control theory explains the monitoring approach to child welfare, which results in the removal of children who could remain with their families. In this case, the system removed Bianca instead of assisting her mother and father with their respective needs, introducing more instability and preventing them from social and economic advancement.

Dominic

Risk Factors. Dominic is safe and has a positive relationship with his mother, who appears to be nurturing. Still, there are some safety concerns, rooted in middle-class standards, that led to the initial child protective services report. This has contributed to some instability for him and his family. The primary risk factor impacting Dominic's stability is poverty. Without resources for childcare, Dominic's mother chose to leave her son home alone. Another risk factor is Dominic's mental health and behavioral issues. Caring for a child with high needs strains parents and increases parenting stress. Finally, Dominic's mother is likely suffering from undiagnosed mental health issues. In fact, she was seeking help for her symptoms when Dominic was left alone.

Theoretical Explanations. From a mujerismo perspective, we might theorize that Daniela's parents judge her for not conforming to more traditional gender roles such as being married, only having children within the context of marriage, and raising her children with a partner so that she does not have to work. These conflicts may contribute to stress within the extended family and may also be exacerbated by issues of acculturation.

Audriana

Risk Factors. Audriana's family lacked the financial means to find housing for just their family unit. Due to the lack of affordable housing and their undocumented status, they had to live with a step-uncle in crowded living conditions. Audriana and her mother had a distant and conflictual relationship because of her own history of trauma. Audriana's behavior changes, including doing poorly in school and withdrawing from activities, are an additional risk factor that contributed to the emotional and physical abuse from her parents following the sexual abuse by her uncle.

Theoretical Explanations. Audriana's mother's choice can be examined within the context of intersectionality and mujerismo theory. Her mother has no resources for housing and likely, no funds to support all the children outside of the step-uncle's home. Historically, women have been blamed and shamed for abuse experienced at the hands of male perpetrators. Both Audriana and her mother are trapped in the same patriarchal society that punishes Audriana and her sister by placing them in foster care without offering her resources to help her, continuing the cycle of oppression.

Closing Summary

Based on the extant literature, Latinx families are not overrepresented in the child welfare system. Nonetheless, Latinx families face unique challenges that impact the occurrence of child maltreatment as well as how it is perceived and managed by the child welfare system. The presence of child maltreatment in the Latinx community may be understood from the perspective of risk factors and theories that speak to the safety, stability, and nurturing within Latinx families. Still, much remains to be learned about the epidemiology of child abuse and neglect in the Latinx population. The next chapter explores trauma and its relationship to maltreatment among Latinx children.

3

Trauma and Its Impact on Latinx Families

> At the end of the day, we can endure
> much more than we think we can.
> —Frida Kahlo

In this chapter, we explore trauma and its impact on Latinx families. We start with a general discussion of trauma and how it impacts individuals, families, and communities. Next, we explore complex trauma and its impact on individual functioning, taking into consideration cultural issues relevant to the Latinx community. We then explain how trauma impacts children and their parents. To conclude, we explore how child welfare practices and policies may promote an antiracist and trauma-informed culture.

Trauma and Child Maltreatment

The discussion of trauma as related to Latinx child maltreatment is important for two primary reasons. First, trauma impacts parenting. As we will discuss, a parent's own history of traumatic experiences may influence their parenting decisions, discipline strategies, and/or attachment with their child (Fonagy et al., 1993; Grand & Salberg, 2021). From a practical perspective, child welfare professionals may be able to prevent maltreatment and/or avoid the removal of a child if they understand the trauma history of the parent and seek help for the parent. Second, trauma impacts child behavior, which can increase the likelihood of maltreatment and entry into the foster care system. As we will discuss, children who have experienced trauma, maltreatment or otherwise, may have troubling behaviors that increase parenting stress. Additionally, we discuss trauma because many Latinx families experience trauma related to migration, transnational families, and structural inequality in the United States, with implications for family functioning and child safety, stability, and nurturing.

Trauma

Trauma is an emotional response "to an event, series of events, or set of circumstances that is experienced by an individual as physically or emotionally harmful or life threatening" (Substance Abuse and Mental Health Services Administration, 2014, p. 7). Trauma can occur at any point in a person's life. Thus, not all trauma stems from child maltreatment, but all child maltreatment can be traumatic. Furthermore, trauma can occur individually or collectively among families, groups, or communities. Every individual experiences trauma differently, with biological, social, and cultural influences impacting how trauma is experienced.

Contemporary conversations about trauma stemmed from early efforts to understand the experiences of veterans of wars (Van der Kolk, 2015). Attention to trauma slowly grew as the women's movement highlighted parallels between veterans' behaviors and survivors of domestic and sexual violence (Herman, 1992). In the 1990s, the Adverse Childhood Experiences (ACE) study was conducted, and the first findings from that study connected exposure to adversity in childhood to physical health outcomes as adults (Hamby et al., 2021). The ACE study asked participants to indicate whether they had experienced any of seven forms of childhood trauma: psychological abuse, physical abuse, sexual abuse, substance use in home, mental illness in the home, domestic violence (mother treated violently), or parent incarceration (Felitti et al., 1998). The study showed a strong link between the number of adversities a person had experienced in childhood and the likelihood that the person would smoke, have heart disease, use drugs, or have cancer, diabetes, or a stroke (Felitti et al., 1998).

The ACE study elevated the importance of incorporating trauma-informed practices into medical, behavioral, and social services by linking trauma to health conditions (Hamby et al., 2021). While attention to childhood adversity is clearly warranted, several cautions have been identified by scholars (Kelly-Irving & Delpierre, 2019). The ACE questionnaire, as an assessment tool, is not an exhaustive list of childhood adversity, and exposure to some ACEs may not constitute trauma in all individuals. It is important to explore the types of events and circumstances that individuals may feel are life threatening. Moreover, events differ in severity and chronicity. Traumatic events can be one-time or acute experiences such as sexual assault victimization, surviving a natural disaster, or surviving a car accident. Trauma can also be prolonged or chronic. Chronic trauma can include ongoing sexual abuse, regularly witnessing violence in the home, or living in a war zone.

Complex trauma refers to chronic and/or severe events that impact a child's attachment, trust, and personality development over time (Van der Kolk, 2015). Depending on the context, complex trauma is also used to describe outcomes that occur due to the repeated exposure to traumatic events (Kliethermes et al., 2014). Complex trauma has been shown to emerge from abuse or profound neglect (Wamser-Nanney & Vandenberg, 2013). These events usually begin early in life and disrupt many aspects of the child's development, including the child's self-concept. Since they often occur in the context of the child's relationship with a caregiver, traumatic experiences can interfere with the child's ability to form a secure attachment bond. Many aspects of a child's healthy physical and mental development rely on a healthy attachment with a caregiver (Perry et al., 1995). Additionally, some developmental periods are marked by periods of brain growth during which trauma can disrupt regulation and the formation of self-identity (Resick et al., 2012).

The impact of complex trauma has also been explored in the context of families across generations. Some of the earliest research examined the impact of large historical events on multiple generations, including the Holocaust (Laub & Hamburger, 2017), enslavement (Graff, 2014), and genocide of Native Americans (Grand, 2018). Among Latinx families, particularly Afro-Latinx families, it is also important to consider how structural violence and oppression may evoke trauma across entire communities. *Historical trauma* refers to the impact of "colonization, cultural suppression, and historical oppression" and has been widely applied to Black and Native American families (Kirmayer et al., 2014, p. 299). In immigrant families, historical trauma may also be related to political violence and migration stressors (Cerdeña et al., 2021).

In parallel, *collective trauma* refers to trauma that an entire group of people experiences, such as a natural disaster, and that produces loss of community, disrupted connections to one's surroundings, and "a sense of separation from other people, difficulty caring for others and loss of a meaningful connection with the self" (Krieg, 2009, p. 29). U.S. immigration policy sometimes recognizes the impact of collective trauma and provides relief through temporary protected status (TPS). As previously noted, TPS allows individuals to work in the United States but does not offer a path to permanent residence or citizenship. As of 2021, four of the twelve countries whose citizens qualify for TPS are Latin American countries: El Salvador, Honduras, Nicaragua, and Venezuela. Because of destructive earthquakes, El Salvadorans were granted TPS in 2001 (Federal Register, 2001). Both Hondurans and Nicaraguans were granted TPS in 2001 due to destruction and flooding caused by Hurricane Mitch (Federal Register, 1999; Federal Register, 1999). Most recently, Venezuelans were given TPS due to a severe economic crisis (Federal Register, 2021). Each of the events leading to TPS designation represents a collective trauma. Another example of a collective trauma is the fear immigrants have had during and from multiple presidential administration's aggressive detainment and deportation protocols (Gramlich, 2020). Over time, collective trauma can lead to mistrust, violence, intergenerational conflict, role diffusion, leadership crisis, and even cultural genocide (Chamberlain et al., 2019).

Contextual Considerations. The experiences and impact of trauma may vary based on race and ethnicity. Some research has found that Latinx children (Felitti et al., 1998; Maguire-Jack et al., 2020) and adults (Maguire-Jack et al., 2020) may experience more ACEs than White individuals. Using a subsample from the National Survey of Children's Health 2016 data, Maguire-Jack and colleagues found that among Latinx children, 51.4 percent have experienced at least one adverse childhood experience compared with 40.9 percent of White children who experienced at least one adverse childhood experience (Maguire-Jack et al., 2020). Despite these high rates, measures of adverse childhood experiences and trauma rarely include experiences faced by

Latinx families, such as discrimination or migration-related trauma (LaBrenz et al., 2020). In this section, we explore adversities that may be shared across generations of Latinx communities, including colonialization and exploitation, migration, transnational families, and structural inequality.

Colonialization and Exploitation

The history of the Latinx population includes colonialization both in the United States and in their home countries. Latin America was largely colonized by Spain or Portugal in the 1500s. Indigenous communities sustained loss of land, exploitation of natural resources, enslavement, violence, and genocide (Gabbert, 2012). In the early 1800s, after years of oppression and rebellion, Latin America gained independence from Spain and Portugal and organized into republics. However, instability has continued to characterize the region, partly because of U.S. intervention (Blanco & Grier, 2009).

Colonialization in the United States involved the taking of land from Mexico and the establishment of the international border between Mexico and United States in the mid-1800s (St. John, 2011). When the border was first established, it was an unmarked line in the desert or the Rio Grande River. There were no restrictions in crossing, and movement across the border was fluid. Expansion of ranching, mining, railroads, and other industrial pursuits created binational communities and families (St. John, 2011). Those communities have since been disrupted through border regulation, and families have been forced to exist across borders or risk migrating to the United States (Hamilton & Hale, 2016).

Migration

Trauma from migration is also a part of the lives of Latinx children, parents, grandparents, and ancestors. Migration may occur for a number of reasons. According to the push-pull theory (Lee, 1966), migration is motivated by push factors such as poverty, lack of opportunities in the home country, or natural disasters. Pull factors attract migrants to a specific destination and include better work, education opportunities, or reunification with family members. For example, migration from Mexico generally follows patterns of peaks in the U.S. economy and growth in the labor market (Passel & Suro, 2005). For Mexicans entering the United States without legal authorization, immigration laws are often selectively ignored to meet labor demands and then used to expel migrants from the country (Gutiérrez, 2019). In contrast, forced migration occurs when individuals must leave their home country due to violence, human rights abuses, or political persecution (Clauss-Ehlers, 2019). Forced migration may also occur when individuals are trafficked into another country and forced to work. Forced migration often has different legal remedies for migrants in that international law requires that those fleeing persecution not be returned to their home countries (Clauss-Ehlers, 2019). In the United States, international trafficking survivors are also entitled to protection not afforded to other migrants (Beale, 2018).

Regardless of the impetus, the migration process, inclusive of the pre-migration, migration, and post-migration phases, may be traumatic. The pre-migration phase is defined by conditions in the home country and departure from the home country, the migration phase is defined by experiences after leaving the home country and before arriving in the receiving country, and the post-migration phase is defined by the conditions in the receiving country (Erdal & Oeppen, 2017). Thus, trauma may unfold in the context of the sociopolitical historical circumstances of the home country and/or the receiving country.

During the 1970s and early 1980s, the U.S. government funded terrorist organizations throughout Latin America to destabilize left-leaning governments and promote U.S. economic interests (Chomsky, 2015). U.S. interventions in Latin America have fueled political instability, which in turn has resulted in mass migration (Rodil, 2019). For example, forced migration from the Northern Triangle countries of El Salvador, Guatemala, and Honduras resulted in a substantial number of migrants entering the United States (Smith, 2020). Scholars attribute this migration to U.S. intervention as well as to the transnational drug trade, which is centered in the Northern Triangle (Smith, 2020). As a result of drug-related gang violence, the region is considered one of the most violent areas in the world outside of war zones (United Nations High Commissioner for Refugees [UNHCR], 2019). The violence, coupled with poverty and lack of resources, pushes many individuals to leave. The trauma of living in an environment that is so unstable and threatening impacts parents and children. Departing the home country is also a potential source of trauma. With forced migration, the decision to leave may be very sudden, and individuals may not be able to speak to family members before leaving (Clauss-Ehlers, 2019).

For Latinx families who have resources and connections, the actual journey to the United States is likely to be safe (e.g., a plane ride). However, migrants who are forced to leave their country often endure more tenuous journeys. Forced migration often requires individuals to use multiple forms of transportation including walking, buses, car rides, boats, or riding on top of trains to pass through Mexico in order to reach the United States (Vega, 2021). Given the journey, migrants are restricted in bringing only what can be carried (Clauss-Ehlers, 2019). The journey might be interrupted as migrants stop to work, deal with Mexican immigration officials, and/or receive shelter (Vega, 2021). The journey is often navigated by a paid guide, or coyote, particularly when travelers reach the U.S. border (Clauss-Ehlers, 2019).

Along the journey, migrants may encounter situations that threaten their lives or the lives of those around them, including lack of medical attention, unsanitary conditions, lack of food and safe drinking water, gangs, environmental hazards, and corrupt government officials (Fernandez, 2019). The likelihood of experiencing violence is high, and women face the risk of sexual assault and kidnapping (Angulo-Pasel, 2018). Estimates suggest that up to 80 percent of women are raped while migrating through Mexico (Bonello & McIntyre, 2014). Children traveling alone are also at a high risk of victimization (DeLuca et al., 2008).

Once migrants reach the U.S. border, they are faced with the uncertainty of what might happen to them. They can choose to present themselves at the border or cross the border without authorization. Coyotes that bring unauthorized migrants across borders are known to abandon groups in deserts (DeLuca et al., 2008). Other migrants who cross by water may drown. For those migrants who present themselves to border patrol or who are apprehended, there are a host of additional stressors that may be traumatic, including border patrol detention, the threat of deportation, the threat of being separated from family, and/or prolonged detention within the United States. Changing policies make it difficult to predict how migrants will be received.

Once in the United States, Latinx individuals may settle in an unwelcoming receiving community where they may experience xenophobia, discrimination, and scapegoating (Quesada et al., 2011). Anti-immigrant rhetoric depicts the Latinx population as a threat (Caraballo, 2020). Additionally, many migrants settle in high-poverty communities with limited resources and economic opportunities. Opportunities may be further limited for migrants who face language barriers, particularly for those who speak an Indigenous language. Acculturative stress, including experiences of isolation and discrimination, are also common. The process of acculturation will include adjustments to new social norms, school systems, and legal processes. Migrants who enter the country without authorization or who have expired visas will have to live "in the shadows" to avoid potential deportation (Cardoso et al., 2018).

Transnational Families

Transnational families are those families who have members living in different countries (Mazzucato & Schans, 2011). Traditionally, transnational families have been viewed as a temporary family structure because the goal of the family would be to reunite in the home or host country. However, restrictive migration policies have forced more transnational families into permanent situations as family members are not able to move as easily across borders (Mazzucato & Schans, 2011). Particularly in cases of forced migration, migrants depart their home country knowing that they may never see certain family members again. Although there are no official governmental estimates or estimates using nationally representative samples, one research study examined demographic data in Latin American countries and found that 7 percent to 21 percent of children live in transnational families due to parental migration (DeWaard et al., 2018).

Parents who migrate without their families often send funds, known as remittances, back to their home countries and children benefit from this financial support (Abrego & LaRossa, 2009). But family separation significantly impacts the parent-child relationship, and children may experience emotional trauma from the separation (Suárez-Orozco et al., 2002). Some research suggests that children separated from their mothers, specifically, have more emotional trauma (Dreby, 2012). Despite the (valid) reasons for the migration of their parents, children may feel abandoned and may develop behavior problems (Dreby, 2012). Even if parents are reunited with their children at a later time, problems may persist. Reunited parents may also have difficulties establishing authority after an extended separation.

Structural Inequality

As previously discussed in chapter 1, Latinx populations in the United States are subjected to various forms of oppression due to their nativity, language, race, and/or gender. Structural inequities result from the disadvantages that groups face because of this oppression (Baciu et al., 2017). Structural inequality limits Latinx families from building protective factors that can buffer effects of trauma. Structural inequality may also be a source of trauma and/or a factor that intensifies the impact of trauma (Williams et al., 2018).

Structural inequities are so deeply embedded in systems that they are not easily observed or addressed. They exist within education, employment, housing, public safety, legal, and transportation sectors. Although these systems exist to promote well-being and can be protective factors against child maltreatment, Latinx families are often structurally excluded. In the domain of education, compared with White students, Latinx students have lower achievement scores, lower high school graduation rates, and lower college enrollment and retention rates (Jang, 2019). This disparity reflects the systemic ways in which socioeconomic status, immigrant status, and primary language impact access to quality schools and educational resources. Within the school system, Latinx youth are also more likely to receive disciplinary referrals (Mitchell et al., 2020). Subsequently, Latinx youth are more likely to have contact with the police, be detained, be formally charged, and be confined longer (Piquero, 2008). Latinx adults are also imprisoned at a higher rate than White adults (Nellis, 2016). The inequities seen in discipline, policing, and imprisonment mirror the reported cases of child maltreatment for Latinx children (Edwards, 2019). In terms of housing, Latinx individuals are less likely to own homes, and when they do, the values of their homes are lower than those of their White counterparts (Squires, 2007). Latinx families who do not own property face challenges in locating housing that is safe, affordable, and easily accessible by public transportation (Ramirez et al., 2019). Immigration status may further limit access to public assistance and health-care programs; immigrants may be unable to rent housing, obtain state identification, work in safe conditions, or ensure that their wages are paid fairly.

The Impact of Trauma on Children

The neuroscience explaining the impact of trauma on the brain is complex and beyond the scope of this book. Briefly, the brain is conceptualized as having four major components: the brainstem, the diencephalon, the limbic, and the cortex (Perry, 2001). The brainstem is responsible for regulating body temperature and heart and lung functions; the diencephalon regulates arousal, sleep, and movement; the limbic area regulates reward, memory, bonding, and emotions; and the cortex regulates higher level thinking and functioning. The brain develops with age, as children are exposed to environmental stimuli that lead to the formation of neural connections (Perry et al., 1995).

Humans receive and process information starting with the most primitive parts of the brain, or the "downstairs" brain (i.e., the brainstem and diencephalon). If the downstairs brain determines that the external stimuli are safe, information is processed by higher levels of the brain. However, if the external stimuli are perceived as a threat, information never reaches the developing limbic and cortex areas. In children who are consistently exposed to threats, those systems that help regulate emotions and thinking remain underdeveloped. Essentially, living in a state of prolonged fear and stress changes brain development; thus, children who are victims of complex trauma often experience problems regulating their emotions and thinking. For a more thorough discussion on the neuroscience of trauma, the reader is directed to Perry et al. (1995).

The behaviors associated with trauma vary greatly and often are related to the developmental period in which the trauma occurred and the type of trauma. For example, research has shown that the stress surrounding domestic violence impacts infants who do not understand what is happening (DeJonghe et al., 2005). These infants may be hypervigilant and unable to attach to caregivers. In preschool children who have experienced violence, trauma may cause increased separation anxiety with caregivers, regression in skills that have previously been mastered (e.g., toileting), increased distress that is manifested through whining and irritability, unexplained angry outbursts, withdrawal from play, and/or not meeting major developmental milestones (National Child Traumatic Stress Network, 2008). Elementary-age children may also express distrust of adults, misread social cues, and overreact to authority and criticism (National Child

Traumatic Stress Network, 2008). At this age, behaviors associated with trauma might be misdiagnosed as ADHD or oppositional disorder because the reactive behaviors, lack of ability to focus, and sensitivity to stimuli may mimic symptoms of those disorders (Dye, 2018). In adolescence, trauma responses might include substance use, suicidal thoughts, difficulty with authority figures, and emotional numbing (National Child Traumatic Stress Network, 2008). None of these behaviors is, in and of themselves, a sign that a child has experienced trauma. Instead, patterns of behaviors or sudden changes in behaviors warrant further exploration and observation.

Challenging behaviors associated with trauma increase parenting stress (Crouch et al., 2019). Parenting stress generally peaks when the child's needs exceed the parent's capacity to meet those needs. Higher levels of parenting stress may result in more chaotic households where child maltreatment is more likely to occur (Gonzalez & MacMillan, 2008). Thus, parents need assistance with understanding trauma and enhancing skills to meet the needs of children who have experienced trauma (Crouch et al., 2019).

Parenting after Trauma

When discussing child maltreatment and trauma, many advocates and practitioners focus solely on children and their outcomes. For example, there are calls for screening children for adverse childhood experiences in pediatric settings (Barnes et al., 2020). However, to prevent child maltreatment, the focus should broaden to include the parents' history of trauma. Although it is not inevitable that parents who experienced trauma will maltreat their own children, traumatic experiences impact the health and well-being of parents and their skills and capacity related to parenting. Sometimes referred to as "ghosts in the nursery," the intergenerational transmission of trauma centers on the parents' childhood experiences and how those experiences impact their relationship with their child (Fonagy et al., 1993).

At its core, trauma impacts a parent's ability to provide consistent caregiving to create a secure environment for the child's neurodevelopment. As described above, trauma elicits a stress response from the body that can shut down the body's ability to engage in high-level cognitive reasoning. Traumatized parents may present as preoccupied, hypervigilant, or as dismissive and detached with their child. More generally, parents may feel that they lack parenting knowledge and supportive relationships and may have a negative sense of self-worth. Attachment theory is most frequently used to study the impact of the parent's history of trauma on parenting, as the ongoing impacts of trauma might decrease the ability of a parent to provide consistent nurturing to their children (Chamberlain et al., 2019). Infants may display disorganized or insecure attachment, particularly if parents have not been able to process their trauma (Chamberlain et al., 2019).

Within Latinx families, parents and children may experience trauma together due to migration, structural inequality, and/or living within a transnational family. When children experience trauma, the impact may be mitigated by the reaction and support they receive from their parents. Positive interactions between children and parents enable children to develop resilience. However, parents who have experienced trauma may be less likely to provide the needed relational support for children.

Resilience and Post-Traumatic Growth

While it is critical to understand behaviors linked to trauma, it is equally critical to understand that trauma does not predestine negative outcomes. There is substantial research examining resilience and post-traumatic growth that suggests individuals can heal and thrive from adversity (Infurna & Jayawickreme, 2019). Resilience refers to an individual's ability to return to a healthy level of functioning after experiencing adversity (Bonanno & Diminich, 2013). Post-traumatic growth is similar conceptually, but refers to a trajectory of increased functioning after a traumatic event that is characterized by improved relationships with others, embracing new possibilities, believing in personal strength, spiritual growth, and appreciation of life (Tedeschi & Calhoun, 1996). In considering child maltreatment prevention, helping parents build resilience and find opportunities for post-traumatic growth is essential. Parents who have experienced trauma report a need for nonjudgmental support to address their mental health and abilities to form trusting relationships (Chamberlain et al., 2019). However, there are few parenting interventions that address the parent's history of trauma. Chapters 5 and 6 focus on interventions that prevent maltreatment or provide support to families who have already experienced maltreatment, while chapter 7 provides a more thorough discussion on resiliency.

Case Illustrations

Trauma is evident in the case histories of Bianca, Dominic, and Audriana, as discussed below. We encourage you to reflect on the myriad impacts of trauma on each child and parent in these cases. We further challenge you to consider how the child welfare system served as a source of healing or alternately exacerbated the effects of trauma on these families.

Bianca

Child Trauma. Bianca's early life in Mexico seems healthy. During that time, she had strong and healthy attachments to her mother and maternal grandmother. Even though the family had few financial resources, there is no indication that her needs were not met. At age four, Bianca migrated to the United States with her mother. Bianca was essentially kidnapped by a coyote who held her until her family could meet his payment demands. Bianca then witnessed her father murder a coyote. Once she began the Head Start program in Arizona, she displayed intense separation anxiety from her mother, which likely stems from this experience. Her mother's engagement and responsiveness to the separation anxiety likely mitigated some of the impact of the trauma Bianca experienced. Later, Bianca witnessed domestic violence perpetuated by her father, and her behaviors at school became more dysregulated. She eventually witnessed her father assault her mother, leading to her placement in a foster home. These experiences undoubtedly serve to exacerbate her separation anxiety.

Parent Trauma. We know little about Bianca's mother's childhood except that she became a mother at a young age and was separated from her partner when she gave birth. Based on her care and attachment to Bianca, there is no reason to believe that she was not cared for as a child. Along with Bianca, her mother experienced the fear and trauma related to their migration and witnessing her partner murder a coyote. She later became a victim of domestic violence by her partner and experienced the separation from her child due to her hospitalization. Still, she engages in nurturing parenting behaviors, and with the right supports, she would likely be able to continue to take care of Bianca.

Dominic

Child Trauma. Dominic had a positive relationship with his half sister's father, but he lost this father figure. He also witnessed his mother get assaulted when she ended her relationship with the half sister's father. Dominic has also been present during a number of heated arguments between his mother and grandparents. It's possible that these events have contributed to Dominic's disruptive behavior problems, something that a mental health professional could explore. Regardless of his behavior, Daniela has demonstrated protective parenting behaviors such as engaging with the school, using behavior modification techniques that she has learned through work, and seeking out help for her own wellness.

Parent Trauma. Daniela experienced domestic violence committed by her daughter's father after she confronted him about his drug use. There are also sources of stress in her life that, although not necessarily traumatic, appear to be causing parenting stress. As a young mother, she lacks certain resources such as childcare, and she has a strained relationship with her own parents. The increased parenting stress may be impacting her physical and mental health. On a positive note, Daniela has sought help for herself.

Audriana

Child Trauma. Before Audriana was born, her father was murdered and her pregnant mother migrated to the United States. We may expect that prenatal stress impacted the developing fetus (Tsao et al., 2019). Later, her mother's depression interfered with the mother-child attachment. When she was older, Audriana was sexually abused by her uncle. The abuse was ongoing, but Audriana was too scared to talk to her mother. Audriana's behavior changes at age fifteen suggest a trauma response; she became withdrawn and disengaged. When the abuse was disclosed, she was physically and verbally abused. Finally, when Audriana's mother had the choice to move in order to keep their family together, she chose to let Audriana enter foster care.

Parent Trauma. Audriana's mother has also experienced trauma. Her husband was murdered and she received death threats. Feeling unsafe, she migrated to the United States while pregnant and with a toddler. During her journey to the United States, she was sexually assaulted. When Audriana and her sister disclosed that they had been sexually abused, Audriana's mother had to choose between secure housing and losing her daughters to foster care. Without affordable housing options, she was separated from two of her children.

Closing Summary

We began this chapter by discussing the importance of trauma in relation to child maltreatment. We postulated that trauma impacts parenting because the parent's own history of trauma may inhibit their well-being and their ability to care for and nurture their child. Children who experience trauma may display challenging behaviors that increase parenting stress and the likelihood of maltreatment. Although there are familiar patterns of behavior for parents and children who have experienced trauma, each family and individual experiences trauma differently. For Latinx families, migration, histories of colonialization, and structural inequality introduce likely sources of trauma that should also be considered when assessing the needs of a child and family. In the next chapter, we provide an examination of the empirical literature on parenting, including discipline practices such as spanking, in Latinx families.

4

Parenting and Discipline in Latinx Families

> She discovered with great delight
> that one does not love one's children
> just because they are one's children
> but because of the friendship
> formed while raising them.
> —Gabriel Garcia Marquez

In U.S. society, we expect that the adult(s) designated as the legal custodian(s) of a child ensure that their basic physical and emotional needs are met; when they are not, the designated adult (typically, the parent) is held socially and criminally responsible. This is the case despite a wealth of evidence that child maltreatment reflects the confluence of a number of socioecological factors, none of which in themselves are necessary or sufficient to cause abuse or neglect (Belsky, 1993; Sturge-Apple et al., 2019). In other words, even though parents are embedded in a web of systems that may impede their ability to provide safety, stability, and nurturance to their child, our society considers parenting at the crux of child welfare issues. There are a number of reasons for this explicit focus on parenting; parents are arguably the most proximal influence on a child, the most invested in the welfare of that child, and, with adequate supports, can modify their approach to parenting to better ensure the well-being of the child. Interventions that promote effective and positive parenting are, indeed, associated with reduced risk of child maltreatment (Kaminski et al., 2008). Thus, the present chapter explores the theoretical and empirical literature on parenting as it relates to child maltreatment, with consideration of the unique social and cultural characteristics of Latinx families.

Parenting in Latinx Populations

Broadly speaking, parenting comprises two primary dimensions: parental responsiveness (i.e., nurturance, acceptance, warmth) and demandingness (i.e., expectations, control, discipline) (Maccoby & Martin, 1983). Responsiveness helps to ensure that a child's needs are met, as parents attend to a child's cues for physical and emotional care. Demandingness promotes developmental growth, as parents encourage and support a child in learning new skills and regulating their behavior and emotions. The way in which demandingness and responsiveness co-occur is indicative of a parenting style: authoritative parents are highly responsive and also demanding, whereas authoritarian parents are low in responsiveness but highly demanding. An important component of parental demandingness is discipline, or the strategies that parents use to correct (mis)behavior. An authoritative approach to discipline includes scaffolding for the sake of fostering growth in the child's social, emotional, and behavioral regulation skills, whereas an authoritarian approach does not attend to the child's need for support in meeting a given demand. In the parenting literature, authoritative parenting has long been considered optimal, and authoritarian parenting maladaptive, conclusions that are broadly supported through empirical studies (Pinquart & Kauser, 2018). Many scholars question the cross-cultural generalizability of past research though, noting that parenting may manifest and impact children differently across cultures (Khaleque & Rohner, 2012).

With Latinx parents, the extant research on parenting styles and child outcomes is inconclusive. Some studies suggest that although parents tend to be authoritarian, their children do not appear to be impacted negatively by this parenting approach (Hillstrom, 2009; Moon et al., 2009; Manongdo & Ramirez Garcia, 2011). Others find Latinx parents to be authoritative, with positive effects on child development (Carlo et al., 2018; Pong et al., 2005; De Von Figueroa-Mosely et al., 2006; Mistry et al., 2010; Driscoll et al., 2008; Merianos et al., 2015). Our own work indicates a more nuanced picture; across a number of longitudinal studies with Latina mothers of young children, we found that although most mothers described themselves as both highly responsive and highly demanding, this authoritative approach was unrelated to child outcomes. Authoritarian parenting, while less common, was associated with negative child outcomes, but only in some domains and only concurrently, not over time (Calzada et al., 2012; Calzada et al., 2017; Calzada et al., 2019). Taken together, the literature to date suggests that the influence of parenting styles may in fact vary across developmental outcomes, time points, and contexts, and that the categorization of authoritarian parenting as a definitive risk factor and authoritative parenting as protective for Latinx children may be premature.

This caution is consistent with current theories that emphasize the dynamic nature of child development, especially for families dealing with social inequalities. As previously discussed, the context in which parenting and child development unfolds is inextricably tied to race, social class, ethnicity, and gender (i.e., their social positionality) (Coll et al., 1996). Parents experience increased and chronic stress when faced with social marginalization, which compromises parental health and positive parenting. At the same time, parents find ways to best protect their children from oppressive forces—for example, by socializing children how to interact with police or immigration authorities. The reality that White children do not need to be socialized on how to appear nonthreatening to police illustrates the unique demands placed on parents as a function of racism. In fact, some scholars argue that even the application of the authoritarian-authoritative typology, which was developed with predominantly White, socioeconomically privileged families (Baumrind, 1966), may be problematic (Ceballo et al., 2012; Domenech-Rodriguez et al., 2009). One proposed solution is to focus on specific manifestations of parental responsiveness and demandingness like warmth and discipline.

Disciplinary Practices

Perhaps the most relevant, and debated, question regarding parenting and child maltreatment is the perceived reliance on harsh disciplinary practices within Latinx (and other non-White) communities. Harsh discipline includes the use of any verbal or physical strategy that is intended to elicit obedience or modify child (mis)behavior through fear, such as yelling, threatening, and spanking (i.e., hitting a child with an open palm). The use of spanking has drawn the most scholarly attention. Indeed, although spanking is distinguishable from abuse in that it is noninjurious, it serves as a risk factor for physical abuse; using the Fragile Families and Child Wellbeing sample, Lee et al. (2014) found that after controlling for maternal depression, education, and family income, spanking in the first year of life was associated with a 36 percent greater possibility of involvement in the child welfare system by the time the child was five years old. Nonetheless, spanking appears to be highly prevalent in the United States. According to data from the National Survey of Children Exposed to Violence (NSCEV), approximately half of all children in the United States under the age of nine are spanked, with the highest rates (65%) among four- and five-year-olds (Finkelhor et al., 2019). Similarly, a 2015 survey by the Pew Research Center (2015) found that 47 percent of all parents with children in the home (e.g., 0–18) reported spanking.

In both the Pew survey and the NSCEV, Black parents reported more spanking than White or Latinx parents, a pattern that has been replicated in other studies (Grogan-Kaylor & Otis, 2007; Silveiria et al., 2020). Retrospective reports with a nationally representative adult sample found a similar pattern: 18 percent of Latinx respondents reported experiencing harsh physical punishment, compared with 21 percent of Black and 17 percent of White respondents (Taillieu et al., 2014). Most studies show no significant differences in the prevalence of spanking between Latinx and White parents, and some evidence suggests less harsh parenting overall. For example, Silveiria et al. (2020) showed that while spanking rates were similar between White and Latinx parents in the Early Childhood Longitudinal Study-Kindergarten, Latinx (and Black) parents were significantly less likely to yell than White parents (Silveiria et al., 2020). Berlin et al. (2009) found that controlling for poverty, Latinx mothers of toddlers were less likely to spank than Black *or* White mothers. On the whole, though, a considerable majority of all U.S. parents appear to find spanking acceptable, and about half discipline their children by spanking at least on occasion and especially when their children are younger.

Spanking from a Sociocultural Perspective. The focus on spanking by child welfare scholars, practitioners, and policy makers centers on two primary concerns: spanking compromises healthy child development, and spanking is a risk factor for physical abuse. Proponents of the anti-spanking movement note that besides being ineffective in correcting child misbehavior (thus serving no purpose), spanking should be conceptualized along the continuum of family violence because (1) it has the same deleterious effects as physical abuse, albeit less severe, and (2) it can escalate to physical abuse (Grogan-Kaylor et al., 2018). Research shows that when parents and children engage in coercive exchanges, the aversive behavior of each (i.e., misbehavior of children; harsh reaction of parents) escalates in the moment and over time, increasing the risk that these exchanges reach the point of verbal or physical violence especially if this is a well-established pattern for the dyad (Patterson, 1982). In response to these arguments, and emphasizing a robust empirical literature documenting the association between spanking and negative academic, social, emotional, and behavioral child outcomes, the American Academy of Pediatrics, the American Psychological Association, and the United Nations' Committee on the Rights of the Child have issued blanket statements discouraging the use of spanking by parents (American Psychological Association, 2019; Sege et al., 2018). Nonetheless, the debate over spanking remains unresolved as a number of scholars caution against overgeneralizing past findings, maintaining that there is evidence of spanking as an effective form of discipline with no clear negative or only minimal impact on child development (Larzelere et al., 2010; Larzelere & Kuhn, 2005; Ferguson, 2013). Most noted are the problematic reliance on cross-sectional data, which limits inferences regarding causality, and the lack of consideration for sociocultural factors, which limits inferences regarding generalizability.

Cultural Norms. Theoretically, the degree to which spanking is perceived as normative within a cultural context, and thus as fair and reasonable, influences both its prevalence and its impact on child developmental outcomes (Lansford et al., 2005). A large cross-national study showed that parents who believe spanking to be necessary were more likely to use corporal punishment (i.e., spank, hit, slap, shake, beat), and that changes in beliefs were related to changes in behaviors (Lansford et al., 2015). Drawing from the same sample, researchers found that while spanking and yelling were associated with negative developmental outcomes regardless of context, impact was mitigated when children perceived these practices to be normative (Gershoff et al., 2010).

Discipline is rooted in ideas about family and parent-child relationships. As previously discussed, Latinx culture espouses familismo, or the centrality of family, where family goals and needs are prioritized over those of individual family members (Sabogal et al., 1987). Underlying familismo is an obligation to reference (e.g., seek advice from, follow the example of) and support (e.g., emotionally, instrumentally) those within the family network. Strong family cohesion ensures close ties (Stein et al., 2014), and parent-child relationships are defined as hierarchical (Calzada et al., 2010). *Respeto*, which calls for unquestioning obedience and deference to adults and elders, serves to maintain these hierarchies and may be enforced through the normative and acceptable use of spanking (Calzada et al., 2013). Importantly, though, culture is dynamic and norms are situated in time and space (Bornstein, 2017), such that ideas about parenting and discipline vary accordingly.

Acculturation. Acculturation, or the adaptation to a new cultural setting (see chapter 1), is one force that leads to shifts in the parenting goals, values, and practices of immigrant populations (Calzada et al., 2010; Fuller & García Coll, 2010). Thus, Latinx who are more acculturated (e.g., English-speaking, less salient ethnic identity) may find the use of spanking and authoritarian parenting less culturally syntonic, as borne out in some studies (Dumka et al., 1997; Parke et al., 2004; Hill et al., 2003; Regalado et al., 2004). But a number of other studies show that foreign-born and Spanish-speaking Latina mothers use spanking and verbal punishment *less* frequently than more acculturated mothers (Altschul & Lee, 2011; Berlin et al., 2009; Taylor et al., 2009), and that "Hispanicism" is associated with more positive parenting and effective discipline (Santisteban et al., 2012). There are a number of explanations for these inconsistencies. First, acculturation is associated with higher levels of formal education, employment, and income (Cabassa, 2003), and this increased access to social and human capital generally lessens parents' reliance on spanking. Second, acculturation is not binary (i.e., acculturated/unacculturated), and many parents may select to preserve aspects of their culture of origin and mainstream culture in adapting to a new social milieu (Berry, 2015). For example, in a study of Mexican-origin parents and adolescents,

Kim et al. (2019) found that the majority of both mothers and fathers reported an integrated approach that emphasized Latinx and mainstream U.S. cultural values simultaneously. Third, acculturation has both costs and benefits. Individuals develop competencies to navigate mainstream culture (e.g., English language skills) and gain access to educational and occupational opportunities, but they may also lose protective aspects of their social connections and identity and become more exposed to structural and interpersonal racism.

Social Positionality. As described by critical race and intersectionality theories, social positionality depends on gender, race, ethnicity, immigrant status, and socioeconomic status. These identities intersect (i.e., every individual has a gender, race, ethnicity, immigrant status, and socioeconomic status) to determine individual experiences of privilege and oppression; the more nondominant identities held by an individual, the more oppression they face. Additionally, discrimination is directed at those with nondominant identities, and Latinx parents typically hold at least two marginalized identities (Latinx, racially non-White) and may hold others (female, poor, immigrant). Experiences of discrimination increase stress and erode health (Paradies et al., 2015), making parenting more challenging for Latinxs (Nomaguchi & House, 2013; Perreira et al., 2006).

At the same time, oppression, racism, and segregation lead parents to adapt their practices to the demands of these ecological forces. From this perspective, spanking and other forms of harsh discipline may be understood as adaptive, serving to secure child compliance in the face of stressors like community violence and unjust policing (Deater-Deckard et al., 2005). For Latinx parents who experience fears related to documentation status, strict and rigid behavioral restrictions of children's daily activities serve to keep family members safe from immigration authorities (Ayón & Garcia, 2019; Brabeck & Xu, 2010; Calzada et al., 2020; Gulbas & Zayas, 2017). However, even adaptive practices may be burdensome. Immigrant parents describe acting with restraint in communicating with their children about immigration histories and in disciplining their children for fear of coming to the attention of authorities; such restraints may weaken the parent-child relationship and undermine the parents' own authority (Parra Cardona et al., 2009; Zayas & Gulbas, 2017).

Empirical Findings. Recognizing that both culture and social position-ality define the parenting context, a number of studies have exam-ined the association between spanking and child outcomes across pan-racial/ethnic groups. Using data from the National Longitudinal Survey of Youth, McLoyd and Smith (2002) found that spanking predicted increases in child behavior problems similarly in Black, White, and Latinx children (i.e., there was no evidence of moderation by race/ethnicity). In a longitudinal study of urban families from twenty U.S. cities, Altschul et al. (2016) found the relation between spanking and child aggression was similar for Latinx and non-Latinx White children from infancy through age five. Using a nationally rep-resentative sample, Gershoff et al. (2012) found that spanking was associated with problem behaviors in both Latinx and non-Latinx kin-dergarteners. In contrast, Stacks et al. (2009) found that spanking at age twenty-four months predicted aggressive behavior at thirty-six months, but only in White—not Black or Latinx—children in the Early Head Start Research and Evaluation study. Barajas-Gonzales et al. (2018) found no association between the use of spanking and child internalizing and externalizing behavior one year later in a large urban sample of Latina mothers and their five-year-old children. Using the same sample, O'Gara et al. (2020) found that spanking was con-currently but not prospectively associated with child behavior prob-lems assessed through age six. In fact, spanking was associated with an increase in child misbehavior only when it was used consistently across time points (i.e., at child ages four, five, and six), suggesting that a "normative" use of spanking that is temporary and in response to specific child misbehaviors may not have long-term negative impacts on children.

Unanswered Questions. Although the extent to which contextual factors moderate associations between spanking and Latinx child development remains unclear from the empirical literature, a number of scholars and professional organizations maintain that spanking and other forms of physical discipline should be discouraged or banned (Afifi et al., 2017). From an ethical perspective, the use of any form of violence toward children should certainly be questioned and, to that end, encouraging the use of alternate forms of discipline is important. Nonetheless, we contend that more research is needed to understand the effects of spanking according to the various and unique ecological conditions of Latinx children. Until then, characterizing spanking as abusive reinforces unjust stereotypes of parents of color as violent and criminal, biases that have been shown to fuel systemic racism within child welfare systems. Since its inception, the child welfare system has been designed to maintain White supremacy, with racism embedded into its structures and policies (Dettlaff & Boyd, 2020). Implicit and explicit biases, specifically, play into the higher rates of referral, substantiation, and removal of children of color relative to White children (Drake et al., 2011; Rivaux et al., 2008). Additionally, perpetuating shame and stigma related to spanking in families and communities where it is culturally acceptable undermines trust of child welfare professionals and contributes to the underutilization of prevention and intervention services that promote alternative (i.e., nonphysical) disciplinary strategies. Finally, the intense focus on spanking and other harsh disciplinary practices fuels a deficit-oriented narrative that overshadows research demonstrating the high levels of responsiveness, nurturance, and warmth of Latinx parents.

Parental Responsiveness

Parental responsiveness encompasses both the awareness of a child's needs and the knowledge and skills to meet those needs in an appropriate and timely way. Consistent with attachment theory, parental responsiveness, nurturance, acceptance, and warmth are associated with better child outcomes across cultures (Khaleque & Rohner, 2012). For example, Rothenberg et al. (2020) found that parental warmth predicted child internalizing and externalizing behavior functioning in twelve samples from nine countries. With U.S. Latinx samples, responsiveness by mothers and fathers, uniquely, has been shown to protect against child mental health problems (Cabrera & Bradley, 2012; Eamon & Mulder, 2005; O'Gara et al., 2019; White et al., 2012; White et al., 2016). Because child mental health problems serve as a risk factor for child maltreatment, parental warmth may indirectly buffer children from risk of abuse and neglect. In addition, warmth and other indicators of responsiveness may buffer against the effects of harsh disciplinary practices, in that harsh discipline may not impact children's emotional or behavioral functioning when parents are also warm and nurturing (Germán et al., 2013). In a national sample that included Latinx families, McLoyd and Smith (2002) found no association between spanking and child behavior as long as mothers showed high emotional support (warmth, responsiveness); the authors speculated that children of supportive mothers interpret discipline as fair and just. A number of other studies, however, have failed to find evidence of moderation by parental warmth (Berlin et al., 2009; Lee et al., 2013; Stacks et al., 2009), possibly because those samples were of younger children who had limited cognitive capacity for such interpretations.

Similar to disciplinary practices, responsiveness is shaped by both culture and context. Consistent with the value of familismo, love, respect, and pride are seen as integral aspects of parenting (Perez-Brena et al., 2012). Parents prioritize communication and recreational time with their children for the sake of strengthening parent-child bonds (Ayón et al., 2015.; Bermúdez et al., 2014; Coltrane et al., 2004; Gonzales et al., 2011; Guilamo-Ramos et al., 2007; Romero & Ruiz, 2007). Warmth is expressed through physical and verbal affection (cariño) and verbal encouragement (Halgunseth & Ipsa, 2012). A number of empirical studies document high levels of physical affection, praise, and parent-child communication by Latinx mothers and fathers of children from early childhood through adolescence (e.g., Calzada & Eyberg, 2002; Calzada et al., 2012; Cabrera et al., 2011; Carlson & Harwood, 2003; Guilamo-Ramos et al., 2007; Perez-Brena et al., 2012; Rodríguez et al., 2014; Sotomayor-Peterson et al., 2012; Taylor & Behnke, 2005; Updegraff et al., 2009).

Some parents show low levels of responsiveness with their children due to contextual stressors. Research suggests that financial stress strains marital relationships, limits social support, and increases the risk of parental depression (Conger et al., 2010). In turn, parents who lack support and are depressed have limited capacity to respond to their children's needs (i.e., be emotionally or physically available to them). Lack of social support, as experienced by Latina mothers, has been linked to higher levels of punitive disciplinary practices (spanking, yelling) (Barajas-Gonzalez et al., 2018) and lower levels of positive parenting (Serrano-Villar et al., 2017). This framework, known as the Family Stress Model, has been tested with Latinx families, in some cases with acculturation stressors included as the exogenous variable, and findings have generally supported the hypothesized mechanisms (Calzada et al., 2019; Davis et al., 2020; Lorenzo-Blanco et al., 2017; White et al., 2009; White et al., 2015).

Belsky (1984; 1993; 2012) likewise theorizes about parenting in context, emphasizing the evolutionary adaptation of humans to the harshness and unpredictability of their environment. He argues that parents who live in challenging environments show lower levels of sensitivity to their offspring, in essence accelerating their independence for the sake of survival. Poverty, in particular, creates harsh and unpredictable environments for families, including the 57 percent of Latinx from families who face poverty or significant financial strain. As one example, neighborhood danger has been shown to compromise Mexican-American youth development by way of harsh parenting (White et al., 2009; 2013; 2015). Notwithstanding the psychological effects, poverty limits the tangible resources that parents are able to provide for their children. Parents need access to adequate housing, food security, health care, and educational, recreational, and occupational opportunities to be responsive to their children's needs. Indeed, child maltreatment prevention models highlight concrete support as one of five domains that allow parents to care for their children (MacLeod & Nelson, 2000).

Case Illustrations

In each of our cases, families were investigated by child protective services and had their children removed because the welfare of children is deemed the sole responsibility of the parent/legal guardian in the United States, except when they fail to meet this responsibility, in which case, the government intervenes. As we discuss discipline and parental responsiveness in each case, reflect on whether each parent was a "good" parent who should retain custody of their child.

Bianca

Discipline. Bianca's family does not disapprove of physical punishment, but they rarely used spanking as discipline. Bianca was spanked once in Mexico by her grandmother after she misbehaved in church. More typically, the adults in Bianca's life would raise their voices to indicate their disapproval. In the United States, Bianca's mother was encouraged to use time-outs, but Bianca's father felt time-outs were an Americanized discipline that was too lenient on children. Still, Bianca was raised primarily with nonphysical forms of punishment.

Parental Responsiveness. Bianca has strong attachments to her mother and grandmother. Since she was very young, her mother spent time with her teaching, playing, gardening, and sewing. In the United States, Bianca's mother was involved with her schooling and engaged with her teachers. In contrast, Bianca spent four years apart from her father and was never attached to him as a young child. Once in the United States, her father's work schedule prevented him from spending time with her. Given the trauma that the family experienced migrating, including her father's shooting of the coyote, Bianca feared her father and remained distant from him. Her father seemed to lack the knowledge and skill to engage with Bianca in ways that would foster a secure attachment with her.

Dominic

Discipline. Daniela, Dominic's mother, was raised in a large family where yelling and guilt induction were the primary means of discipline. There is no indication that her parents used physical discipline. With Dominic, Daniela does not yell or use guilt but instead relies on tools from her work as a day care teacher. It's possible that these parenting strategies are viewed as culturally incongruent by Dominic's grandparents and highlight how differential acculturation may impact parenting.

Parental Responsiveness. Daniela is clearly struggling with her health and/or mental health when Dominic is removed from her care. She had become more withdrawn and disengaged, apparently due to symptoms of depression. However, there is no indication that her parenting was unresponsive to Dominic in the past. Rather, she appeared to be actively engaged with doctors, the school, and family to help ensure all his needs were met.

Audriana

Discipline. Audriana's parents are strict and they rely on physical discipline to correct misbehaviors. When her brothers were caught by police for stealing candy, her parents whipped them with a belt. It is possible that their fear of coming to the attention of law enforcement influences their disciplinary practices, including their perceived need to punish their children severely for risking problems with immigration authorities. Similarly, when Audriana and her sister are verbally and physically abused for reporting their uncle's abusive behavior, their parents may have been driven by fear of having government authorities in the home. This fear can be understood as a reflection of the extreme violence they witnessed in Honduras.

Parental Responsiveness. Audriana's mother has never been responsive to or warm with Audriana. There is no indication that her step-father has a strong relationship with her either. Audriana has been cared for by her aunt. It is likely that the trauma Audriana's mother has experienced since before Audriana was born has impeded her ability to act in warm and nurturing ways to her children.

Closing Summary

The welfare of children is first and foremost the responsibility of their parent or legal guardian. While few would argue with this notion, a wealth of theoretical and empirical research shows that how parents care for and interact with their children is a function of complex social systems. These systems (e.g., health, education, justice) serve to oppress non-White populations, as illustrated by the disproportionate risk for poverty, segregation, limited educational attainment, unemployment, incarceration, poor physical and mental health, and interpersonal racism faced by Latinx and other communities of color in the United States. From a systems perspective, parenting unfolds as a reaction and adaptation to these stressors. It is impossible to know what parenting of Latinx children raised in the United States might be in the absence of these oppressive forces, but cultural studies offer important insights. Latinx culture promotes values that prioritize family and hierarchical parent-child relationships, and in alignment with these values, Latinx parenting is warm, involved, responsive, demanding, and strict. In the next chapter, we explore child maltreatment prevention approaches, including various home visiting and parent education programs, that reduce risk of maltreatment in Latinx populations.

5

Preventing Child Maltreatment among Latinx Families in the United States

> La paz no es solamente la ausencia de la guerra; mientras haya pobreza, racismo, discriminación y exclusion difícilmente podremos alcanzar un mundo de paz.
> —Rigoberta Menchu

Child maltreatment prevention often includes identification of factors that may place families and communities at risk, and addressing these early on, before neglect or abuse occurs. In this chapter, we explore child maltreatment prevention among Latinx families. To start, we review risk factors that have been addressed in child maltreatment prevention efforts. Next, we explore practices that have been developed to prevent child maltreatment. To conclude, we examine the cultural responsiveness of various practices and interventions, as well as evidence of their effectiveness with Latinx families.

Risk and Protective Factors

As discussed in chapter 2, child maltreatment is defined in federal legislation as "any recent act or failure to act on the part of a parent or caregiver that results in death, serious physical or emotional harm, sexual abuse, or exploitation, or an act or failure to act that presents an imminent risk of serious harm" (Child Abuse Prevention and Treatment Act of 2010, P.L. 111–320). When assessing risk of maltreatment, it is important to consider *risk factors*, or factors that increase the likelihood that a child experiences maltreatment, and *protective factors*, or factors that decrease the likelihood of maltreatment. According to the developmental-ecological model (Bronfenbrenner, 1974), factors at levels of a child's ecology play a role in shaping risk of maltreatment. We highlight two salient factors at the societal level: poverty and discrimination.

Poverty is a known risk factor for child maltreatment (Drake & Jonson-Reid, 2014), and 19 percent of Latinx adults and 27 percent of Latinx families with children live below the official poverty line (Cabrera et al., 2021; Noe-Bustamante & Flores, 2019). Data from a national database of child protective service referrals found a strong association between county-wide disparities in poverty and county-wide disparities in maltreatment of Latinx children, particularly in large urban cities (Maguire-Jack et al., 2015). Indicators of poverty at the neighborhood level, such as community-wide unemployment rates (Freisthler et al., 2007), community-wide proportion of female-headed families (Freisthler et al., 2007), residential instability (Klein & Merritt, 2014), and neighborhood impoverishment (Klein & Merritt, 2014), have also been linked to higher rates of child maltreatment referrals for Latinx children. Latinx children are more likely to live in poor neighborhoods and, specifically, in urban poverty (Acevedo-Garcia et al., 2020). Freisthler et al. (2007) found that community poverty rates, unemployment, and female-headed households were associated with higher child maltreatment rates among Latinx youth in California. Racial and ethnic makeup of neighborhoods has also been linked to child maltreatment referral and substantiation (Freisthler et al., 2007).

As discussed in chapter 2, Latinx populations face discrimination, a form of violence that negatively impacts child development and mental health (Sanders-Phillips, 2009). Research with youth and young adults from urban, low-income neighborhoods suggests that discrimination is more commonly identified as a stressful experience than mental illness or other commonly measured adverse childhood experiences (Wade et al., 2014). Given that the World Health Organization includes psychological attacks in their definition of violence and child maltreatment (Krug et al., 2002), some experts have argued that race- and ethnic-based discrimination should be considered a form of violence and maltreatment when it is directed at a child (Sanders-Phillips, 2009; Sanders-Phillips & Kliewer, 2020). Reports of discrimination among Latinx individuals vary, with recent studies suggesting that between 55 percent (Garnett et al., 2014) and 94 percent (Zeiders et al., 2021) of Latinx adolescents may be subjected to discrimination. Among Latinx adults, between 38 percent (Gonzalez-Barrera & Lopez, 2020) and 58 percent (Horowitz et al., 2019) reported discrimination in the past year. A recent Pew Research Study found that Latinx adults with darker skin tones were more likely to report racial discrimination (Horowitz et al., 2019), highlighting intersectionality and disparate experiences among Latinx individuals based on other identities such as race.

Beyond interpersonal discrimination, systemic forms of discrimination, including police brutality and violence during Immigration and Customs Enforcement (ICE) raids, have long been documented and are considered by some to be state-sanctioned child maltreatment. For example, the Migrant Protection Protocol ("Remain in Mexico" policy) enacted by the Trump administration forced asylum seekers transiting through Mexico to reach the United States to stay in Mexico while their asylum cases were being processed (Garrett, 2020). This policy sought to criminalize and stigmatize asylum seekers and served to dehumanize families coming from the southern border. Between April 2019 and January 2021, over 70,000 migrants were sent to Mexico under the Migrant Protection Protocol (TRAC Reports, Inc., 2021), including over 16,000 Latinx children (Cooke et al., 2019).

The Zero-Tolerance Policy, also enacted during the Trump administration, forced families to separate when apprehended crossing the U.S.-Mexico border. Under this policy, over 3,000 children were separated from their parents between May 7, 2018, and June 20, 2018 (U.S. Department of Justice, 2021). Although the Trump administration largely stopped the practice of forced separation (due in large part to criticism and ongoing advocacy), the lack of coordination and planning prior to its enactment led to challenges locating the children and parents who had been separated. In response to this, the Biden administration signed an executive order on February 2, 2021, to establish an interagency task force to continue to reunify children and parents separated intentionally through the Zero-Tolerance Policy (Biden Jr., 2021; Executive Order No. 14011, 2021). Still, family detention and centers for unaccompanied minors continue to be overcrowded. Reports of lack of soap, toothbrushes, and access to medical care among families in immigrant detention centers (Physicians for Human Rights, 2021) would constitute neglect if they were to occur in a family setting and has drawn harsh criticism from professional groups such as the American Academy of Pediatrics and the American Psychological Association. Anti-immigrant policies and practices have been linked to poorer child developmental and mental health outcomes (Stacciarini et al., 2015).

Additionally, experts have raised concern about failure-to-protect laws that may disproportionately impact immigrant parents, some of whom may face legal repercussions related to their immigrant status for making reports to law enforcement (Rogerson, 2012). Failure-to-protect laws hold parents accountable for "harm caused to children in their care by finding them liable for what the law views as passive parental inaction" (Rogerson, 2012, p. 581). These are commonly assessed as neglect or child endangerment due to a parent's inaction, but do not consider external factors that may impede a parent's ability to report and seek help.

In parallel, some experts have raised concerns that higher levels of parental stress or trauma among Latinx immigrants may increase the risk of child maltreatment (Dettlaff & Finno-Velasquez, 2013), particularly when they have experienced trauma in their countries of origin (Mendoza et al., 2017) or on the journey to the United States (Dettlaff & Finno-Velasquez, 2013). One study found that 54 percent of Latinx asylum seekers experienced political violence, including torture, severe physical harm, or violent death of a loved one, in their countries of origin (Eisenman et al., 2003). Moreover, Latinx immigrants who cross the southern border to arrive in the United States may face increased risk of sexual violence, assaults, and beatings (Infante et al., 2012).

On the other hand, the immigrant paradox documents better mental health and behavioral functioning in foreign-born adults relative to U.S.-born Latinx adults (LaBrenz et al., 2020; Salas-Wright et al., 2015). Additionally, a systematic review found evidence of an immigrant paradox in child abuse, with immigrant children less likely to experience physical abuse than their U.S.-born peers, and immigrant parents less likely to be reported to CPS (Millett, 2016). But the same systematic review found that according to community data outside of CPS, immigrant children were more likely to experience physical neglect and lack of supervision (Millett, 2016). Notably, the specific types of maltreatment more likely to be experienced by immigrant youth include those more highly correlated with poverty and cultural norms, such as child supervision.

Child Maltreatment Prevention from an Ecological Framework

To be effective, prevention efforts must attend to factors that place families at risk for maltreatment, and protective factors that may be leveraged to mitigate such risk. From an ecological framework, factors at all levels—such as child age and ability status, parental factors such as mental health or substance use issues, family factors such as overall stress and functioning, community factors such as violent crime rates or lack of access to quality education, and larger structural factors such as systemic bias and racism—intersect in complex and dynamic ways (Cicchetti et al., 2000; Scannapieco & Connell-Carrick, 2005). Thus, a multipronged or multilevel approach to prevention is warranted. Figure 5.1 presents some of the initiatives that have been developed to target different levels of the child's ecological niche.

Community Approaches to Child Maltreatment Prevention

Although several programs and interventions have been developed to target child or family risk factors associated with child maltreatment, there has been a recent push to tackle child maltreatment prevention as a public health issue that requires community-wide responses (He et al., 2020; Roygardner et al., 2021). For example, as part of their National Center for Injury Prevention and Control's Division of Violence Prevention, the Centers for Disease Control and Prevention (2021) has focused on preventing childhood adversity (including child maltreatment) via community programs, after-school activities, education on adverse childhood experiences, affordable child

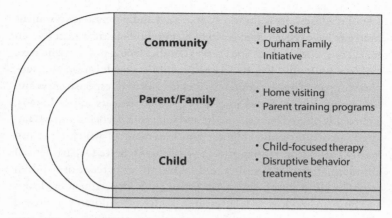

FIGURE 5.1. Child Maltreatment Prevention by Level

care programs, and child tax credits, among other strategies. Some partnerships have explored linkages of child welfare data with other public health data to provide child maltreatment surveillance that can identify risk factors and lead to large-scale prevention (Putnam-Hornstein et al., 2011). One specific community-level initiative is the Durham Family Initiative (DFI) in Durham County, North Carolina, which combined a Community Collaborative and System of Care Council, neighborhood development intervention, and family-centered interventions to address community child maltreatment rates (Rosanbalm et al., 2010). The program initially focused on community-based supports for families with children in underserved neighborhoods and expanded to include universal home visiting for new parents. Between its launch in 2002 and its culmination in 2014, community maltreatment rates decreased by 50 percent. Although the larger initiative was terminated in 2014, a universal home visiting program emerged from DFI that has been implemented by Durham County. Other communities have implemented similar initiatives, including the Hampton Healthy Families Partnership in Virginia and Annie E. Casey's Rebuilding Communities Initiative (Child Welfare Information Gateway, n.d.).

Another community-wide approach to improving outcomes for children has been the development and implementation of Head Start programs. Although Head Start initially was developed to promote school readiness, its community approach and parental involvement strategies have proven effective in reducing child maltreatment (Green et al., 2014, 2020). Head Start serves families facing poverty who have children under five by offering early childhood education and supports for parenting. Its key tenets include cultural responsiveness and community buy-in. Head Start has expanded since its launch in 1995, is currently offered in 1,600 public and nonprofit agencies, and has tailored opportunities for migrant families, many of which serve primarily Latinx communities (e.g., Washington State Department of Children, Youth & Families, n.d.). Overall, 37 percent of children served by Head Start in 2017 were Latinx (U.S. Department of Health and Human Services, 2019). Research has found children who attend Head Start experience lower rates of spanking (Zhai et al., 2011), lower rates of child welfare involvement during elementary school (Green et al., 2014), and reductions in overall maltreatment (Green et al., 2020).

In addition to these efforts, we argue that federal policy changes are also needed to prevent state-sanctioned child maltreatment that occurs in immigrant detention centers and when migrant parents and children are forcibly separated. Policies that provide opportunities for family unity and prevent separation are crucial to promote intergenerational mobility and social well-being, which serve to prevent maltreatment (Gubernskaya & Dreby, 2017). Family unity can be enhanced through policies that allow family visas to permit children and their parents to enter the United States together, alternatives to immigrant detention for families awaiting hearings, and opportunities for undocumented parents of U.S.-born children to obtain a visa and remain in the United States. Even among Latinx individuals who are permanent residents or U.S. citizens, more restrictive immigration policies have been linked to service underutilization, increasing the chance that risk factors for maltreatment remain unaddressed (Latz et al., 2019). In parallel, efforts to address the root causes of migration, particularly among Latinx individuals, could help address trauma exposure in one's country of origin and its subsequent impact on maltreatment. Since 2021, Vice President Harris has initiated efforts to address instability and other root causes of migration in Central America and Mexico (Congressional Research Service, 2021). As these efforts unfold, it will be important to explore their impact on trauma, migration, and maltreatment.

Family- and Child-Centered Approaches to Child Maltreatment Prevention

While community and societal approaches to child maltreatment prevention have largely emerged from public health or education frameworks, many child welfare services have continued to focus on family- or child-centered prevention. Several federal policies targeting child maltreatment require the provision of evidence-based services (i.e., services that have been rigorously evaluated through intervention trials). In child welfare, the California Evidence-Based Clearinghouse for Child Welfare (CEBC) and the Title IV-E Prevention Services Clearinghouse have rated various programs that target child maltreatment prevention based on the level and quality of evaluation and evidence of each program's effectiveness in preventing child maltreatment. Notably, with the Families First Prevention Services Act of 2018 (HR 1892), child welfare agencies became eligible to receive funds to provide maltreatment prevention services that are evidence-based. Thus, state agencies are incentivized to implement programs that have already received ratings from the CEBC or the Title IV-E Prevention Services Clearinghouse (Torres & Mathur, 2018). These programs include behavioral parent training programs such as SafeCare; home visiting programs such as Nurse-Family Partnership, and child treatment programs such as Multisystemic Therapy. Table 5.1, adapted from the CEBC, displays the programs in each of these categories, as rated by the CEBC.

Of the programs rated by the CEBC, most target the parents or entire family unit and provide parent education. Some parent education programs, such as The Period of PURPLE Crying or Parents as Teachers, are specific to parents of young children. The Period of PURPLE Crying, for example, provides education about typical infant crying to parents of children under six months of age in an effort to reduce shaken baby syndrome (Barr et al., 2009). Parents as Teachers provides education on early childhood development to parents of children under age six (Pfannenstiel & Seltzer, 1989). Many programs, such as Parents as Teachers, Adults and Children Together (ACT) Raising Safe Kids, and the Incredible Years, have been translated and administered in Spanish, though relatively few have been culturally adapted or tested specifically for validity among Latinx families.

Table 5.1

Child Maltreatment Prevention Programs Rated by the California Evidence-Based Clearinghouse for Child Welfare

	Home Visiting	Primary Prevention	Secondary Prevention	Population
Adults and Children Together (ACT) Raising Safe Kids		X		English & Spanish language; Latinx participants in studies
Body Safety Training Workbook		X		English & Spanish language; Latinx participants in studies
C.A.R.E.S. (Coordination, Advocacy, Resources, Education, and Support)			X	English & Spanish language; Latinx participants
Child First	X		X	English & Spanish language; Latinx participants in studies
Circle of Security (COS)-Home Visiting 4	X			English only; Latinx participants in studies
Combined Parent-Child Cognitive Behavioral Therapy (CPC-CBT)			X	English & Spanish language; Latinx participants in study
Exchange Parent Aide	X		X	English & Spanish language; Latinx participants in study
Family Connections (FC)			X	English & Spanish language
Healthy Families America (HFA)	X			English & Spanish language; Latinx participants in study

Table 5.1 Continued

Child Maltreatment Prevention Programs Rated by the California Evidence-Based Clearinghouse for Child Welfare

	Home Visiting	Primary Prevention	Secondary Prevention	Population
The Incredible Years			X	English & Spanish language; Latinx participants in study
Nurse-Family Partnership (NFP)	X	X		English & Spanish language; Latinx participants in study
Nurturing Parenting— Parents & Their School-Age Children 5–11 (NP1)			X	English & Spanish language; Latinx participants in study
Parents Anonymous®		X	X	English & Spanish language; Latinx participants in study
Parents as Teachers (PAT)	X	X		English & Spanish language; Latinx participants in study
The Period of Purple Crying®		X		English & Spanish language
SafeCare®	X		X	English & Spanish language; Latinx participants
Safe Child Program		X		English & Spanish language
Safe Environment for Every Kid (SEEK)		X	X	English & Spanish language; Latinx participants in study
Safe Touches©		X		English only; Latinx participants in studies
Step-by-Step Parenting Program®			X	No Spanish language or Latinx participants

(Continued)

Table 5.1   Continued
Child Maltreatment Prevention Programs Rated by the California Evidence-Based Clearinghouse for Child Welfare

	Home Visiting	Primary Prevention	Secondary Prevention	Population
Stewards of Children®		X		English & Spanish language
Strong Communities for Children		X		English only; Latinx participants in studies
Triple P— Positive Parenting Program® System		X		English & Spanish language; Latinx participants in study
"Who Do You Tell?"™ ("WDYT"™)		X		No Spanish language or Latinx participants

Note: Table adapted from the California Evidence-Based Clearinghouse (CEBC) website (https://www.cebc4cw.org/), accessed on May 3, 2021.

Other programs offer peer support, such as Parents Anonymous®. Parents Anonymous is guided by core components of mutual support, parent leadership, shared leadership, and personal growth/change to foster well-being (Polinsky et al., 2010, 2011). In two studies, parent participants reported fewer risk factors for child maltreatment at program completion compared with when they began Parents Anonymous. However, neither of the previous studies examined the impact specifically on Latinx families.

One limitation of evidence-based practices is the reliance on randomized controlled trials or quasi-experimental designs that require multiple points of contact and follow-up. Researchers have found a lag in recruitment, enrollment, and retention strategies to encourage participation in research by Latinx and other families of color (George et al., 2014). Latinx immigrants may face barriers to participate in randomized controlled trials due to language barriers, lack of insurance coverage, or immigration status (Adulin et al., 2019). Therefore, some experts have called for more cultural adaptations of child maltreatment prevention programs, many of which were developed and tested among predominantly White samples (Kumpfer et al., 2002; Molnar et al., 2016). It could also be beneficial to use a community-based approach to engage Latinx families in processes to develop programs specifically to meet their needs and reflect their strengths and values.

Culturally Responsive Child Maltreatment Prevention Programs

The CEBC rates programs for the general U.S. population but provides limited information about cultural responsiveness or the effectiveness of each program for diverse racial and ethnic groups. One way to make programs more responsive to diverse family needs is through adaptations. Cultural adaptation is defined as "the systematic modification of an evidence-based treatment or intervention protocol to consider language, culture, and context in such a way that it is compatible with the client's cultural patterns, meanings, and values" (Bernal et al., 2009, p. 362). Importantly, though, practitioners and researchers must weigh model fidelity with adaptation, identifying which core components are essential to maintain, and which can be adapted to better meet child, family, or community needs (Castro et al., 2004). It is also important to attend to the heterogeneity of Latinx families based on national origin, immigration status, family composition, and socioeconomic status, and avoid stereotyping and oversimplifying the cultural context (Baumann et al., 2015; Kreuter et al., 2003). Examples of cultural adaptation for Latinx families include facilitation in Spanish and the use of bilingual program staff (Castro et al., 2004; Mejia et al., 2016; Valdez et al., 2018), use of culturally relevant language (D'Angelo et al., 2009), and attention to cultural beliefs, values, or norms (Castro et al., 2004; Elder et al., 2009). Considering familismo, for instance, programs may be adapted to include broader assessment of family members, family cohesion and conflict, and family support or to include the larger family unit in the intervention (Bailey et al., 2015). Cultural adaptation can also extend to the community, to include activities to increase community buy-in and infrastructure (Castro et al., 2004).

Evidence in support of cultural adaptations is mixed. Efforts to adapt child maltreatment prevention programs, such as the Strengthening Families Program (SFP), may increase retention (Kumpfer et al., 2002), but other literature suggests that unadapted evidence-based practices work as well with youth of color as with White youth (Huey Jr. & Polo, 2008). However, a more recent meta-analysis of psychotherapy found that culturally adapted psychotherapy was more effective than unadapted psychotherapy in improving psychological functioning (Benish et al., 2011). Similarly, two recent meta-analyses of cultural adaptations of psychological interventions found a medium effect size for culturally adapted interventions over unadapted versions (Griner & Smith, 2006; Hall et al., 2016). There is a need for similar studies of cultural adaptations of child maltreatment prevention programs, such as the ones rated favorably by the CEBC.

Despite these recommendations, there is a growing critique of the push for evidence-based programming that relies on a "gold standard" of strict study design and quantitative methods (Kerrigan & Johnson, 2019) and promotes colonial and oppressive methods (Shahjahan, 2011). Evidence-based practices emerge from a positivist framework (Thyer, 2008; White & Willis, 2002) that fail to address larger systemic root causes of child maltreatment. Indeed, many of the evidence-based programs for child maltreatment prevention focus on the individual child or parent, which risks overpathologizing families and distracting from the need for larger structural changes such as community-wide poverty alleviation and access to employment or education (Hansen et al., 2014). Child maltreatment efforts must expand to include larger, systemic root causes of maltreatment, particularly among families of color. Specifically, anti-oppressive frameworks are needed to promote strategies that challenge manifestations of power and the status quo that maintains social inequities (French et al., 2020; Rogers, 2012).

Case Illustrations

In revisiting the cases of Bianca, Dominic, and Audriana, we consider how prevention efforts may have altered the course of events leading up to the child's removal from the home. We ask you to identify other avenues of prevention that would have supported the well-being of each child. We also challenge you to consider the ways in which our society invests (or does not invest) in prevention efforts for the sake of child safety, stability, and nurturing.

Bianca

Family- and Child-Centered Prevention. Bianca's parents could have benefited from a home visiting program to help the family transition after Bianca and her mother joined her father in Arizona. The three of them had never lived together in Mexico, and they faced several other stressors such as lack of access to health care, Bianca's father's accident and injury, parental substance use, and, ultimately, domestic violence. Furthermore, a comprehensive psychosocial assessment could have revealed stressors related to immigration or legal status that may have contributed to the maladaptive coping techniques Bianca's father presented. In Bianca's case, she was enrolled in a local Head Start program. When the center staff noticed behaviors such as Bianca crying and hitting her mother and teachers at drop-off, lack of engagement with other children, and banging her head against the wall, there were missed opportunities to provide support and engage Bianca's family to understand the root cause of these behavior changes.

Community-Centered Prevention. In parallel, systemic changes, such as more equitable immigration policies, could have helped increase service accessibility for Bianca's parents and reduce family stress. For example, workers' compensation could have stabilized the family after her father's injury, but these funds were not available because of their immigration status. Going back further into the family's history, more humane and equitable immigration policies would not have divided the family across borders. Moreover, it is possible that U.S. foreign policy contributed to the instability that Bianca and her family faced prior to migrating to the United States. Had the family been able to migrate together, Bianca likely would have been more attached to her father, strengthening the family unit.

Dominic

Family- and Child-Centered Prevention. The supposedly "neglectful" supervision that led to Dominic's removal from the home reflected several risk factors, such as maternal mental health problems, parenting stress due to his disruptive behaviors, and challenges in the grandparent-parent relationship. There are several early intervention options that could have been provided to Daniela after Dominic's diagnosis of ADHD, particularly since medication was not acceptable. A culturally responsive early intervention for ADHD (Malkoff et al., 2019) could help reduce Dominic's disruptive behaviors and mitigate their impact on stress in his mother, his mother's partner, and his grandparents. A culturally responsive intervention could honor Daniela's decision to not medicate her child and provide alternatives such as Cogmed Working Memory Training (Chacko et al., 2013). Several in-home services could have been offered after the initial child maltreatment referral instead of rushing to remove Dominic from his mother's care. For example, ACT Raising Safe Kids and Triple P are both evidence-based child maltreatment prevention programs that have included Latinx families in prior studies.

Community-Centered Prevention. More accessible medical care for single mothers that includes childcare or childcare that has nontraditional hours and is affordable could have prevented his removal. Moreover, Dominic's case highlights protective factors in his neighborhood that could have been further utilized, such as the presence of neighbors concerned for his well-being. Strategies to build community support within their building and within Dominic's school could provide his mother with more concrete support.

Audriana

Family- and Child-Centered Prevention. For Audriana, prevention programs could have been offered to her family prior to her disclosure of sexual abuse given the other risk factors present in this case, such as the violent death of her father, her mother and sister's exposure to community violence and death threats in Honduras, and stress related to the migration to the United States. Although these experiences were not likely known to many outside the family, the church could serve an important role in identifying and referring families like Audriana's for services while honoring their need for privacy. To our knowledge, the unique needs of asylum seekers are not considered in any of the current evidence-based practices for child maltreatment prevention, but are critical for serving Latinx populations.

Community-Centered Prevention. Prevention at the community level in Audriana's case could have included partnering with the church to provide education programs for parents, including how to provide safety, stability, and nurturing to children, and how to identify and prevent sexual and other forms of abuse. Programs that make safe housing accessible may have helped Audriana's mother better support her daughters without risking her own stability and that of her other children. Additionally, the system did nothing to punish the perpetrator of the sexual abuse and instead punished the children by removing them from their family.

Closing Summary

This chapter examined diverse strategies for child maltreatment prevention. Using an ecological framework, child, family, and community factors were identified that contribute to maltreatment, and programs to address these factors were presented. Although community-level issues such as poverty or discrimination may disproportionately impact Latinx families, most evidence-based practices target child and family factors, such as parenting and child behavior problems. Furthermore, the review of programs and policies highlighted a need to evaluate how child maltreatment prevention can be more culturally responsive and anti-oppressive. There is a clear need, particularly among child welfare programs, to target larger, systemic factors that may be more prevalent among Latinx families and to ensure that services offered reflect the cultural norms and values of the families served. The next chapter will explore alternative response, foster care, and other interventions for Latinx children and families after a report has been made to CPS.

6

Providing Targeted
Child Maltreatment
Interventions to
Latinx Families

> We all have an unsuspected reserve
> of strength inside that emerges
> when life puts us to the test.
> —Isabel Allende

In this chapter, we explore culturally responsive child maltreatment programs for Latinx families who have been referred to Child Protective Services (CPS). We build upon the framework from the previous chapter in which we explored child maltreatment prevention to consider experiences of Latinx families once they are referred to CPS. We pay special attention to alternative response and family preservation for Latinx families, as well as their experiences with foster care and culturally responsive practices to prevent recurrences of maltreatment. We provide an overview of programs and interventions that have been evaluated specifically for Latinx families. To conclude, we offer a guide for future intervention efforts.

Referrals to Child Protective Services for Maltreatment among Latinx Families

In 2019, there were approximately 3.4 million referrals to CPS for alleged maltreatment that were investigated. Of these, approximately 23.4 percent of children referred were Latinx (U.S. Department of Health & Human Services, 2021). Once referred to CPS and screened for investigation, cases can be routed to alternative response, family preservation services, or removal, depending on the level of risk assessed. After adjusting for sociodemographic factors, some research has found Latinx children to have a lower risk of referrals for child maltreatment than White children (Putnam-Hornstein et al., 2013). However, other research has found that Latinx families involved in child welfare may experience race-based inequities due to oversurveillance and bias (Merritt, 2021). Thus, it is important to understand how Latinx families may experience their journeys through the child welfare system.

Although Latinx families are not overrepresented in CPS referrals at a national level, experts have found there to be mismatches between the child welfare system and Latinx culture (Davidson et al., 2019). During the investigation, the incongruence between the bureaucracy of the child welfare system and the value on interpersonal relationships (*personalismo*) typical in Latinx communities, along with the use of unannounced visits that undermine the parent-worker relationship, alienates Latinx families (Ayón & Aisenberg, 2010; Schraufnagel et al., 2006). One study of 1,754 children across four states found that caseworkers were less likely to contact and engage fathers in Latinx families than fathers in White families (Arroyo et al., 2019). Another study found that some caseworkers avoided considering the child or family's ethnicity when developing the case plan because of the Multiethnic Placement Act (MEPA) of 1994 (U.S. Public Law 103-82), which could prevent referrals to bilingual services or bilingual foster homes (Suleiman, 2003). Thus, during the referral and investigation stages, it is critical to understand how the child welfare system can be responsive and best meet the needs of diverse Latinx families, considering the multiple identities, beliefs, and values they may hold.

Latinx Children in Foster Care

Removal from the home is the most severe outcome following a CPS investigation. Latinx children are not overrepresented in foster care, except in certain states such as Maine, where there are over four times the number of Latinx children in foster care as in the child population (LaBrenz et al., 2021). Although it is unclear why this variation may occur, some prior research with Black youth in foster care has found that states with more children of color tend to have lower rates of overrepresentation than states with fewer children of color (Foster, 2012). Moreover, rates may vary due to state variation in definitions of child maltreatment, expectations for mandated reporters, and services accessible to prevent foster care entries. Notably, Latinx families in foster care face disparities in service referrals and utilization. In one study, Latinx infants and toddlers of immigrant parents who were in foster care had the lowest rates of referrals to early childhood intervention services out of all racial/ethnic groups (Johnson-Motoyama et al., 2016). These findings appear to generalize to all Latinx children in foster care (Leslie et al., 2000). Another study found that Latinx families involved in child welfare were not referred to services to meet basic needs, such as housing, as often as other racial/ethnic groups (Lovato-Hermann et al., 2017).

Although there are few recent national estimates of the proportion of children in foster care who are immigrants or children of immigrants, one study from 2012 found that 8.6 percent of all children referred to CPS were children of immigrants (Dettlaff & Earner, 2012). Not surprisingly, immigrant or mixed-status Latinx families may face additional barriers with the child welfare system. Although unaccompanied minors or those separated from their parents at the border are traditionally served by the Office of Refugee Resettlement (ORR) (Monico et al., 2019), Latinx children living in the United States may be taken into the child welfare system if a parent is taken into custody by Immigration and Customs Enforcement (Applied Research Center, 2011; Carr, 2018). In these cases, Latinx children whose parents are undocumented may enter the foster care system not because of child maltreatment but because of immigration policies that criminalize undocumented parents. This issue has been raised in cases tried at the Texas Supreme Court and Nebraska Supreme Court, both of which ruled that parents have a right to parent their children, regardless of immigration and/or documentation status (Carr, 2018). More recently, though, the Trump administration's Zero-Tolerance Policy forcibly separated families crossing at the border as discussed in chapter 5. Though the majority of children separated under the Zero-Tolerance Policy were taken into the ORR system (Monico et al., 2019), some migrant children, particularly those under the age of thirteen, may be placed in transitional foster care to comply with federal policy that requires children to be placed in the least restrictive setting (Roth et al., 2018). Among children who enter the foster care system because of parental deportation or detainment, an estimated 15,000 remain in care for over five years (Applied Research Center, 2011). In these cases, the child welfare system may petition to terminate parental rights (American Immigration Council, 2021), depriving children of connections to their families despite no actual child maltreatment having occurred. For those children who were separated from their parents but were not placed in foster care, collaboration with immigration specialists, consulates, and border liaisons can help achieve permanency (Cabrera et al., 2019).

Family Preservation and Alternative Response Programs

Recently, there has been a push to preserve families at risk for child maltreatment and to invest more resources in prevention or alternative response programs instead of traditional child welfare involvement (Center for the Study of Social Policy, 2020). Alternative response, also referred to as differential response, offers an alternative to traditional investigation when a child welfare agency receives a referral of alleged maltreatment (Osterling et al., 2008). In cases where there is not an imminent safety risk, alternative response can provide families with services in a less adversarial way instead of a traditional CPS investigation (Hughes et al., 2013; Schene, 2001). This allows the child welfare system to support families referred to CPS without removing the child or conducting an in-depth investigation (Whittaker & Tracy, 2017). Traditional CPS investigations tend to be adversarial, punitive, and accusatory in nature (Loman & Siegel, 2005). Therefore, alternative response provides opportunities for families to engage with services and build relationships with professionals without fear of removal.

Many families that are deferred to alternative response receive family preservation services. Family preservation can include prevention or early intervention services, such as home visiting that can prevent future child maltreatment reports (Johnson et al., 2005). Family preservation services also include general and community support services for families at risk or in crisis such as respite, parenting classes, mental health services, substance use treatment services, assistance to address domestic violence, and peer-to-peer mentoring (Capacity Building Center for States, 2016; Chaffin et al., 2001). One goal of family preservation services is to avoid child removals (Logan, 2018), which could help address racial disparities in foster care entries and subsequent outcomes (Lothridge et al., 2012; Raymond & Griffith, 2008; Semanchin Jones, 2014).

Although family preservation or other alternative response models vary, some research has found that Latinx families are referred to these kinds of programs more often than other families (Jones, 2015). For example, in the 2020 fiscal year, Latinx children represented 51.9 percent of children who received family preservation services in Texas (Texas Department of Family and Protective Services, n.d.). This may be due to lower parental risk among Latinx families referred to CPS, as one national study found that Latinx parents had the lowest rates of substance use or mental health issues when compared with Native American, White, or Black parents (Libby et al., 2006). Family preservation programs encompass a wide range of interventions, such as intensive preservation, parent education/training, or home visiting, to improve child well-being and safety within their family unit. Some family preservation services have been tested with Latinx families, with promising results. For example, Ayón and Lee (2005) found that Latinx families who received family preservation services reported more positive outcomes related to child academic adjustment and externalizing behavior compared with White families who received the same services (Ayón & Lee, 2005). Another study found that Latinx families who received intensive family preservation services had slightly higher rates of successful program completion than White participants (Bagdasaryan, 2005).

On the other hand, a number of studies suggest that Latinx parents receive fewer services, especially culturally responsive services, compared with White parents (Garcia et al., 2012; Libby et al., 2006). There may also be cultural norms that stigmatize mental health service utilization (De Silva et al., 2020). This is particularly true for immigrant families, who may be less likely to choose or have the means to access CPS services, especially if a parent is undocumented (Finno-Velasquez, 2013; Finno-Velasquez et al., 2016; Merritt, 2021). McCue Horwitz et al. (2012) found that Latinx children referred to family preservation services received less support than their White peers who had been referred.

Evidence-Based Practices for Child Maltreatment among Latinx Families

When children enter foster care, child welfare practitioners develop a case plan that considers family risk and protective factors, child safety, and a plan for permanency (D'Andrade, 2015). Per federal legislation, child welfare agencies are required to make reasonable efforts and provide timely, targeted services to parents to support family reunification (Berrick et al., 2008). Considering the factors that often lead to a child's removal (e.g., parental substance use, mental health issues, domestic violence, and lack of parenting skills), services often include parent training or other parent skill-building interventions, substance use treatment, or mental health services (LaBrenz et al., 2021). There are two clearinghouses that review and rate the evidence base for child welfare programs: The California Evidence-Based Clearinghouse for Child Welfare (CEBC) and the Title IV-E Prevention Services Clearinghouse. The Title IV-E Prevention Services Clearinghouse was developed in accordance with the Family First Prevention Services Act (FFPSA) to rate programs based on findings related to child welfare outcomes in published studies. As FFPSA is rolled out and implemented across state and county child welfare systems, federal funding will be limited to programs that have been ranked as well supported, supported, or promising. Thus, it is particularly important to understand how evidence-based practices have been developed, and whether they have been adequately adapted and/or tested with Latinx families.

One recent project was undertaken by Fettes et al. (2020) to culturally adapt SafeCare+®, an evidence-based intervention for child-welfare-involved families and families at risk of maltreatment. Recruiting Latinx families from an urban child welfare system, Fettes et al. (2020) examined barriers that Latinx families may face when seeking support, such as challenges in connecting with community resources, fear of contact with the authorities, and for some Latinx families, limited command of English. Integrating knowledge about potential barriers, Fettes et al. (2020) published a protocol to implement the cultural adaptation of SafeCare+® along with a timeline for evaluation. This includes a planning and implementation phase to establish and formalize partnerships, conducting community outreach, conducting an assessment of family needs, and gathering feedback from key community members.

Other evidence-based programs eligible for Title IV-E funds that have been culturally adapted include Triple P®, Parent-Child Interaction Therapy, The Incredible Years, and Parent Management Training—the Oregon Model (PMTO™; Baumann et al., 2015). However, in their systematic review of cultural adaptations and implementations of parent training programs, Baumann et al. (2015) critiqued much of the literature and concluded that there is an ongoing need to examine how programs are culturally adapted and implemented. For example, a study of cultural adaptations of the Strengthening Families Program (SFP) for families of color found that adaptations that reduced the number of sessions or changed core components of the intervention for the sake of participant retention also served to reduce positive outcomes (Kumpfer et al., 2002).

In contrast to the programs rated by the Title IV-E Clearinghouse, which were not specifically developed for Latinx families or other non-White families, a few interventions have been developed specifically to serve families of color. For example, the Family to Family practice model was developed to address the needs of Black families involved in child welfare (Lothridge et al., 2012). Part of the Family to Family practice model entails building community partnerships to link families with services and creating tools for community partners to identify strengths and areas to improve. As part of this self-evaluation process, community stakeholders identified the need for more targeted trainings on racial disparities and responses. Although the trainings initially focused on reducing disparities among Black youth, researchers also observed improved outcomes among Latinx families who participated in the adapted and community-responsive practice model (Lothridge et al., 2012).

As described in chapter 5, culturally adapted programs consider language, culture, and context to fit with the clients' cultural patterns and values (Bernal et al., 2009). Cultural adaptation starts with an intervention developed for a specific population and modifies it to meet the needs of a unique community. This process is complex, time-consuming, and costly. One of the major challenges is adapting a program to an entire population, given its diversity. Demographic characteristics like immigrant status (Dettlaff & Johnson, 2011), national origin (Johnson-Motoyama et al., 2015), socioeconomic status (Nadan et al., 2015), child age (Palusci, 2011), child gender (Alzate & Rosenthal, 2009), and disabilities or other developmental delays (Johnson-Motoyama et al., 2016) influence risk for maltreatment, as well as outcomes due to maltreatment. This is because well-being is so intricately linked with social identities. For example, experiences of discrimination among Latinx individuals are both gendered and racialized (Uzogara, 2019). Moreover, intersectional identities are situated in a broader context of ethnic networks, social relations, and public policies that further influence risk of maltreatment (Johnson, 2007). According to Núñez (2014), organizational factors (e.g., anti-immigration laws, anti-bilingual education policies), representational factors (e.g., immigrant, citizenship), intersubjective factors (e.g., gender, class), and experiential factors (e.g., internalized beliefs and own narrative) are foundational to the study of intersectionality. The feasibility of undertaking adaptations that attend to all of these nuances is questionable. One possible approach to create more culturally responsive and nuanced programs could be to engage in community-based research to develop programs specifically for the target population, and with their active participation. Indeed, French et al. (2020) recently identified five anchors of radical healing that could include collectivism, critical consciousness, radical hope, strength and resistance, and cultural authenticity and self-knowledge, all of which could be integrated into community-based research with Latinx communities.

Another major challenge is that "evidence-based" programs often lack evidence of their effectiveness with Latinx families. For example, the Iowa Parent Partner program is an evidence-based intervention for families whose children are in foster care. In the Iowa Parent Partner program, parents are matched with a mentor to provide support and help navigate the child welfare system and other services required as part of the case plan. Yet, in one of the largest evaluation studies to date, only 9 percent of participants identified as Latinx and there were no sub-group analyses conducted to examine the treatment effect specifically for Latinx parents (Chambers et al., 2019). Similarly, the

Sobriety Treatment and Recovery Teams (START) was reviewed by the Title IV-E Clearinghouse and rated as a promising practice for families with substance use disorders whose children are in foster care. However, as with Iowa Parent Partner, the empirical evidence for START comes from largely White samples (Hall et al., 2015; Huebner et al., 2012), with less than 1 percent of Latinx participants. Research is needed to adapt and rigorously evaluate these programs with diverse samples (e.g., immigrant and nonimmigrant) of Latinx families.

Cultural Responsiveness of Child Welfare Systems

As the proportion of children in the United States who are Latinx continues to grow (Child Trends, 2018), experts have called for *culturally responsive* child welfare systems and services (Ayón & Aisenberg, 2010; LaLiberte et al., 2015; Leake et al., 2010; Mindell et al., 2003). Cultural responsiveness is defined as "the idea that child welfare professionals need to identify and nurture the unique cultural strengths, beliefs, and practices of each family with whom [they] work and integrate that knowledge into the intervention approaches [they] employ" (LaLiberte et al., 2015, p. 2). Programs that are culturally responsive are guided by eight main principles: (1) communication of high expectations; (2) active delivery methods; (3) practitioner as a facilitator; (4) inclusion of culturally and linguistically diverse clients; (5) cultural sensitivity; (6) reshaping curriculum or delivery of services; (7) client-controlled discourse; and (8) small group instruction (Ladson-Billings, 1994). More recently, additional components of culturally responsive services or programs have been identified, such as explicitly naming White privilege (Hopson, 2009), understanding historical oppression and resilience of clients (Fraizer-Anderson et al., 2012), and understanding diverse communication and relational styles (Frierson et al., 2010; Hood et al., 2015). These components align with mujerismo. In the process of integrating culturally responsive services and systems, it is important to develop collaboration based on family and community assets, such as identification of community resources and building relationships with key community partners (Rivera, 2002). Given systemic discrimination and bias, it is important for community providers administering child maltreatment prevention programs to consider policies and practices in the larger community that lead to disparate experiences and outcomes among Latinx families (Fontes, 2011).

A few studies have examined trainings for child welfare agencies to improve cultural responsiveness, such as the Culturally Competent Systems of Care with Latino Children and Families (Dettlaff & Rycraft, 2010), and a simulation training for child welfare agencies (Leake et al., 2010). In both of these projects, training modules were developed to prepare practitioners and other child welfare workers to better engage and serve Latinx families referred to CPS. In Dettlaff and Rycraft's (2010) study, there were eight training modules that were delivered in an in-person, full-day training; the curriculum included modules related to cultural values and traditions of Latinx families, immigration and acculturation, systems of care, engaging Latinx families, understanding cultural factors in assessment, and a case simulation. In their study, Leake et al. (2010) utilized a simulation training to give practitioners hands-on experience integrating culturally responsive practices into their typical tasks. Although other culturally responsive models have been developed to better serve families (Chow & Austin, 2008; Ortega & Faller, 2011), few have specifically focused on the intersubjective, organizational, representational, and experiential factors unique to Latinx families.

Goodman et al. (2004) explored ways to integrate multicultural and feminist tenets in service delivery, leading to six key principles. These principles encourage "(a) ongoing self-examination, (b) sharing power, (c) giving voice, (d) facilitating consciousness raising, (e) building on strengths, and (f) leaving clients the tools to work toward social change" (p. 793). More recently, French et al. (2020) offered a similar framework for Black, Indigenous, and People of Color (BIPOC) communities (e.g., Latinx families), focusing on "radical healing." These scholars borrow from several frameworks, including ethnopolitical psychology, Black psychology, Liberation psychology, and intersectionality theory to promote healing from detrimental patriarchal forces and foster culturally aligned transformation. The scholars identified five anchors to guide efforts in research, practice, and training, including collectivism, critical consciousness, radical hope, strength, and resistance, as well as cultural authenticity and self-knowledge. As researchers, practitioners, and policy makers consider the development of Latinx-centered child welfare services, they are encouraged to keep these principles in mind, as they not only urge reflexivity across the various stakeholders but also promote empowerment within Latinx communities.

Case Illustrations

This section will apply the concepts in this chapter related to alternative response and cultural responsiveness in Bianca's, Dominic's, and Audriana's cases from the introduction. Readers are encouraged to consider what biases might inform the assessment and decision-making process and explore cultural values and familial strengths that could be leveraged to prevent mismanagement of these cases.

Bianca

Alternative Response. In Bianca's case, alternative response instead of a traditional CPS investigation and immediate removal could have allowed for her to remain with her mother while her family received services to address domestic violence. Although Bianca's case does not give details about the length of time she has been in foster care, or whether this was a temporary measure, it does state that her mother was deemed "unable to protect her." It is unclear how the child welfare investigator arrived at that determination, or if the possibility of alternative response and/or other family preservation services were explored. An alternative response could have been to work with Bianca's mother to find her own housing and refer the father to domestic violence services. Removing Bianca added an additional trauma to her life, which was likely unnecessary based on the facts of the case.

Cultural Responsiveness. A culturally responsive practitioner in Bianca's case would have identified her and her family's strengths, beliefs, and practices, and selected services that best aligned with those. Bianca's parents, especially her mother, showed resilience and a number of strengths. An exploration of the oppression, trauma, and structural barriers to accessing public assistance and social services is equally important. Such an assessment would allow the caseworker to identify and address the true underlying causes for Bianca's removal.

Dominic

Alternative Response. Alternative response is often considered in cases where there are allegations of neglect that are not severe and are not co-occurring with physical or sexual abuse allegations. In Dominic's case, instead of removing him from his mother's care (Daniela), alternative response could have given her and the rest of the family support options to address the challenges in providing him with consistent supervision. In-home, family preservation support services could have included a home visiting program to assist Daniela with expectations and behavior management for Dominic and his sister, support groups that Dominic's mother could attend with other parents of children with ADHD, and counseling for Daniela.

Cultural Responsiveness. A culturally responsive practitioner would consider family strengths and supports when making a decision about a placement with his maternal grandparents. There was some reported tension between Daniela (Dominic's mother) and her parents, but they were living in the same building and had provided childcare in the past. An assessment of family dynamics, possibly strained due to differing cultural beliefs and acculturation between Daniela and her parents, and family expectations related to Daniela's role and responsibilities as a mother, would help ensure the success of the temporary placement. In Dominic's case, there are several protective factors and strengths present, so it would be important to build upon these. The caseworker could also explore how safety and neglectful supervision may be conceptualized differently from Daniela's perspective.

Audriana

Cultural Responsiveness. In Audriana's case, a culturally responsive framework would be important to use in the initial meetings between the caseworker and the family. When Audriana's counselor at school referred the case to CPS, her mother was given the option of having her children removed, having the uncle (and alleged perpetrator of sexual abuse) leave the home, or moving with her children to a new home. Building a trusting and strong partnership with Audriana's mother would be critical. Furthermore, there was no mention of the stepfather and his role in making family decisions. Audriana's case mirrors findings in Arroyo et al.'s 2019 study, in that Latinx father or paternal figures tend to be engaged less frequently in CPS investigations than White father/paternal figures. Given the mixed documentation status of Audriana's family (e.g., her stepfather overstayed a work visa), it is also possible that her parents were hesitant to engage with child welfare authorities, which could be mitigated with sensitivity. In addition, Audriana's family was very engaged in the Pentecostal Church and had strict values for their daughters. Sleepovers with friends were also prohibited. As such, the removal and placement of Audriana and her sister in an emergency shelter could be particularly challenging, as it could conflict with many of the family's cultural and religious beliefs.

Finally, it is not clear if the practitioner adequately assessed the intersectional identities of this family. By forcing the mother to choose between finding a new housing arrangement and having her children removed, the practitioner is assuming that the family has the resources to immediately secure new housing. The case clearly states that her parents moved in with her step-uncle because of the high cost of living and housing in Los Angeles, which could inhibit the parents' ability to leave without housing and/or other financial supports. The lack of housing services offered to Audriana's family also reflects Lovato-Hermann et al.'s (2017) findings that Latinx parents are less likely to be referred to basic needs services, such as housing, than White families. In Audriana's case, a more critical, culturally responsive engagement and assessment of her family could have provided the family with more appropriate services to meet safety needs while avoiding a removal.

Closing Summary

This chapter reviewed Latinx families' experiences with the child welfare system once referred for alleged maltreatment. As with child maltreatment prevention programs, there is an overall lack of adaptation and cultural responsiveness in the evidence-based programming offered to Latinx children in foster care. Despite robust literature on their effectiveness, some programs have had less than 1 percent of participants identify as Latinx. The neglect of Latinx families in the literatures has serious repercussions: Latinx families are underserved or mis-served by the child welfare system. We also highlight how state-sanctioned violence contributes to the separation of children from loving and nurturing parents because of their immigrant status. This is one illustration of how systemic oppression contributes to child maltreatment in Latinx families. In the next chapter, we integrate a strengths-based perspective to explore resilience and healing among Latinx families in the aftermath of maltreatment.

7

Promoting Resilience and Healing in Latinx Families

My choice isn't what I breathe in, it's what I exhale and right now, I feel a need for all of us to breathe fire.

—Alexandria Ocasio-Cortez

In this chapter, we explore resilience and well-being in Latinx families. We start with a review of measures to capture strengths-based policies and practices among Latinx families. Next, using an ecological framework, we examine individual, family, and community strategies to build resilience. Then, we explore how practitioners can use a cultural competence, cultural humility, and critical humility approach to foster resilience and healing among Latinx families. To conclude, we explore resilience and healing specifically in Latinx families.

Strengths-Based Policies and Practices

Although child welfare has traditionally focused on *risk factors* or family problems that may increase the likelihood of child maltreatment, more recent literature has taken a strengths-based approach to identify *protective factors* or factors that build family resilience and reduce the risk of child maltreatment (Center for Study of Social

Policy, 2004). The shift away from risk-focused programs may decrease stigmatization that families feel when accessing support services, which, in turn, can improve family engagement and participation (Asawa et al., 2008; Counts et al., 2010). In fact, Baglivio and Wolff (2021) recently proposed a Positive Childhood Experiences (PCE) cumulative resilience scale as a strengths-based alternative to the traditional Adverse Childhood Experiences (ACE) scale that measures cumulative risk and adversity. PCEs encompass protective factors such as effective family-child communication, feeling supported by one's family, and having adult mentors (Slopen et al., 2017).

The assessment of protective factors and resilience allows practitioners to develop a strengths-based understanding of families to inform case planning. Two measures that capture protective factors and are widely used with Latinx families at-risk for maltreatment are the Strengthening Families framework (CSSP, 2004) and the FRIENDS National Research Center's Protective Factors Survey (PFS) (Bailey et al., 2015). Both of these measures include protective factor subscales related to social connections, concrete support, and knowledge of parenting and child development. Other protective factors include family functioning, nurturing and attachment, and the child's social development. Protective factors are often categorized as *assets* (e.g., positive internal factors such as self-esteem or coping skills) or *resources* (e.g., external factors such as community infrastructure or schools) (Fergus & Zimmerman, 2005).

The Parents' Assessment of Protective Factors (PAPF), a measure developed from the Strengthening Families framework, has been tested and validated among Spanish-speaking families at risk for child maltreatment (LaBrenz et al., 2020). The PFS has been translated and validated among a Latinx sample (Conrad-Hiebner et al., 2015). Through the Strengthening Families (SF) framework, some research has examined protective factors such as nurturing, attachment, knowledge of parenting and child development, and social support among Latinx families (Bailey et al., 2015). Parental nurturing (Thornberry et al., 2013), knowledge of child development (McMillin et al., 2016), and social support (Thompson, 1995) are all associated with lower risk of child maltreatment.

Other scales assess resilience. One such scale is the Mexican Measurement Scale of Resilience (RESI-M) (Palomar Lever & Gomez Valdez, 2010), which was developed and tested on a sample of Mexican young adults from diverse sociodemographic backgrounds and includes dimensions of family support, social support, family structure, and social competence (Palomar Lever & Gomez Valdez, 2010). The Connor-Davidson Resilience Scale (CD-RISC; Connor & Davidson, 2003; Moreno et al., 2019) and the Brief Resilience Scale (BRS) (Karaman et al., 2019; Smith et al., 2008) were developed to measure resilience among the general U.S. population, but have since been tested and validated among Latinx populations in the United States and abroad. In general, theory and measure development of protective factors and of resilience reinforce strengths-based policy and practice.

Protective Factors in Latinx Families

A number of protective factors have been documented in Latinx families, including family involvement, supervision of children, positive communication, presence of extended family, and biculturalism (Cardoso & Thompson, 2010). Mariscal (2020) found that maternal monitoring served as a protective factor that buffered the relationship between exposure to violence and mental health problems among Latinx youth. Other research conducted on Latinx families has found father involvement (Gaxiola-Romero & Frias Armenta, 2012; Nair et al., 2020), parental involvement (Mogro-Wilson, 2011), shared family rituals (Santander et al., 2008), positive relationships with adults outside of one's family (Flores et al., 2005), and social support (Lázaro & Lopez, 2010) serve as protective factors among Latinx families at risk for maltreatment. Familismo is often cited as a central and protective factor for Latinx children (but see chapter 1 for a more nuanced discussion); and living in a two-parent household and family stability are generally high among Latinx families, even compared with White families (National Research Center on Hispanic Children and Families, 2017). Preservation of Latinx culture (e.g., Spanish language, traditional values and traditions) is also considered protective, as shown in the literatures on family functioning (see chapter 4) and the immigrant paradox (see chapter 1). In the context of differential acculturation between parents and children, Buckingham and Brodsky (2015) identified protective factors such as effective communication and problem-solving strategies that helped families build resilience when confronted with acculturation gaps. Protective factors represent opportunities to engage and empower Latinx families to build strengths and support healthy development.

Resilience in Latinx Families

Resilience is defined as "the capacity to overcome adversity resulting from the interplay between risk and protective factors, embedded in multidimensional interconnected systems, including the individual, family, community, and culture" (Mariscal, 2020, p. 2). At the community level, resilience can be considered a way to resist oppression instead of assimilating "to oppressive systems" (Sonn & Fisher, 1998, p. 457). As previously discussed, Latinx populations face significant oppression within U.S. society that marginalizes those who are not White, U.S.-born, English-speaking, and middle class.

Resilience can be impacted by individual factors (e.g., cognitive skills, self-regulation, spirituality) and environmental factors (e.g., access to resources, relationships) (Bernard, 2004). The American Psychological Association (2017) lists building resilience as part of its multicultural guidelines to respond to trauma among diverse populations. Using an ecological framework, Gómez and Kotliarenco (2010) identified a wide range of factors that contribute to resilience, including cognitive processing, attachment, emotional regulation, self-esteem, family cohesion and roles, peer relationships, and cultural values, traditions, and rituals. Gannotti et al. (2004) documented the role of underlying values, specifically allocentrism, familism, simpatia, power, distance, personal space, time orientation, and gender roles, in building resilience. Morelato's (2011) work emphasized the interaction between internal factors (e.g., psychological, biological, etc.) and external factors (e.g., contextual, environmental). Similarly, Vesely et al. (2017) highlighted the importance of considering the broader context of Latinx families, including structural barriers such as immigration laws and discrimination that could impede a family's ability to positively adapt to adversity. Research shows that societal attitudes toward Latinx immigrants undermine individual and collective resilience (Suárez-Orozco et al., 2018).

The literature aligns with the theory of intersectionality, or the interconnectedness of social identities such as race/ethnicity and gender (Bryant-Davis & Comas-Diaz, 2016; Crenshaw, 1991), in illustrating how some social identities increase relative privilege, thereby

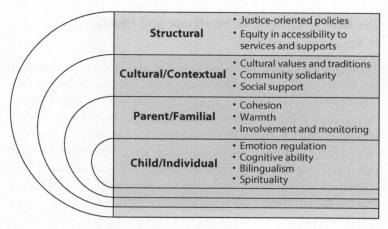

Structural	• Justice-oriented policies • Equity in accessibility to services and supports
Cultural/Contextual	• Cultural values and traditions • Community solidarity • Social support
Parent/Familial	• Cohesion • Warmth • Involvement and monitoring
Child/Individual	• Emotion regulation • Cognitive ability • Bilingualism • Spirituality

FIGURE 7.1. Integrative Model of Resilience

facilitating resilience (Buckingham & Brodsky, 2020). Indeed, one critique of resilience models is the overemphasis on individual and family factors that fail to recognize the role of social structures that maintain deeply embedded inequities (Walsh, 2015). Thus, consistent with the integrative model of child development (Coll et al., 1996) and mujerismo (Bryant-Davis & Comas-Diaz, 2016), we consider how factors at the child, parent, community, and structural levels facilitate resilience (see Fig. 7.1).

In support of this ecological perspective, prior research has found that resilience in Latinx communities can be fostered by investing in community centers, after-school programs, and programs to partner mentors with youth (Shetgiri et al., 2009). Renfroe (2020) found that Latinx immigrant involvement with community organizations partially mitigated the impacts of xenophobic policies and systems. One model, the Restorative Integral Support (RIS), was developed as a whole-person approach to building resilience after experiencing trauma (Larkin et al., 2012). At the community level, RIS includes steps such as engaging the community, utilizing local resources to address needs, and building partnerships (Larkin & Park, 2012). Therefore, an understanding of structural barriers and facilitators is important to build more resilient communities and connect Latinx families with resources that can help them cope with stressors related to child welfare involvement.

The Role of Cultural Competence and Humility in Fostering Resilience

The identification and promotion of protective factors and resilience in Latinx families require that caseworkers fully and deeply understand the range of strengths and challenges they face in navigating their everyday realities. Traditionally, human and social service disciplines have focused on *cultural competence* for providers to become competent or knowledgeable about another group's cultural values and practices (Fong, 2004). Cultural competence has been defined as "the acquisition of knowledge, values, and skills needed [. . .] to work with persons from different ethnic cultural backgrounds" (Fong, 2004, p. 351). Social work, a discipline that has been central to child welfare practice, has implemented standards and indicators for cultural competence among practitioners (National Association of Social Workers, 2015). Cultural competence may entail language proficiency and understanding of cultural beliefs (Fernandez et al., 2004). Specific to Latinx families, some studies have evaluated cultural adaptations of mental health (Soto et al., 2018) or parenting interventions (Haralson et al., 2020) by measuring professional competence.

In child welfare, cultural competence has often included training materials to raise professional knowledge of disproportionality, disparities, and unjust policies such as the Indian Child Welfare Act (Lawrence et al., 2012; McPhatter, 1999; Pierce & Pierce, 1996). For Latinx families involved in child welfare, professionals may demonstrate cultural competence by understanding acculturation and immigration issues and how these may impact family processes (Dettlaff, 2008; Hancock, 2005). Cultural competence can also be assessed via responses to children of color in the child welfare system, caseworker-family interactions, and agency policies (Pierce & Pierce, 1996). However, scholars note inconsistencies in how cultural competence is conceptualized, measured, and assessed among child welfare agencies (Nybell & Gray, 2004). Moreover, some have critiqued cultural competence, as it focuses more on professional knowledge than effectiveness in serving clients (Beagan, 2018) and may not actively challenge structural inequalities (Fischer-Borne et al., 2015).

In contrast to cultural competence, in which the practitioner presents mastery of cultural knowledge of groups with whom they work (Fischer-Borne et al., 2015), cultural humility posits that professionals are "flexible and humble enough to let go of the false sense of security that stereotyping brings" (Tervalon & Murray-Garcia, 1998, p. 119). Cultural competence has been deemed product-focused (e.g., mastery of knowledge), while cultural humility is process-focused (e.g., engaging in lifelong learning; Yancu & Farmer, 2017). Cultural humility, which is aligned with mujerismo, requires professionals to engage in self-reflection, consider their own positionality (Tinkler & Tinkler, 2016), and shift away from the professional as the expert (Ross, 2010). Thus, cultural humility is a micro-level approach that promotes ongoing self-reflection and lifelong learning. Corey (2021) identified three main components of cultural humility that nicely involve a mujerismo stance: self-reflection, attention to power imbalances between professionals and clients, and developing nonpaternalistic partnerships.

In child welfare, cultural humility results in practitioners drawing "on the cultural expertise of the families with whom they work" and recognizes that the family is the expert of their own story and experience (Ortega & Faller, 2011, p. 33). From a cultural humility perspective, child welfare practitioners can use strategies such as active listening, reflecting, and reserving judgment to engage and assess their clients (Ortega & Faller, 2011). Moreover, cultural humility requires child welfare practitioners to critically assess their own positionality and intersecting identities, such as ethnicity, gender, and socioeconomic status to build trust and "make visible" the privilege inherent in many practitioner-client relationships (Mallon, 2020, p. vi). The intersectional approach of cultural humility can help practitioners recognize the heterogeneity of Latinx families and shift away from stereotypes or sweeping generalizations (Fontes, 1993; Meléndez Guevara et al., 2021). Furthermore, cultural humility can help strengthen the relationship between providers and Latinx clients (Mosher et al., 2017).

In light of the critique that cultural humility does not adequately disrupt privilege or address structural inequalities, as recommended by mujerismo, some disciplines have embraced *critical humility*. Critical humility includes self-reflection on positionality but also includes strategies to interrupt privilege (Barlas et al., 2017). It builds upon the three principles that Corey (2021) identified for *cultural humility* to include a critical understanding of and actions to deconstruct structural barriers and advance towards liberation. Critical humility includes "a commitment to social justice and positioning oneself in an ethical stance toward equity and non-neutrality" (Terrazas et al., 2020, p. 363).

Healing and Resilience among Latinx Families

Given the multiple dimensions and factors that can impact resilience among Latinx families, it is important to consider multipronged approaches that target protective factors at the individual, family, and community levels to foster resilience and healing. One important component is education and outreach about various community services and how to access each one; this could help address some disparities in service utilization (Shetgiri et al., 2009). At the family level, some strengths-based interventions have been developed or adapted for Latinx families that promote family functioning. A recent strengths-based intervention, *Confía en Mi, Confío en Ti* (Trust in Me, Trust in You), was developed specifically for Latinx families to improve parent-child relationships via attachment security, self-efficacy, and empathy (Borelli et al., 2021). This intervention targets several factors associated with resilience in prior studies, such as empathy and self-efficacy. Furthermore, it seeks to foster resilience through parent-child connection, encouragement, and security. The group format of *Confía en Mi, Confío en Ti* allows Latinx mothers to build their own resilience through self-efficacy and empathy, as well as collective resilience through shared experiences among parent participants (Borelli et al., 2021). Parent management training is another family-level intervention that focuses on positive parenting approaches and improving the parent-child relationship. In a study with seventy-three Spanish-speaking Latinx parents, families that received a specific type of parent management training, *Nuestras Familias: Andando Entre Culturas* (Our Families: Moving Between Cultures), had increases in effective parenting, skill encouragement, and overall quality of parenting (Martinez Jr & Eddy, 2005).

Although much of the literature on resilience among Latinx families in child welfare focuses on child or family factors, the current influx of unaccompanied minors and the lingering effects of the Zero-Tolerance Policy and family separation have highlighted the need for policy changes and macro-level advocacy to support resilience in Latinx immigrant families, as advised by the mujerismo framework (Ataiants et al., 2018). The Building Migrant Resilience in Cities project at York University (2021) explored the concept of *transformative resilience* to examine adaptation and coping among immigrant communities through challenging power dynamics. Transformative resilience recognizes inequalities and power differentials in the social structure and, utilizing a framework of interdependence among individuals and their environments, focuses on structural changes that can build resilient systems (DeVerteuil & Golubchikov, 2016). Through transformative resilience, community members may organize and advocate for public policy and programming that builds community infrastructure and resources. For example, policies that extend childcare benefits may improve employment and education accessibility for parents who could not afford childcare without assistance (Shields & Abu Alrob, 2020).

For providers or professionals that work with Latinx clients, transformative resilience can include shared solidarity and advocacy to challenge racism and nativism. For example, Muñoz et al. (2018) found that resilience among Latinx youth on college campuses during the Trump administration increased when there was solidarity and advocacy to support Deferred Action for Childhood Arrivals (DACA) students. More generally, programs that foster a sense of community have been linked to higher resilience among Latinx immigrants (Buckingham & Brodsky, 2020). Transformative resilience embraces the tenets of mujerismo by fostering activism, promoting collective liberation from oppressive structures, and ensuring transformation that is attentive to the intersecting identities of the Latinx community (Bryant-Davis & Comas-Diaz, 2016).

Case Illustrations

Like all families, and particularly families who persevere in the face of oppressive experiences related to poverty and immigration, the cases of Bianca, Dominic, and Audriana demonstrate how the child welfare system can recognize strengths and promote resilience and healing. They also illustrate the opportunities to engage in meaningful advocacy that challenges inequities and insists on just and humane systems for all families. We challenge you to draw parallels to the communities with which you work and to develop your own commitments to strength-based and transformative approaches grounded in critical humility and mujerismo.

Bianca

Strengths-Based Practices. Strengths-based practices could focus on building upon the protective factors identified in the case, such as the mother's employment, Bianca's participation in Head Start, and connections with neighbors who made the initial report when they were concerned for Bianca and her mother's safety. A case plan could include opportunities to increase social support, possibly in her neighborhood, at Bianca's school, or among her co-workers.

Critical Humility. In Bianca's case, a critical humility perspective could help the practitioners understand the unique circumstances and experiences of Bianca and her parents while also recognizing structural inequities and challenges that may have increased family stress. This would include exploring cultural beliefs and expectations with Bianca's family and how these may have impacted the events that led to Bianca's removal. Furthermore, structural factors such as health-care accessibility, disability benefits, services for English-language learners, and documentation status all could have impacted Bianca's mother's ability to create a safety plan and separate from Bianca's father, as well as her father's ability to access supportive services.

Transformative Resilience. There are several opportunities that could help foster transformative resilience in Bianca and her family. For example, given that Bianca's mother was the victim of a crime in the United States, a practitioner could refer her to a center for crime victim support to help her apply for a crime victim's visa. This could help her mother access more services and connect with resources such as a separate apartment, at least temporarily, depending on Bianca's father's willingness to engage in therapy. Practitioners can also engage in advocacy to help address inept policies and structural concerns.

Dominic

Strengths-Based Practices. Protective factors in Dominic's case include consistently living with his mother for the first six years of life; the presence of Rodrigo, a father figure in the household; his mother's use of resources in the community (e.g., day care center, behavioral health services for Dominic and herself); the presence of extended family; and concerned neighbors. The practitioner could work with Dominic's mother and Rodrigo to expand their own support networks within the community, which could facilitate a safety plan to avoid any future instances of neglectful supervision. Given Daniela's openness to social services, the practitioner could also facilitate referral to sites that may provide low-cost and after-hours childcare.

Critical Humility. Using a critical humility perspective, the practitioner in Dominic's case could critically assess structural barriers that Dominic and his family may have experienced, situate their own positionality, and then explore the family's cultural context from a strengths-based perspective (Gannotti et al., 2004). It would also be important for the practitioner to consider the family's prior experience with different systems, such as the schools and health care, and how this might impact their perception of the child welfare system.

Transformative Resilience. The practitioner could critically examine agency policies that could be changed to focus on resilience instead of deficits. In Dominic's case, the issue of a onetime neglectful supervision, especially when the grandparents lived in the apartment above, would have been better addressed by working with the family to create a safety plan and better utilize their own support networks, rather than by removing the child. Part of healing and resilience in this case might include advocating for more accessible childcare and health-care service options.

Audriana

Strengths-Based Practices. In Audriana's case, strengths include her citizenship status; the legal status of her mother and siblings; the presence of several important family figures, including her mother and stepfather; the presence of a religious community; her involvement in school and extracurricular activities; and her relationship with other adults including her aunt, the pastor at her family's church, and the school counselor. To leverage the family's connection to the Pentecostal church, for example, a practitioner could explore whether the pastor may participate in discussions with the family. This could provide the family with opportunities to reframe their daughters' behavior and revelation of abuse while still respecting and validating their religious beliefs. The presence of their maternal aunt is also a strength that was unexplored by the practitioner. The aunt might have served as a viable placement for the girls to keep them out of an institutional placement.

Critical Humility. A practitioner could use a critical humility perspective by exploring the family's cultural beliefs, experiences, and perceptions of the current situation. Given the parents' strict religious beliefs, it could be important to explore their belief that the girls were lying. In doing so, it would be important for practitioners to understand how topics like sexual initiation and sexual abuse are perceived in the family's culture, to self-reflect on their own biases and beliefs related to the family's culture and religiosity, and to consider the structural policies and practices that are impacting the family.

Transformative Resilience. Transformative resilience could focus on addressing the structural barriers that Audriana's family faces. This could include advocating for and identifying housing opportunities for Audriana's mother and stepfather that would enable them to leave the step-uncle's house. In addition, gender inequities could be explored in this case to unpack the family's beliefs about sexual intercourse and to dispel myths of sexual abuse.

Closing Summary

This chapter examined resilience and healing in Latinx families. An integrative model of resilience can help us identify risk and protective factors at the child, family/parent, community, and structural levels. For Latinx families, a multilevel integrative model of resilience may be particularly useful, as it can encompass the complex cultural and contextual considerations that may promote or impede resilience. Practitioners can engage in cultural and critical humility to foster resilience and empower Latinx clients. In addition to exploring multilevel factors, it is also important to consider ways to promote transformative resilience among Latinx families, through strategies such as community organization and advocacy for socially just policies. In the next chapter, we conclude the book by reimagining each of the cases from the introduction through a lens of critical humility, mujerismo, and equity.

8

Conclusion

Future Directions

> We cannot seek achievement
> for ourselves and forget about
> progress and prosperity for our
> community. . . . Our ambitions
> must be broad enough to include
> the aspirations and needs of others,
> for their sakes and for our own.
> —Cesar Chavez

In this book, we have explored issues relevant to Latinx populations in the United States to advance understanding of how the child welfare system can meet its goal of providing services "to promote the well-being of children by ensuring safety, achieving permanency, and strengthening families" for *all* children (Child Welfare Information Gateway, 2020, p. 2). We argue that the mission of strengthening families and communities and keeping children safe requires dismantling systems of oppression and building equitable and inclusive systems. Among Latinx families, this can include an approach rooted in mujerismo that integrates diverse cultural values and beliefs to transform families and communities (Gloria & Castellanos, 2016).

We dedicate this final chapter to Bianca's, Dominic's, and Audriana's cases. In this chapter, building upon mujerismo and antiracist frameworks, we reconceptualize and reimagine the cases through a lens of empowerment, equity, and transformation. In each case, there are multiple examples of how oppression impacts the lives of families. There are also multiple points where practice interventions and policies could have supported families to avoid removal from the home while still ensuring that the children have safe, stable, and nurturing environments.

In chapter 2, we discussed the public health model for healthy child development. The model identifies three basic needs of children: (1) safety, or the physical and psychological well-being of a child within their social and physical environment; (2) stability, or the extent to which children have consistent and reliable social and physical environments for their optimal development; and (3) nurturing, or the extent to which developmental needs of a child are met through responsive caregiving (Fortson et al., 2016). Through this lens, we examine points where practice and policy changes could have altered the trajectory of the family.

Bianca

Bianca is an eight-year-old Mexican girl who has been removed from her parents in Arizona after her father physically assaulted her mother. Bianca's mother was hospitalized and Bianca was placed into foster care.

Stability

The first opportunity to reimagine Bianca's case begins with her parents in Mexico. The stability of the family has been impacted by U.S. interventions in Latin America that have created multigenerational poverty, community violence, and corruption. Bianca's family does not want to migrate to the United States and does not want to be a transnational family. In a reimagined scenario, socially just policies from the United States would provide Bianca's family real opportunities to provide a stable home for her. Taking a mujerista approach, local communities would be empowered to identify their members' needs and be given autonomy to use reparations to address the needs they identify. With opportunities for financial stability, Bianca's family has options to stay together in their hometown because there would be enough work for her father to provide for the family.

Another opportunity to reimagine Bianca's case is the family's situation in the United States. Once Bianca and her mother are in the United States, the family is forced to live "in the shadows" because of their undocumented status. When her father is injured and cannot work, there are no services available to help the family financially, as they are barred from public welfare programs due to their lack of documentation. Thus, U.S. immigration policy directly creates instability for Bianca and her family by denying them access to public services that could stabilize their family. In a reimagined case, Bianca's father could access health care for his injury as well as financial support while he heals from his injury. Bianca's mother could have options to work or train for work that did not pay her "under the table." Both parents would then be afforded the same rights as other parents to be protected in the workplace and access programs to stabilize their family.

Nurturing

A strength of Bianca's case is that she has had many adults in her life who have shown warmth and kindness. Before coming to the United States, Bianca was cared for by a grandmother with whom she had a strong attachment. After migrating to the United States, Bianca could not see her grandmother or talk to her by phone on a regular basis. In all likelihood, Bianca will never physically visit with her grandmother again because border crossings are too risky. In a reimagined scenario, Bianca would be able to safely visit her grandmother, and when (if) she was removed from her mother, her grandmother could safely get to her to provide care. U.S. policy shifts could value families by allowing for safe entry and exit across the U.S.-Mexico border. As discussed in chapter 3, restricted movement across the border is a recent phenomenon. Historically, unrestricted movement across the border fostered industry and growth for border communities.

Another strength of Bianca's case is her enrollment in the Head Start program. This is one of the few programs that is available to undocumented children. Bianca's mother received parenting advice related to discipline. However, the programs targeted mothers and, as such, Bianca's father missed opportunities to learn about ways to support Bianca's development. In a reimagined case, minor adjustments to that programming could improve nurturing. First, the program could receive additional financial support to offer educational opportunities for parents outside of regular childcare hours. Opportunities would be available for Bianca's father to attend the parenting classes and a support group for Spanish-speaking fathers. These could be offered in the evenings with free childcare and dinner. Bianca's parents could meet other Latinx immigrant families, some of whom are also in the process of regularizing their immigration status. The facilitators would conduct the classes in Spanish and have developed curriculums specific to common cultural and parenting beliefs, incorporating concepts such as *familismo* and *respeto* into the materials. Bianca's father could learn about developmental stages, appropriate expectations, and discipline strategies, and connect with other fathers who have attended the parenting classes. The informal parent networks would help Bianca's parents provide and receive support within their community.

Another strength in Bianca's life is the nurturing and dedication provided by her mother. Bianca's removal from her mother's care disrupts that nurturing and is a source of additional trauma for Bianca. In a reimagined scenario, Bianca's mother can receive support from Bianca's school. In this scenario, the teachers at Bianca's school note the change in her behavior early on. They ask both of Bianca's parents to come in for a conference. At the conference, Bianca's parents report feeling overwhelmed and stressed due to her father's injury, unemployment, and subsequent increased alcohol consumption. The teachers are nonjudgmental and supportive. They refer Bianca's parents to a school-based social worker who works with the parents to co-construct a support plan. The social worker refer Bianca's family to a pro bono immigration support center to help her parents regularize their status, as this will allow her parents to seek employment and obtain healthcare benefits. In the meantime, the social worker refers her father to a public clinic that serves undocumented immigrants so that he can receive treatment for the injury he suffered at his construction job.

As alcohol abuse and domestic violence are often interrelated (Shorey et al., 2013; Taft et al., 2010), the social worker discusses support and safety options with Bianca's parents. Bianca's father commits to attending weekly Alcoholics Anonymous meetings, and together, her parents can anonymously call the National Domestic Violence Hotline, where the advocate refers them to a family support center. At the family support center, a team of professionals conducts an assessment and creates a safety plan with Bianca's family. The professionals recognize the structural factors that have added stress to Bianca's family, and should have experience advocating for parents with limited English and who are undocumented. Furthermore, they incorporate *personalismo* into their work by taking the time to get to know Bianca's parents and establish rapport.

Safety

Prior to her placement in foster care, Bianca had experienced a traumatic event that threatened her safety. After crossing the border with her mother, Bianca was separated from her mother and held hostage when a coyote demanded more money before her release. She witnessed her father kill the coyote when he refused to release Bianca. This event was traumatic for the whole family. In a reimagined scenario where border crossing is safe and unrestricted, this tragedy would not have occurred. While that would be the ideal scenario, we can also reimagine Bianca's case in terms of the assistance her family could have received after the trauma. In this scenario, having lived in Phoenix for four years, Bianca's father has become familiar with several support services for Latinx immigrants. He recognizes the danger that Bianca was in, and the trauma she may have experienced on her journey to the United States. After getting Bianca and her mother back to his place in Phoenix, he reaches out to an organization that provides legal assistance with U Visas for undocumented immigrants who have been victims of crime in the United States. Within twenty-four hours of calling the center to ask for assistance, the intake team meets with Bianca and her parents. The intake team uses a critical humility approach, in which they explore and validate the family's beliefs, concerns, and strengths. Bianca's parents identify their two main concerns: getting proper documentation to remain in the country legally, and providing support to Bianca and her mother given the trauma they endured on the journey to the United States. Based on the areas of support Bianca's parents mention in the intake interview, the team assigns a pro bono lawyer to the case, who files a U Visa for all three members of the family. The intake team also refers the family to a therapist who will conduct an assessment and help the family process the separation, trauma related to the situation with the coyote, and the family's subsequent reunification and adaptation. These services are offered to the family pro bono. The therapist is fluent in Spanish and has expertise working with families seeking asylum and undocumented crime victims. Through the services they are provided at the center, Bianca's mother can also have weekly calls with her family back in Mexico. This provides Bianca and her mother with a sense of support and connectedness.

The second safety concern in Bianca's case relates to her placement in foster care. If Bianca's case were reimagined as discussed above, there would be no need for her to be placed into foster care. In a reimagined scenario, Bianca's family would already receive support from the school social worker, family violence program, and Alcoholics Anonymous. The professionals involved in the case work with Bianca and her mother to develop a safety plan and support and validate her beliefs and decisions in the process. With an understanding of all her options, Bianca's mother chooses to stay with Bianca's father, and her decision is respected. Bianca's father recognizes the need to get help and is able to participate in the elaboration of the safety plan. When her parents argue, Bianca and her mother activate their safety plan, which involves them leaving the apartment to stay with a friend who has become part of their informal support network. Bianca's mother also notifies the father's sponsor at Alcoholics Anonymous.

Bianca's Reimagined Ending

Like many children, Bianca entered foster care because she had witnessed domestic violence. She was never physically abused. The child welfare system alleges that Bianca's mother is unable to care for her and keep her safe. However, Bianca's mother is the primary source of stability and nurturing for Bianca, and their separation will inevitably harm Bianca. Our reimagining of Bianca's case begins with her family never having to come to the United States. Indeed, that decision point would have changed the course of the entire story, and Bianca would have never witnessed her father murder a coyote and never entered foster care. Her family may have still experienced domestic violence, but there would have been more familial supports available to them.

We conclude our journey with Bianca imagining that her family was never forced to migrate to the United States. Rather, policies changed so that violence, corruption, and poverty were mitigated in her community through fair labor practices that benefited her father. The United States provided reparations to communities negatively impacted by U.S. policies. Using funds, Bianca's community can build schools and a medical clinic. Bianca thrives at school and grows up with the safety, stability, and nurturing needed by every child.

Dominic

Dominic is a six-year-old Puerto Rican boy who lives in New York City. He is in kindergarten and was recently diagnosed with ADHD. Dominic lives with his mother, her boyfriend, and his infant sister. He was placed into foster care because he was left home alone.

Stability

Dominic's case can be reimagined starting before he was born. While Daniela has many strengths as a mother, she had Dominic at a young age when she did not have access to resources such as high-quality health care (e.g., prenatal and perinatal) and other supports that could have helped stabilize the family. Given Daniela's young age, home visiting services would have helped ensure that she had the skills and confidence to nurture and care for her newborn; provide for him financially; manage her own health and well-being; and build up her social support. Services would be guided by a thorough assessment of Daniela's background, values, social networks, and parenting goals. Home visiting services would coach Daniela to proactively engage Dominic's grandparents and biological father. With adequate support, such as co-parenting classes, Dominic's father may have remained involved in Dominic's upbringing and his sister's father may have received substance use treatment before his substance use escalated to the point that he was doing drugs in the home.

Another point of instability in Dominic's life has been school. Dominic was asked to leave his day care because of his disruptive behavior, and his behavior issues have continued into kindergarten. He was diagnosed with ADHD. In a reimagined case, Dominic's day care center would be well resourced, and its staff trained on how to identify and deal with challenging behaviors. The curriculum is focused on building social and emotional learning skills. The diverse staff are intentional and proactive in building positive relationships with parents. Feedback on how the children are doing in the day care setting is given frequently using a strengths-based perspective. In Dominic's case, Daniela is invited to observe how he is doing, set goals for his adjustment to school, reward him for his progress, and reinforce positive behaviors outside of school. When a referral becomes necessary, the day care staff helps explain the process of seeking pediatric consultation and ensures that Daniela has a pediatrician that she feels comfortable seeing. She is also offered a referral to a mental health professional and empowered to choose the professional that best fits her needs. When she chooses not to use medication to treat Dominic's ADHD, her day care offers her psychoeducational and psychosocial resources that are accessible to her. Daniela chooses to work with a social worker, who helps her make a plan for managing Dominic's symptoms and also meets with the family members who help care for him. Daniela also attends a parenting group for caregivers of young children with ADHD. Once in kindergarten, Dominic's teacher partners with Daniela to manage his ADHD. They set behavior and learning goals that are developmentally appropriate and leverage Dominic's strengths. Rodrigo is explicitly included in the plan, helping to ease some of the burden on Daniela.

Nurturing

A strength of Dominic's case is the multiple supportive adults who nurture him. Daniela is attached to and protective of both her children. Daniela's parents are also engaged with Dominic and his sister; and Daniela's current partner, Rodrigo, has been acting as a father figure. Dominic's current teacher is also supportive.

Daniela has been experiencing fatigue, sadness, and lack of motivation. Given her strained relationship with her parents and the demands of working to help Dominic with his behaviors, these symptoms suggest she may struggle with depression, which can interfere with her ability to continue to nurture and support Dominic and his sister. In reimagining Dominic's case, we see an opportunity for nurturing Daniela. Recognizing the importance of the family system, especially in multigenerational Latinx families, Daniela and her parents are offered family therapy. Services are nearby, are available outside of traditional business hours, provide childcare, and are available for a nominal fee. Therapists are Latinx and bilingual. Issues of familismo (beliefs, expectations, and family roles and responsibilities) and acculturation (differential acculturation, shifting cultural values) are explored to build understanding and respect for each caregiver's parenting approach.

Safety

Despite the strengths of Dominic's family, there are two instances where his safety is threatened. In the first instance, his sister's father uses drugs in the home and physically assaults his mother. Dominic witnesses this violence. In terms of safety, Daniela removed her children from a living situation where they were likely to witness or experience more violence. While she decided to protect her children, there is no indication that either she or Dominic received help to process their experience. In a reimagined scenario, Daniela would have the means to leave and to secure safe housing where she was not dependent on anyone for financial support. Through a local family violence program, she would learn how to talk with and support Dominic in dealing with the experience.

The second safety issue involves Dominic being left home alone while Daniela seeks treatment for her symptoms of depression. In a reimagined scenario, once Daniela experiences these depressive symptoms, she has a strong family network. She feels comfortable confiding in her parents and other family members to get support in meeting her daily needs (e.g., cooking, caring for the children). She is also familiar with mental health services because of her experience with family therapy and parenting groups. When Daniela makes an appointment to see a doctor about her depressive symptoms, she has a thorough understanding of Dominic's needs as a child with ADHD. He can be impulsive and energetic and cannot be left unsupervised. When she learns that neither her parents nor Rodrigo is available at the time of her appointment, she knows she has other options, including extended family who may be available and a job that allows her to take time off for a doctor's appointment. She talks through the situation with Rodrigo, who calls their network to find childcare for Dominic. Daniela gets an appropriate diagnosis for her depression and is referred for psychotherapy and she gradually improves with the help of her support network.

Dominic's Reimagined Ending

Dominic entered foster care because his mother left him unsupervised. He never experienced abuse. Rather, he was removed based on allegations of neglect. In taking a closer look at Dominic's case, he had a childhood where his mother tried very hard to provide stability and nurturing. In our opinion, Dominic's removal from her care should never have happened. Our reimagining of his case involves an informal and formal support system for Daniela that steps in to help at key points in her life, including when Dominic is born and as soon as Daniela identifies she is feeling depressed. With the right help, Daniela can care for herself and her children without a need for intervention from the child welfare system.

Audriana

Audriana is a fifteen-year-old girl living in Los Angeles with her mother, older sister, stepfather, and three younger half brothers. They live in a home owned by her step-uncle, who lives in the home as well. Audriana and her sister were sexually abused by the uncle. After disclosing the abuse, they were placed into an emergency shelter.

Audriana's case is the only case in our series where the child actually experienced abuse. This was deliberate because most entries into foster care are due to neglect rather than abuse. In Bianca's and Dominic's cases, there are clear pathways to prevent entry into foster care. With Audriana, there is a clear safety concern that requires intervention. We contend that with the right supports in place, the intervention would not have to separate the family. Thus, we reimagine Audriana's case in the context of stability, nurturing, and safety both before and after the abuse to understand how her case outcome could be different.

Stability

Audriana's family has many strengths. Her mother and stepfather work hard. The family is connected to their community through church and the children are involved in school activities. The main issue threatening the family's stability is housing. They are forced to live in their uncle's home because of the extraordinary cost of living in Los Angeles. In reimagining Audriana's case, housing seems to be the issue that may have prevented her from living with a predatory step-uncle. Ideally, Audriana's family would earn a living wage that would allow them to afford a safe home for themselves. Audriana's stepfather would not have issues finding work despite his status as undocumented. Fair and just immigration policies would allow him access to jobs where his rights as a worker are protected.

Nurturing

Audriana has a distant relationship with her mother, likely due to the trauma her mother experienced pre-migration and during migration. While pregnant with Audriana, her mother experienced the murder of her husband in Honduras. Audriana's mother then migrated to the United States while pregnant. She was sexually assaulted during the journey. All of these experiences were incredibly traumatic. In reimagining Audriana's case, there are many points that could be changed to alter the course of her life. To begin with, U.S. intervention in Latin America, particularly related to the drug trade and law enforcement, would cease and pathways for economic growth would decrease violence. Audriana's father would never have been a victim of violence.

Another point of intervention could be the family's migration to the United States. Just immigration policies would have allowed Audriana's mother to realistically apply for and receive refugee status in the United States. She could then journey by plane directly to Los Angeles. Such a journey would have prevented the sexual violence she experienced. Once in the United States, Audriana's mother would have access to services to help her process the trauma she experienced so she would be able to maintain healthy attachments with her daughters and support them throughout their development, including when (if) they disclosed abuse.

Safety

The sexual abuse committed by the step-uncle is the foremost safety concern in Audriana's case. In reimagining Audriana's case, the abuse might have been prevented if the family had their own housing and were not living with a predatory individual. Once the abuse was disclosed, Audriana's family could have prevented the removal of the girls if they were able to find housing of their own. Ideally, Audriana's mother would have worked on her own trauma history so that she was emotionally available to provide the support that the girls needed once they disclosed the abuse. The family would be connected to professionals who could provide therapy and psychoeducation about sexual assault and parenting children who have experienced trauma. The girls would also receive medical care to ensure they have not contracted sexually transmitted infections and/or become pregnant. A medical provider could address the girls' concerns and answer any questions they may have. These services are available in Spanish and the service providers are attuned to the cultural and contextual nuances of the girls' cases.

Audriana's Reimagined Ending

Despite the serious abuse Audriana and her sister have endured, there is opportunity for her family to heal. Perhaps most importantly, we reimagine a scenario where Audriana's mother can get help for her own trauma years before this event, and when her daughters disclose the abuse, she is able to support them in their healing and protect them from further harm. Audriana and her sister are not separated from their half siblings because the family finds their own housing that allows all the children to remain in their current schools. The entire family then receives support through therapy as needed. Building upon strengths and protective factors, Audriana's family can foster transformative resilience to liberate the family from oppressive structures they have faced based on their intersecting identities.

Closing Summary

As we reach the end of our reimagined cases and this book, we revisit some of our professional beliefs that guided this book. We are committed to social justice and to the dismantling of systems that perpetuate racism, sexism, xenophobia, classism, and ableism. The child welfare system is a critical safeguard for the well-being of children, but it can serve to further stress, harm, and, in some cases, traumatize families that face these oppressive forces. Thus, a full understanding of child maltreatment in Latinx families must be guided by an assessment of families in the context of their social identities and lived experiences. The cases we presented are fictional, but they reflect common scenarios that we have encountered in our professional practice. As illustrated by these cases, there are a variety of injustices and constraints that families face that make them more likely to come to the attention of and to be misserved by the child welfare system. We contend that systemic changes that provide support to families are the best solution to preventing and healing from child maltreatment.

References

Abidin, R. R. (1992). The determinants of parenting behavior. *Journal of Clinical Child Psychology, 21*(4), 407–412. https://doi.org/10.1207 /s15374424jccp2104_12

Abraído-Lanza, A. F., Armbrister, A. N., Flórez, K. R., & Aguirre, A. N. (2006). Toward a theory-driven model of acculturation in public health research. *American Journal of Public Health, 96*(8), 1342–1346. https:// doi.org/10.2105/AJPH.2005.06498

Abrego, L., & LaRossa, R. (2009). Economic well-being in Salvadoran transnational families: How gender affects remittance practices. *Journal of Marriage and Family, 71*(4), 1070–1085. https://www.jstor.org/stable /27752519.

Acevedo-Garcia, D., Noelke, C., & McArdle, N. (2020). *The geography of child opportunity: Why neighborhoods matter for equity.* Brandeis: The Heller School for Social Policy and Management. https://www .diversitydatakids.org/sites/default/files/file/ddk_the-geography-of-child -opportunity_2020v2_0.pdf

Adulin, G., Cyrus, J. W., Asare, M., & Sabik, L. M. (2019). Barriers and facilitators to breast and cervical cancer screening among immigrants in the United States. *Journal of Immigrant and Minority Health, 21*(3), 606–658. https://doi.org/10.1007/s10903-018-0794-6

Afifi, T. O, Ford, D., Gershoff, E. T., Merrick, M., Grogan-Kaylor, A., Ports, K. A., MacMillan, H. L., Holden, G. W., Taylor, C. A., Lee, S. J., & Peters Bennett, R. (2017). Spanking and adult mental health impairment: The case for the designation of spanking as an adverse childhood experience. *Child Abuse & Neglect, 71*, 24–31. https://doi.org/10.1016/j .chiabu.2017.01.014

Ai, A. L., Lee, J., Solis, A., & Yap, C. (2016). Childhood abuse, religious involvement, and substance abuse among Latino-American men in the United States. *International Journal of Behavioral Medicine, 23*(6), 764–775. https://doi.org/10.1007/s12529-016-9561-z

Alegría, M., Canino, G., Shrout, P. E., Woo, M., Duan, N., Vila, D., Torres, M., Chen, C. N., & Meng, X. L. (2008). Prevalence of mental illness in immigrant and non-immigrant U.S. Latino groups. *The American Journal of Psychiatry, 165*(3), 359–369. https://doi.org/10.1176/appi.ajp .2007.07040704

Alegría, M., Canino, G., Stinson, F. S., & Grant, B. F. (2006). Nativity and DSM-IV psychiatric disorders among Puerto Ricans, Cuban Americans, and non-Latino whites in the United States: Results from the National Epidemiologic Survey on Alcohol and Related Conditions. *The Journal of Clinical Psychiatry, 67*(1), 56–65. https://doi.org/10.4088 /jcp.v67n0109

Altschul, I., & Lee, S. J. (2011). Direct and mediated effects of nativity and other indicators of acculturation on Hispanic mothers' use of physical aggression. *Child Maltreatment, 16*(4), 262–274. https://doi.org/10.1177 /1077559511421523

Altschul, I., Lee, S. J., & Gershoff, E. T. (2016). Hugs, not hits: Warmth and spanking as predictors of child social competence. *Journal of Marriage and Family, 78*(3), 695–714. https://doi.org/10.1111/jomf.12306

Alzate, M. M., & Rosenthal, J. A. (2009). Gender and ethnic differences for Hispanic children referred to child protective services. *Children and Youth Services Review, 31*(1), 1–7. https://doi.org/10.1016/j.childyouth .2008.05.002

American Immigration Council (2021, June). *U.S.-citizen children impacted by immigration enforcement.* https://www.americanimmigrationcouncil .org/sites/default/files/research/us_citizen_children_impacted_by _immigration_enforcement_0.pdf

American Psychological Association (2017). *Multicultural guidelines: An ecological approach to context, identity, and intersectionality.* http://www .apa.org/about/policy/multicultural-guidelines.pdf

American Psychological Association (2019, February 15). *Resolution on physical discipline of children by parents.* Retrieved from https://www.apa .org/about/policy/physical-discipline.pdf

Anguiano, R. M. (2018). Language brokering among Latino immigrant families: Moderating variables and youth outcomes. *Journal of Youth and Adolescence, 47*(1), 222–242. https://doi.org/10.1007/s10964-017 -0744-y

Angulo-Pasel, C. (2018). The journey of Central American women migrants: Engendering the mobile commons. *Mobilities, 13*(6), 894–909. https:// doi.org/10.1080/17450101.2018.1498225

Applied Research Center (2011, November 8). Shattered families: The perilous intersection of immigration enforcement and the child welfare system. *The Atlantic Philanthropies.* atlanticphilanthropies.org/research -reports/report-shattered-families-perilous-intersection-immigration -enforcement-and-child-welfare-s

Arroyo, J., Zsembik, B., & Peek, C. W. (2019). Ain't nobody got time for dad? Racial-ethnic disproportionalities in child welfare casework practice with nonresident fathers. *Child Abuse & Neglect, 93*, 182–196. https://doi.org/10.1016/j.chiabu.2019.03.01

Asawa, L. E., Hansen, D. J., & Flood, M. F. (2008). Early childhood intervention programs: Opportunities and challenges for preventing child maltreatment. *Education and Treatment of Children, 31*(1), 73–110. http://www.jstor.org/stable/42899964.

Ataiants, J., Cohen, C., Riley, A. H., Lieberman, J. T., Reidy, M. C., & Chilton, M. (2018). Unaccompanied children at the United States border, a human rights crisis that can be addressed with policy change. *Journal of Immigrant and Minority Health, 20*(4), 1000–1010. https://doi.org/10.1007/s10903-017-0577-5

Ayón, C. (2015). *Economic, social, and health effects of discrimination on Latino immigrant families*. Migration Policy Institute. https://www.immigrationresearch.org/system/files/FCD-Ayon.pdf

Ayón, C. (2016). Talking to Latino children about race, inequality, and discrimination: Raising families in an anti-immigrant political environment. *Journal of the Society for Social Work and Research, 7*(3), 449–477. https://doi.org/10.1086/686929

Ayón, C., & Garcia, S. J. (2019). Latino immigrant parents' experiences with discrimination: Implications for parenting in a hostile immigration policy context. *Journal of Family Issues, 40*(6), 805–831. https://doi.org/10.1177/0192513X19827988

Ayón, C., & Aisenberg, E. (2010). Negotiating cultural values and expectations within the public child welfare system: A look at familismo and personalismo. *Child & Family Social Work, 15*(3), 335–344. https://doi.org/10.1111/j.1365-2206.2010.00682.x

Ayón, C., & Lee, C. D. (2005). A comparative analysis of child welfare services through the eyes of African American, Caucasian, and Latino parents. *Research on Social Work Practice, 15*(4), 257–266. https://doi.org/10.1177/1049731505274673

Ayón, C., Williams, L. R., Marsiglia, F. F., Ayers, S., & Kiehne, E. (2015). A latent profile analysis of Latino parenting: The infusion of cultural values on family conflict. *Families in Society: The Journal of Contemporary Human Services, 96*(3), 203–210. https://doi.org/10.1606/1044-3894.2015.96.25

Baciu, A., Negussie, Y., Geller, A., & Weinstein, J. N. (2017). *The root causes of health inequity*. Communities in Action: Pathways to Health Equity. National Academies Press (US). https://www.ncbi.nlm.nih.gov/books/NBK425845/

Bagdasaryan, S. (2005). Evaluating family preservation services: Reframing the question of effectiveness. *Children and Youth Services Review, 27*(6), 615–635. https://doi.org/10.1016/j.childyouth.2004.11.014

Baglivio, M. T., & Wolff, K. T. (2021). Positive childhood experiences (PCE): Cumulative resiliency in the face of adverse childhood experiences. *Youth Violence and Juvenile Justice, 19*(2), 139–162. https://doi.org/10.1177/1541204020972487

Bailey, A. M., Brazil, A. M., Conrad-Hiebner, A., & Counts, J. (2015). Protective factors among Latino families involved with child welfare: A review of Spanish protective factor research on child maltreatment prevention in seven countries. *Children and Youth Services Review, 55*, 93–102. https://doi.org/10.1016/j.childyouth.2015 .05.013

Barajas-Gonzales, R. G., Calzada, E., Huang, K. Y., Covas, M., Castillo, C. M., Linares Torres, H., & Brotman, L. M. (2018). Parent spanking and verbal punishment, and young child internalizing and externalizing behaviors in Latino immigrant families: Test of moderation by context and culture. *Parenting, 18*(4), 219–242. https://doi.org/10.1080/15295192 .2018.1524242

Barlas, C., Kasl, E., MacLeod, A., Paxton, D., Rossenwasser, P., & Sartor, L. (2017). White on white: Communicating about race and white privilege with critical humility. *Understanding & Dismantling Privilege, 2*(1). http://www.wpcjournal.com/article/view/10106

Barnes, A. J., Anthony, B. J., Karatekin, C., Lingras, K. A., Mercado, R., & Thompson, L. A. (2020). Identifying adverse childhood experiences in pediatrics to prevent chronic health conditions. *Pediatric Research, 87*, 362–370. https://doi.org/10.1038/s41390-019-0613-3

Barr, R. G., Barr, M., Fujiwara, T., Conway, J., Catherine, N., & Brant, R. (2009). Do educational materials change knowledge and behaviour about crying and shaken baby syndrome? A randomized controlled trial. *Canadian Medical Association Journal, 180*(7), 727–733. https://doi.org /10.1503/cmaj.081419

Bauer, G. R. (2014). Incorporating intersectionality theory into population health research methodology: Challenges and the potential to advance health equity. *Social Science & Medicine, 110*, 10–17. https://doi.org /10.1016/j.socscimed.2014.03.022

Baumann, A. A., Powell, B. J., Kohl, P.L., Tabak, R. G., Penalba, V., Proctor, E. K., Domenech-Rodriguez, M. M., & Cabassa, L. J. (2015). Cultural adaptation and implementation of evidence-based parent-training: A systematic review and critique of guiding evidence. *Children and Youth Services Review, 53*, 113–120. https://doi.org/10.1016 /j.childyouth.2015.03.02.

Baumrind, D. (1966). Effects of authoritative parental control on child behavior. *Child Development, 37*(4), 887–907. https://doi.org/10.2307 /1126611

Beagan, B. L. (2018). A critique of cultural competence: Assumptions, limitations, and alternatives. In C. L. Frisby & W. T. O'Donohue (Eds.), *Cultural Competence in Applied Psychology* (pp. 123–138). Springer Link. https://link.springer.com/chapter/10.1007/978-3-319 -78997-2_6#citeas

Beale, S. S. (2018). The Trafficking Victim Protection Act: The best hope for international human rights litigation in the U.S. courts? *Case Western Reserve Journal of International Law, 50*, 17–47. https://scholarship.law .duke.edu/cgi/viewcontent.cgi?article=6605&context=faculty _scholarship

Bekteshi, V., & Kang, S. (2020). Contextualizing acculturative stress among Latino immigrants in the United States: A systematic review. *Ethnicity & Health, 25*(6), 897–914. https://doi.org/10.1080/13557858 .2018.1469733

Belsky, J. (1984). The determinants of parenting: A process model. *Child Development, 55*(1), 83–96. https://doi.org/10.2307/1129836

Belsky, J. (1993). Etiology of child maltreatment: A developmental-ecological analysis. *Psychological Bulletin, 114*(3), 413–434. https://doi.org/10.1037 /0033-2909.114.3.413

Belsky, J. (2012). The development of human reproductive strategies: Progress and prospects. *Current Directions in Psychological Science, 21*(5), 310–316. https://doi.org/10.1177/0963721412453588

Benish, S. G., Quintana, S., & Wampold, B. E. (2011). Culturally adapted psychotherapy and the legitimacy of myth: A direct-comparison meta-analysis. *Journal of Counseling Psychology, 58*(3), 279–289. https://doi.org /10.1037/a0023626

Berger, L., & Waldfogel, J. (2011). 'Economic determinants and consequences of child Maltreatment.' *OECD Social, Employment and Migration Working Papers*, No. 111, OECD Publishing. https://doi.org /10.1787/5kgfo9zj7h9t-en

Berlin, L. J., Ispa, J. M., Fine, M. A., Malone, P. S., Brooks-Gunn, J., Brady-Smith, C., Ayoub, C., & Bai, Y. (2009). Correlates and consequences of spanking and verbal punishment for low-income White, African American, and Mexican American toddlers. *Child Development, 80*(5), 1403–1420. https://doi.org/10.1111/j.1467-8624.2009.01341.x

Bermúdez, J. M., Zak-Hunter, L. M., Stinson, M. A., & Abrams, B. A. (2014). "I am not going to lose my kids to the streets": Meanings and experiences of motherhood among Mexican-origin women. *Journal of Family Issues, 35*(1), 3–27. https://doi.org/10.1177/0192513X12462680

Bernal, G., Jimenez-Chafey, M. I., & Domenech Rodriguez, M. M. (2009). Cultural adaptation of treatments: A resource for considering culture in evidence-based practice. *Professional Psychology: Research and Practice, 40*(4), 361–358. https://doi.org/10.1037/a0016401

Bernard, B. (2004). *Resiliency. What we have learned*. WestEd.

Berrick, J. D., Young, C., D'Andrade, A. C., & Frame, L. (2008). Reasonable efforts? Implementation of the reunification exception provisions of ASFA. *Child Welfare, 87*(3), 163–182. https://scholarworks.sjsu.edu/cgi/viewcontent .cgi?referer=&httpsredir=1&article=1007&context=social_work_pub

Berry, J. W. (1997). Immigration, acculturation, and adaptation. *Applied Psychology, 46*(1), 5–34. https://doi.org/10.1111/j.1464-0597.1997 .tb01087.x

Berry, J. W. (2015). Acculturation. In J. E. Grusec & P. D. Hastings (Eds.), *Handbook of socialization: Theory and research* (pp. 520–538). The Guilford Press.

Biden, J. R., Jr. (2021, February 2). *Executive order on the establishment of interagency task force on the reunification of families*. The White House.

https://www.whitehouse.gov/briefing-room/presidential-actions/2021/02/02/executive-order-the-establishment-of-interagency-task-force-on-the-reunification-of-families/

Blanco, L., & Grier, R. (2009). Long live democracy: The determinants of political instability in Latin America. *Journal of Development Studies, 45*(1), 76–95. https://doi.org/10.1080/00220380802264788

Bonanno, G. A., & Diminich, E. D. (2013). Annual research review: Positive adjustment to adversity—trajectories of minimal–impact resilience and emergent resilience. *Journal of Child Psychology and Psychiatry, 54*(4), 378–401. https://doi.org/10.1111/jcpp.12021

Bonello, D., & McIntyre, E. S. (2014, September 10). *Is rape the price to pay for migrant women chasing the American Dream?* https://splinternews.com/is-rape-the-price-to-pay-for-migrant-women-chasing-the-1793842446

Borelli, J. L., Yates, T. M., Hecht, H. K., Cervantes, B. R., Russo, L. N., Arreola, J., Leal, F., Torres, G., & Guerra, N. (2021). Confía en mi, confio en ti: Applying developmental theory to mitigate sociocultural risk in Latinx families. *Development and Psychopathology, 33*(2), 581–597. https://doi.org/10.1017/S0954579420001364

Bornstein, M. H. (2017). The specificity principle in acculturation science. *Perspectives on Psychological Science, 12*(1), 3–45. https://doi.org/10.1177/1745691616655997

Boyle, C. A., Boulet, S., Schieve, L. A., Cohen, R. A., Blumberg, S. J., Yeargin-Allsopp, M., Visser, S. & Kogan, M. D. (2011). Trends in the prevalence of developmental disabilities in US Children, 1997–2008. *Pediatrics, 127*(6), 1034–1042. https://doi.org/10.1542/peds.2010-2989

Brabeck, K., & Xu, Q. (2010). The impact of detention and deportation on Latino immigrant children and families: A quantitative exploration. *Hispanic Journal of Behavioral Sciences, 32*(3), 341–361. https://doi.org/10.1177/0739986310374405.

Breslau, J., Borges, G., Hagar, Y., Tancredi, D., & Gilman, S. (2009). Immigration to the USA and risk for mood and anxiety disorders: Variation by origin and age at immigration. *Psychological Medicine, 39*(7), 1117–1127. https://doi.org/10.1017/S0033291708004698

Breslau, J., Kendler, K. S., Su, M., Gaxiola-Aguilar, S., & Kessler, R. C. (2005). Lifetime risk and persistence of psychiatric disorders across ethnic groups in the United States. *Psychological Medicine, 35*(3), 317–327. https://doi.org/10.1017/s0033291704003514

Bridges, A. J., de Arellano, M. A., Rheingold, A. A., Danielson, C. K., & Silcott, L. (2010). Trauma exposure, mental health, and service utilization rates among immigrant and United States-born Hispanic youth: Results from the Hispanic family study. *Psychological Trauma: Theory, Research, Practice, and Policy, 2*(1), 40–48. https://doi.org/10.1037/a0019021

Bronfenbrenner, U. (1974). Developmental research, public policy, and the ecology of childhood. *Child Development, 45*(1), 1–5. https://doi.org/10 .2307/1127743

Bryant-Davis, T., & Comas-Díaz, L. (2016). Introduction: Womanist and mujerista psychologies. In T. Bryant-Davis & L. Comas-Díaz (Eds.), *Womanist and mujerista psychologies: Voices of fire, acts of courage* (pp. 3–25). American Psychological Association. https://doi.org/10.1037 /14937-001

Buckingham, S. L., & Brodsky, A. E. (2015). "Our differences don't separate us": Immigrant families navigate intrafamilial acculturation gaps through diverse resilience processes. *Journal of Latina/o Psychology, 3*(3), 143–159. https://doi.org/10.1037/lat0000042

Buckingham, S. L., & Brodsky, A. E. (2020). Relative privilege, risk, and sense of community: Understanding Latinx immigrants' empowerment and resilience processes across the United States. *American Journal of Community Psychology.* https://doi.org/10.1002/ajcp.12486

Bywaters, P., Scourfield, J., Webb, C., Morris, K., Featherstone, B., Brady, G., Jones, C., & Sparks, T. (2019). Paradoxical evidence on ethnic inequities in child welfare: Towards a research agenda. *Children and Youth Services Review, 96*, 145–154. https://doi.org/10.1016/j.childyouth .2018.11.042

Cabassa, L. J. (2003). Measuring acculturation: Where we are and where we need to go. *Hispanic Journal of Behavioral Sciences, 25*(2), 127–146. https://doi.org/10.1177/0739986303025002001

Cabrera, J., Roberts, Y. H., Lopez, A., Lopez, L., Zepeda, A., Sanchez, R., Punske, C., Gonzalez, G., Nuño, M., Garay-Castro, L., Lopez, I., Aguilera-Flemming, T., & Pelezarski, Y. (2019). Working across borders: Effective permanency practices at the intersection of child welfare and immigration. *Child Welfare, 96*(6), 1–24. https://www.jstor.org/stable/48623633

Cabrera, N., Hennigar, A., Chen, Y., West, J., Fagan, J., & Wildsmith, E. (2021, February 10). *Programs can build on the strengths of Latino families with low incomes to improve outcomes.* National Research Center on Hispanic Children & Families. https://www.hispanicresearchcenter.org /research-resources/programs-can-build-on-the-strengths-of-latino -families-with-low-incomes-to-improve-outcomes/

Cabrera, N. J., & Bradley, R. H. (2012). Latino fathers and their children. *Child Development Perspectives, 6*(3), 232–238. https://doi.org/10.1111 /j.1750-8606.2012.00249.x

Cabrera, N. J., Hofferth, S. L., & Chae, S. (2011). Patterns and predictors of father-infant engagement across race/ethnic groups. *Early Childhood Research Quarterly, 26*(3), 365–375. https://doi.org/10.1016/j.ecresq.2011 .01.001

Calzada, E., Barajas-Gonzalez, R. G., Huang, K. Y., & Brotman, L. (2017). Early childhood internalizing problems in Mexican- and Dominican-origin children: The role of cultural socialization and parenting practices. *Journal of Clinical Child & Adolescent Psychology, 46*(4), 551–562. https://doi.org/10.1080/15374416.2015.1041593

Calzada, E. J., Basil, S., & Fernandez, Y. (2013). What Latina mothers think of evidence-based parenting practices: A qualitative study of treatment acceptability. *Cognitive and Behavioral Practice, 20*(3), 362–374. https://doi.org/10.1016/j.cbpra.2012.08.004

Calzada, E. J., & Eyberg, S. M. (2002). Self-reported parenting practices in Dominican and Puerto Rican mothers of young children. *Journal of Clinical Child and Adolescent Psychology, 31*(3), 354–363. https://doi.org/10.1207/153744202760082612

Calzada, E. J., Fernandez, Y., & Cortes, D. E. (2010). Incorporating the cultural value of respeto into a framework of Latino parenting. *Cultural Diversity and Ethnic Minority Psychology, 16*(1), 77–86. https://doi.org/10.1037/a0001607.

Calzada, E. J., Gulbas, L. E., Hausmann-Stabile, C., Kim, S. Y., & Berger Cardoso, J. (2020). Mental health issues within Latinx populations: Evaluating the state of the field. In A. D. Martínez & S. D. Rhodes (Eds.), *New and Emerging Issues in Latinx Health* (pp. 45–62). Springer International Publishing. https://doi.org/10.1007/978-3-030-24043-1_3

Calzada, E. J., Huang, K. Y., Anicama, C., Fernandez, Y., & Brotman, L. M. (2012). Test of a cultural framework of parenting with Latino families of young children. *Cultural Diversity and Ethnic Minority Psychology, 18*(3), 285–296. https://doi.org/10.1037/a0028694

Calzada, E. J., Huang, K. Y., Linares-Torres, H., Singh, S. D., & Brotman, L. (2014). Maternal familismo and early childhood functioning in Mexican and Dominican immigrant families. *Journal of Latina/o Psychology, 2*(3), 156–171. https://doi.org/10.1037/lat0000021

Calzada, E. J., Kim, Y., & O'Gara, J. L. (2019). Skin color as a predictor of mental health in young Latinx children. *Social Science & Medicine, 238*, 112467. https://doi.org/10.1016/j.socscimed.2019.112467

Calzada, E. J., Roche, K. M., White, R.M.B., Partovi, R., & Little, T. D. (2020). Family strengths and Latinx youth externalizing behavior: Modifying impacts of an adverse immigration environment. *Journal of Latinx Psychology, 8*(4), 332–348. https://doi.org/10.1037/lat0000162

Calzada, E. J., Sales, A., & O'Gara, J. L. (2019). Maternal depression and acculturative stress impacts on Mexican-origin children through authoritarian parenting. *Journal of Applied Developmental Psychology, 63*, 65–75. https://doi.org/10.1016/j.appdev.2019.05.001

Calzada, E. J., Tamis-LeMonda, C. S., & Yoshikawa, H. (2013). Familismo in Mexican and Dominican families from low-income, urban communities. *Journal of Family Issues, 34*(12), 1696–1724. https://doi.org/10.1177/0192513X12460218

Camacho-Rivera, M., Kawachi, I., Bennett, G. G., & Subramanian, S. V. (2015). Revisiting the Hispanic health paradox: The relative contributions of nativity, country of origin, and race/ethnicity to childhood asthma.

Journal of Immigrant and Minority Health, 17, 826–833. https://doi.org /10.1007/s10903-013-9974-6

Campesino, M., Belyea, M., & Schwartz, G. (2009). Spirituality and cultural identification among Latino and non-Latino college students. *Hispanic Health Care International: The Official Journal of the National Association of Hispanic Nurses, 7*(2), 72. https://doi.org/10.1891/1540-4153.7.2.72

Campesino, M., & Schwartz, G. E. (2006). Spirituality among Latinas/os implications of culture in conceptualization and measurement. *Advances in Nursing Science, 29*(1), 69–81. https://doi.org/10.1097/00012272 -200601000–00007

Capacity Building Center for States (2016). *Promoting safe and stable families.* Children's Bureau. https://capacity.childwelfare.gov/states/resources /promoting-safe-stable-families/

Caraballo, K. (2020). From victim to criminal and back: The minority threat framework's impact on Latinx immigrants. *City & Community, 19*(2), 315–322. https://doi.org/10.1111/cico.12495

Cardoso, J. B., Dettlaff, A. J., Finno-Velasquez, M., Scott, J., & Faulkner, M. (2014). Nativity and immigration status among Latino families involved in the child welfare system: Characteristics, risk, and maltreatment. *Children and Youth Services Review, 44,* 189–200. https://doi.org/10.1016 /j.childyouth.2014.06.008

Cardoso, J. B., Scott, J. L., Faulkner, M., & Lane, L. B. (2018). Parenting in the context of deportation risk. *Journal of Marriage and Family, 80*(2), 301–316. https://doi.org/10.1111/jomf.12463

Cardoso, J. B., & Thompson, S. J. (2010). Common themes of resilience among Latino immigrant families: A systematic review of the literature. *Families in Society, 91*(3), 257–265. https://doi.org/10.1606/1044-3894 .4003

Carlo, G., White, R.M.B., Streit, C., Knight, G. P., & Zeiders, K. H. (2018). Longitudinal relations among parenting styles, prosocial behaviors, and academic outcomes in U.S. Mexican adolescents. *Child Development, 89*(2), 577–592. https://doi.org/10.1111/cdev.12761

Carlson, V. J., & Harwood, R. L. (2003). Attachment, culture, and the caregiving system: The cultural patterning of everyday experiences among Anglo and Puerto Rican mother–infant pairs. *Infant Mental Health Journal, 24*(1), 53–73. https://doi.org/10.1002/imhj.10043

Carr, P. B. (2018). Parental detention and deportation in child welfare cases. *Child Welfare, 96*(5), 81–101.

Castillo, L. G., Perez, F. V., Castillo, R., & Ghosheh, M. R. (2010). Construction and initial validation of the Marianismo Beliefs Scale. *Counselling Psychology Quarterly, 23*(2), 163–175. https://doi.org/10.1080 /09515071003776036

Castro, F. G., Barrera, M., & Martinez, C. R. (2004). The cultural adaptation of prevention interventions: Resolving tensions between fidelity and fit. *Prevention Science, 5*(1), 41–45.

Ceballo, R., Kennedy, T. M., Bregman, A., & Epstein-Ngo, Q. (2012). Always aware (Siempre pendiente): Latina mothers' parenting in high-risk neighborhoods. *Journal of Family Psychology, 26*(5), 805–815. https://doi.org/10.1037/a0029584

Center for Study of Social Policy (2004). *Protecting children by strengthening families: A guidebook for early childhood programs.*

Center for the Study of Social Policy (2020, June 19). *New movement seeks to upend the child welfare system and create anti-racist supports for children and families.* cssp.org/about-us/connect/press-room/new-movement -seeks-to-upend-the-child-welfare-system-and-create-anti-racist-supports -for-children-and-families/

Centers for Disease Control and Prevention (2019). *Youth risk behavior survey: Data summary & trends report 2009–2019.* https://www.cdc.gov /healthyyouth/data/yrbs/pdf/YRBSDataSummaryTrendsReport2019 -508.pdf

Centers for Disease Control and Prevention (2021, June 30). *We can prevent childhood adversity.* https://vetoviolence.cdc.gov/apps/aces-infographic /home

Cerdeña, J. P., Rivera, L. M., & Spak, J. M. (2021). Intergenerational trauma in Latinxs: A scoping review. *Social Science & Medicine, 270,* 113662. https://doi.org/10.1016/j.socscimed.2020.113662

Cervantes, R. C., Padilla, A. M., Napper, L. E., & Goldbach, J. T. (2013). Acculturation-related stress and mental health outcomes among three generations of Hispanic adolescents. *Hispanic Journal of Behavioral Sciences, 35*(4), 451–468. https://doi.org/10.1177 /0739986313500924

Chacko, A., Feirsen, N., Bedard, A. C., Marks, D., Uderman, J. Z., & Chimiklis, A. (2013). Cogmed working memory training for youth with ADHD: A closer examination of efficacy utilizing evidence-based criteria. *Journal of Clinical Child & Adolescent Psychology, 42*(6), 769–783. https://www.ncbi.nlm.nih.gov/books/NBK142924/

Chaffin, M., Bonner, B. L., & Hill, R. F. (2001). Family preservation and family support programs: Child maltreatment outcomes across client risk levels and program types. *Child Abuse & Neglect, 25*(10), 1269–1289. https://doi.org/10.1016/S0145-2134(01)00275-7

Chamberlain, C., Gee, G., Harfield, S., Campbell, S., Brennan, S., Clark, Y., Mensah, F., Arabena, K., Herrman, H., & Brown, S. (2019). Parenting after a history of childhood maltreatment: A scoping review and map of evidence in the perinatal period. *PLOS ONE, 14*(3), e0213460. https:// doi.org/10.1371/journal.pone.0213460

Chambers, J. M., Lint, S., Thompson, M. G., Carlson, M. W., & Graef, M. I. (2019). Outcomes of the Iowa Parent Partner program evaluation: Stability of reunification and re-entry into foster care. *Children and Youth Services Review, 104,* 104353. https://doi.org/10.1016/j.childyouth .2019.05.030

Chemtob, C. M., Gudiño, O. G., & Laraque, D. (2013). Maternal posttraumatic stress disorder and depression in pediatric primary care: Association with child maltreatment and frequency of child exposure to traumatic events. *JAMA Pediatrics, 167*(11), 1011–1018. https://doi.org /10.1001/jamapediatrics.2013.2218

Cheng, T. L., Goodman, E., Bogue, C. W., Chien, A. T., Dean, J. M., Kharbanda, A. B., Peeples, E. S., & Scheindlin, B. (2015). Race, ethnicity, and socioeconomic status in research on child health. *Pediatrics, 135*(1), 225–237. https://doi.org/ 10.1542/peds.2014-3109

Child Trends (2018). *Racial and ethnic composition of the child population.* https://www.childtrends.org/indicators/racial-and-ethnic-composition -of-the-child-population

Child Welfare Information Gateway (n.d.). *Cross-system collaboration in prevention services.* https://www.childwelfare.gov/topics/preventing /developing/collaboration/cross-system-collaboration-in-prevention -services/

Child Welfare Information Gateway. (2020). *How the child welfare system works.* U.S. Department of Health and Human Services, Children's Bureau, an Office of the Administration for Children and Families. https://www.childwelfare.gov/pubpdfs/cpswork.pdf

Chomsky, N. (2015). Impacts of free market and US foreign policy on Colombian and Latin American revolution. *Revista Científica Guillermo de Ockham, 13*(1), 21–25.

Chow, J.C.C., & Austin, M. J. (2008). The culturally responsive social service agency: The application of an evolving definition to a case study. *Administration in Social Work, 32*(4), 39–64. https://doi.org /10.1080/03643100802293832

Cicchetti, D., Toth, S. L., & Maughan, A. (2000). An ecological-transactional model of child maltreatment. In A. J. Sameroff, M. Lewis, & S. M. Miller (Eds), *Handbook of developmental psychopathology* (pp. 698–722). Kluwer Academic Publishers. https://doi.org /10.1007/978-1-4615-4163-9_37

Clarke, W., Turner, K., & Guzman, L. (2017, October). *One quarter of Hispanic children in the United States have an unauthorized immigrant parent.* National Research Center on Hispanic Children & Families. https://www.hispanicresearchcenter.org/wp-content/uploads/2019/08 /Hispanic-Center-Undocumented-Brief-FINAL-V21.pdf

Clauss-Ehlers, C. S. (2019). Forced migration among Latinx children and their families: Introducing trilateral migration trauma as a concept to reflect a forced migratory experience. *Journal of Infant, Child, and Adolescent Psychotherapy, 18*(4), 330–342. https://doi.org/10.1080 /15289168.2019.1686742

Cohn, D. (2010, March 3). *Census history: Counting Hispanics.* Pew Research Center. https://www.pewresearch.org/social-trends/2010/03/03/census -history-counting-hispanics-2/

Coll, C. G., Lamberty, G., Jenkins, R., McAdoo, H. P., Crnic, K., Wasik, B. H., & García, H. V. (1996). An integrative model for the study of developmental competencies in minority children. *Child Development, 67*(5), 1891–1914. https://doi.org/10.1111/j.1467-8624.1996.tb01834.x

Coltrane, S., Parke, R. D., & Adams, M. (2004). Complexity of father involvement in low-income Mexican American families. *Family Relations, 53*(2), 179–189. http://www.jstor.org/stable/3700261

Conger, R. D., Conger, K. J., & Martin, M. J. (2010). Socioeconomic status, family processes, and individual development. *Journal of Marriage and Family, 72*(3), 685–704. https://doi.org/10.1111/j.1741-3737.2010.00725.x

Congressional Research Service (2021, December 3). *Latin America and the Caribbean: U.S. policy overview.* fas.org/sgp/crs/row/IF10460.pdf

Connor, K. M., & Davidson, J.R.T. (2003). Development of a new resilience scale: The Connor-Davidson Resilience Scale (CD-RISC). *Depression and Anxiety, 18*(2), 76–82. https://doi.org/10.1002/da.10113

Conrad-Hiebner, A., Schoemann, A. M., Counts, J. M., & Chang, K. (2015). The development and validation of the Spanish adaptation of the Protective Factors Survey. *Children and Youth Services Review, 52*, 45–53. https://doi.org/10.1016/j.childyouth.2015.03.006

Conron, K. J., Beardslee, W., Koenen, K. C., Buka, S. L., & Gortmaker, S. L. (2009). A longitudinal study of maternal depression and child maltreatment in a national sample of families investigated by Child Protective Services. *Archives of Pediatric and Adolescent Medicine, 163*(10), 922–930. https://doi.org/10.1001/archpediatrics.2009.176

Coohey, C. (2001). The relationship between familism and child maltreatment in Latino and Anglo families. *Child Maltreatment, 6*(2), 130–142. https://doi.org/10.1177/1077559501006002005

Cooke, K., Rosenberg, M., & Levinson, R. (2019, October 11). *Exclusive: U.S. migrant policy sends thousands of children, including babies, back to Mexico.* Reuters. reuters.com/article/us-usa-immigration-babies-exclusive-idUSKBN1WQ1H1

Corey, E. (2021). *Questioning cultural humility.* National Affairs. https://www.nationalaffairs.com/publications/detail/questioning-cultural-humility

Counts, J. M., Buffington, E. S., Chang-Rios, K., Rasmussen, H. N., & Preacher, K. J. (2010). The development and validation of the protective factors survey: A self-report measure of protective factors against child maltreatment. *Child Abuse & Neglect, 34*(10), 762–772. https://doi.org/10.1016/j.chiabu.2010.03.003

Crenshaw, K. (1989). Demarginalizing the intersection of race and sex: A black feminist critique of antidiscrimination doctrine, feminist theory and anti-racist politics. *University of Chicago Legal Forum, 14*, 538–554. https://chicagounbound.uchicago.edu/cgi/viewcontent.cgi?article=1052&context=uclf

Crenshaw, K. (1991). Mapping the margins: Intersectionality, identity politics, and violence against women of color. *Stanford Law Review, 43*(6), 1241–1299.

Cross, T. P., & Casanueva, C. (2009). Caseworker judgements and substantiation. *Child Maltreatment, 14*(1), 38–52. https://doi.org/10.1177/1077559508318400

Crouch, E., Radcliff, E., Brown, M., & Hung, P. (2019). Exploring the association between parenting stress and a child's exposure to adverse childhood experiences (ACEs). *Children and Youth Services Review, 102,* 186–192. https://doi.org/10.1016/j.childyouth.2019.05.019

Crouch, J. L., & Behl, L. E. (2001). Relationships among parental beliefs in corporal punishment, reported stress, and physical child abuse potential. *Child Abuse & Neglect, 25*(3), 413–419. https://doi.org/10.1016/S0145-2134(00)00256-8

Cuevas, A. G., Dawson, B. A., & Williams, D. R. (2016). Race and skin color in Latino health: An analytic review. *American Journal of Public Health, 106*(12), 2131–2136. https://doi.org/10.2105/AJPH.2016.303452

Cumming-Potvin, W. (2013). "New basics" and literacies: Deepening reflexivity in qualitative research. *Qualitative Research Journal, 13*(2), 214–230, https://doi.org/10.1108/QRJ-04-2013-0024

D'Andrade, A. C. (2015). Parents and court-ordered services: A descriptive study of service use in child welfare reunification. *Families in Society, 96*(1), 25–34. https://doi.org/10.1606/1044-3894.2015.96.5

D'Angelo, E. J., Llerena-Quinn, R., Shaprio, R., Colon, F., Rodriguez, P., Gallagher, K., & Beardslee, W.R. (2009). Adaptation of the preventive intervention program for depression for use with predominantly low-income Latino families. *Family Process, 48*(2), 269–291. https://doi.org/10.1111/j.1545-5300.2009.01281.x

Darity, W. A., Jr., Dietrich, J., & Hamilton, D. (2005). Bleach in the rainbow: Latin ethnicity and preference for whiteness. *Transforming Anthropology, 13*(2), 103–109. https://doi.org/10.1525/tran.2005.13.2.103

Davidson, R. D., Morrissey, M. W., & Beck, C. J. (2019). The Hispanic experience of the child welfare system. *Family Court Review, 57*(2), 201–216. https://doi.org/10.1111/fcre.12404

Davis, A. N., Carlo, G., & Crockett, L. J. (2020). The role of economic stress in parents' depression and warmth and adolescents' prosocial behaviors among U.S. Latino/as. *Peace and Conflict: Journal of Peace Psychology, 26*(2), 162–170. https://doi.org/10.1037/pac0000406

De Silva, L.E.D., Ponting, C., Ramos, G., Guevara, M.V.C., & Chavira, D. A. (2020). Urban Latinx parents' attitudes towards mental health: Mental health literacy and service use. *Children and Youth Services Review, 109,* 104719. https://doi.org/10.1016/j.childyouth.2019.104719

Deater-Deckard, K., Dodge, K., & Sorbring, E. (2005). Cultural differences in the effects of physical punishment. In M. Tienda (Author) & M. Rutter (Ed.), *Ethnicity and causal mechanisms* (pp. 204–226). Cambridge University Press. https://doi.org/10.1017/CBO9781139140348.010

Deater-Deckard, K., Lansford, J. E., Malone, P. S., Alampay, L. P., Sorbring, E., Bacchini, D., Bombi, A.S., Bornstein, M. H., Chang, L., Di Giunta, L.,

Dodge, K. A., Oburu, P., Pastorellii, C., Skinner, A. T., Tapanya, S., Tirado, L.M.U., Zelli, A., & Al-Hassan, S. M. (2011). The association between parental warmth and control in thirteen cultural groups. *Journal of Family Psychology, 25*(5), 790–794. https://doi.org/10.1037/a0025120

DeJonghe, E. S., Bogat, G. A., Levendosky, A. A., von Eye, A., & Davidson II, W. S. (2005). Infant exposure to domestic violence predicts heightened sensitivity to adult verbal conflict. *Infant Mental Health Journal, 26*(3), 268–281. https://doi.org/10.1002/imhj.20048

DeLuca, L. A., McEwen, M. M., & Keim, S. M. (2008). United States–Mexico border crossing: Experiences and risk perceptions of undocumented male immigrants. *Journal of Immigrant and Minority Health, 12*(1), 113. https://doi.org/10.1007/s10903-008-9197-4

Dettlaff, A. J. (2008). Immigrant Latino children and families in child welfare: A framework for conducting a cultural assessment. *Journal of Public Child Welfare, 2*(4), 451–470. https://doi.org/10.1080/15548730802523257

Dettlaff, A. J. (2015, Winter). Racial disproportionality and disparities in the child welfare system. *CW360°*, 4–5. http://cascw.umn.edu/wp-content/uploads/2015/03/CW360-Winter2015.pdf#page=4

Dettlaff, A. J., & Boyd, R. (2020). Racial disproportionality and disparities in the child welfare system: Why do they exist, and what can be done to address them? *The Annals of the American Academy of Political and Social Science, 692*(1), 253–274. https://doi.org/10.1177/0002716220980329

Dettlaff, A. J., & Earner, I. (2012). Children of immigrants in the child welfare system: Characteristics, risk, and maltreatment. *Families in Society: The Journal of Contemporary Social Services, 93*(4), 295–303. https://doi.org/10.1606/1044-3894.4240

Dettlaff, A. J., Earner, I., & Phillips, S. D. (2009). Latino children of immigrants in the child welfare system: Prevalence, characteristics, and risk. *Children and Youth Services Review, 31*(7), 775–783. https://doi.org/10.1016/j.childyouth.2009.02.004

Dettlaff, A. J., & Finno-Velasquez, M. (2013). Child maltreatment and immigration enforcement: Considerations for child welfare and legal systems working with immigrant families. *Children's Legal Rights Journal, 33*(1), 37–63. https://lawecommons.luc.edu/cgi/viewcontent.cgi?article=1009&context=clrj

Dettlaff, A. J., & Johnson, M. A. (2011). Child maltreatment dynamics among immigrant and U.S. born Latino children: Findings from the National Survey of Child and Adolescent Well-being (NSCAW). *Children and Youth Services Review, 33*(6), 936–944. https://doi.org/10.1016/j.childyouth.2010.12.017

Dettlaff, A. J., Rivaux, S. L., Baumann, D. J., Fluke, J. D., Rycraft, J. R., & James, J. (2011). Disentangling substantiation: The influence of race, income, and risk on the substantiation decision in child welfare.

Children and Youth Services Review, 33(9), 1630–1637. https://doi.org/10.1016/j.childyouth.2011.04.005

Dettlaff, A. J., & Rycraft, J. R. (2010). Adapting systems of care for child welfare practice with immigrant Latino children and families. *Evaluation and Program Planning, 33*(3), 303–310. https://doi.org/10.1016/j.evalprogplan.2009.07.003

DeVerteuil, G., & Golubchikov, O. (2016). Can resilience be redeemed? Resilience as a metaphor for change, not against change. *City Analysis of Urban Change, Theory, Action, 20*(1), 143–151. https://doi.org/10.1080/13604813.2015.1125714

De Von Figueroa-Mosely, C., Ramey, C. T., Keltner, B., & Lanzi, R. G. (2006). Variations in Latino parenting practices and their effects on child cognitive developmental outcomes. *Hispanic Journal of Behavioral Sciences, 28*(1), 102–114. https://doi.org/10.1177/0739986305284036

DeWaard, J., Nobles, J., & Donato, K. M. (2018). Migration and parental absence: A comparative assessment of transnational families in Latin America. *Population, Space and Place, 24*(7), e2166. https://doi.org/10.1002/psp.2166

DiLillo, D., Tremblay, G. C., & Peterson, L. (2000). Linking childhood sexual abuse and abusive parenting: the mediating role of maternal anger. *Child Abuse & Neglect, 24*(6), 767–779. https://doi.org/10.1016/S0145-2134(00)00138-1

Dishion, T. J., Patterson, G. R., & Kavanagh, K. A. (1992). An experimental test of the coercion model: Linking theory, measurement, and intervention. In J. McCord & R. E. Tremblay (Eds.), *Preventing antisocial behavior: Interventions from birth through adolescence* (pp. 253–282). Guilford Press.

Dixon, A. R., & Telles, E. E. (2017). Skin color and colorism: Global research, concepts, and measurement. *Annual Review of Sociology, 43*(1), 405–424. https://doi.org/10.1146/annurev-soc-060116-053315

Domenech-Rodriguez, M. M., Donovick, M. R., & Crowley, S. L. (2009). Parenting styles in a cultural context: Observations of "protective parenting" in first-generation Latinos. *Family Process, 48*(2), 195–210. https://doi.org/10.1111/j.1545-5300.2009.01277.x

Drake, B., & Jonson-Reid, M. (2014). Poverty and child maltreatment. In J. E. Korbin & R. D. Krugman (Eds), *Handbook of child maltreatment* (pp. 131–148). Springer.

Drake, B., Jolley, J. M., Lanier, P., Fluke, J., Barth, R. P., & Jonson-Reid, M. (2011). Racial bias in child protection? A comparison of competing explanations using national data. *Pediatrics, 127*(3), 471–478. https://doi.org/10.1542/peds.2010-1710

Dreby, J. (2012, August 20). *How today's immigration enforcement policies impact children, families, and communities.* Center for American Progress. https://www.americanprogress.org/issues/immigration/reports

/2012/08/20/27082/how-todays-immigration-enforcement-policies
-impact-children-families-and-communities/

Driscoll, A. K., Russell, S. T., & Crockett, L. J. (2008). Parenting styles and youth well-being across immigrant generations. *Journal of Family Issues, 29*(2), 185–209. https://doi.org/10.1177/0192513X07307843

Dumka, L. E., Roosa, M. W., & Jackson, K. M. (1997). Risk, conflict, mothers' parenting, and children's adjustment in low-income, Mexican immigrant, and Mexican American families. *Journal of Marriage and Family, 59*(2), 309–323. https://doi.org/10.2307/353472

Dunn, M. G., Tarter, R. E., Mezzich, A. C., Vanyukov, M., Kirisci, L., & Kirillova, G. (2002). Origins and consequences of child neglect in substance abuse families. *Clinical Psychology Review, 22*(7), 1063–1090. https://doi.org/10.1016/S0272-7358(02)00132-0

Dye, H. (2018). The impact and long-term effects of childhood trauma. *Journal of Human Behavior in the Social Environment, 28*(3), 381–392. https://doi.org/10.1080/10911359.2018.1435328

Eamon, M. K., & Mulder, C. (2005). Predicting antisocial behavior among Latino young adolescents: An ecological systems analysis. *American Journal of Orthopsychiatry, 75*(1), 117–127. https://doi.org/10.1037/0002-9432.75.1.117

Edelman, P. (2019). *Not a crime to be poor: The criminalization of poverty in America.* New Press.

Edwards, F. (2019). Family surveillance: Police and the reporting of child abuse and neglect. *RSF: The Russell Sage Foundation Journal of the Social Sciences, 5*(1), 50–70. https://doi.org/10.7758/rsf.2019.5.1.03

Eisenman, D. P., Gelberg, L., Liu, H., & Shapiro, M. F. (2003). Mental health and health-related quality of life among adult Latino primary care patients living in the United States with previous exposure to political violence. *JAMA, 290*(5), 627–634. https://doi.org/10.1001/jama.290.5.627

Elder, J. P., Ayala, G. X., Parra-Medina, D., & Talavera, G. A. (2009). Health communication in the Latino community: Issues and approaches. *Annual Review of Public Health, 30*, 227–251. https://doi.org/10.1146/annurev.publhealth.031308.100300

Erdal, M. B., & Oeppen, C. (2017). Forced to leave? The discursive and analytical significance of describing migration as forced and voluntary. *Journal of Ethnic and Migration Studies, 44*(6), 981–998. https://doi.org/10.1080/1369183X.2017.1384149

Falicov, C. J. (1998). *Latino families in therapy: A guide to multicultural practice.* The Guilford Press.

Falicov, C. J. (2010). Changing constructions of machismo for Latino men in therapy: "The devil never sleeps." *Family Process, 49*(3), 309–329. https://doi.org/10.1111/j.1545-5300.2010.01325.x

Featherstone, B., & Fawcett, B. (1994). Feminism and child abuse: opening up some possibilities? *Critical Social Policy, 14*(42), 61–80. https://doi.org/10.1177/026101839401404205

Federal Register. (1999). Designation of Honduras Under Temporary Protected Status, 64(2), 524–526. https://www.govinfo.gov/content/pkg /FR-1999-01-05/pdf/98-34849.pdf

Federal Register. (1999). Designation of Nicaragua Under Temporary Protected Status, 64(2), 526–528. https://www.govinfo.gov/content/pkg /FR-1999-01-05/pdf/98-34848.pdf

Federal Register. (2001). Designation of El Salvador Under Temporary Protected Status Program, 66(47), 14214–14216. https://www.govinfo .gov/content/pkg/FR-2001-03-09/pdf/01-5818.pdf

Federal Register. (2010). Designation of Haiti for Temporary Protected Status, 75(13), 3476–3479. https://www.govinfo.gov/content/pkg/FR -2010-01-21/pdf/2010-1169.pdf

Federal Register. (2021). Designation of Venezuela for Temporary Protected Status, 86(44), 13574–13581. https://www.govinfo.gov/content/pkg/FR -2021-03-09/pdf/2021-04951.pdf

Feldman, S. R., Vallejos, Q. M., Quandt, S. A., Fleischer Jr., A. B., Schulz, M. R., Verma, A., & Arcury, T. A. (2009). Health care utilization among migrant Latino farmworkers: The care of skin disease. *The Journal of Rural Health, 25*(1), 98–103. https://doi.org/10.1111/j.1748-0361.2009.00205.x

Felitti, V. J., Anda, R. F., Nordenberg, D., Williamson, D. F., Spitz, A. M., Edwards, V., Koss, M. P., & Marks, J. S. (1998). Relationship of childhood abuse and household dysfunction to many of the leading causes of death in adults: The Adverse Childhood Experiences (ACE) Study. *American Journal of Preventive Medicine, 14*(4), 245–258. https://doi.org /10.1016/S0749-3797(98)00017-8

Fergus, S., & Zimmerman, M. A. (2005). Adolescent resilience: A framework for understanding healthy development in the face of risk. *Annual Review of Public Health, 26,* 399–419. https://doi.org/10.1146/annurev .publhealth.26.021304.144357

Ferguson, C. J. (2013). Spanking, corporal punishment and negative long-term outcomes: A meta-analytic review of longitudinal studies. *Clinical Psychology Review, 33*(1), 196–208. https://doi.org/10.1016 /j.cpr.2012.11.002

Fernandez, A., Shillinger, D., Grumbach, K., Rosenthal, A., Stewart, A. L., Wang, F., & Perez-Stable, E. J. (2004). Physician language ability and cultural competence. *Journal of General Internal Medicine, 19,* 167–174. https://doi.org/10.1111/j.1525-1497.2004.30266.x

Fernandez, H. (2019). Entering the United States: The differing views from the Northern Triangle, Cuba and Puerto Rico. *Hispanic Journal of Law & Policy,* 66–97. http://stcl.edu/Journals/HispanicLaw/2019 /2019Fernandez66-97.pdf

Fernández-Esquer, M. E., Agoff, M. C., & Leal, I. M. (2017). Living *sin papeles*: Undocumented Latino workers negotiating life in "illegality." *Hispanic Journal of Behavioral Sciences, 39*(1), 3–18. https://doi.org /10.1177/0739986316679645

Ferrari, A. M. (2002). The impact of culture upon child rearing practices and definitions of maltreatment. *Child Abuse & Neglect, 26*(8), 793–813. https://doi.org/10.1016/s0145-2134(02)00345-9

Fettes, D. L., Aarons, G. A., Brew, V., Ledesma, K., & Silovsky, J. (2020). Implementation of a trauma-informed, evidence-informed intervention for Latinx families experiencing interpersonal violence and child maltreatment: A protocol for a pilot randomized control trial of SafeCare+®. *Pilot and Feasibility Studies, 6*(1), 153, 1–9. https://doi.org/10.1186/s40814-020-00681-3

Finch, B. K., & Vega, W. A. (2003). Acculturation stress, social support, and self-rated health among Latinos in California. *Journal of Immigrant Health, 5*, 109–117. https://doi.org/10.1023/A:1023987717921

Finkelhor, D., Turner, H., Wormuth, B. K., Vanderminden, J., & Hamby, S. (2019). Corporal punishment: Current rates from a national survey. *Journal of Child and Family Studies, 28*, 1991–1997. https://doi.org/10.1007/s10826-019-01426-4

Finno-Velasquez, M. (2013). The relationship between parent immigration status and concrete support service use among Latinos in child welfare: Findings using the National Survey of Child and Adolescent Well-being. *Children and Youth Services Review, 35*(12), 2118–2127. https://doi.org/10.1016/j.childyouth.2013.10.013

Finno-Velasquez, M., Cardoso, J. B., Dettlaff, A. J., & Hurlburt, M. S. (2016). Effects of parent immigration status on mental health service use among Latino children referred to child welfare. *Psychiatric Services, 67*(2), 192–198. https://doi.org/10.1176/appi.ps.201400444

Fischer-Borne, M., Montana Cain, J., & Martin, S. L. (2015). From mastery to accountability: Cultural humility as an alternative to cultural competence. *Social Work Education, 34*(2), 165–181. https://doi.org/10.1080/02615479.2014.977244

Flores, A. (2017, September 18). *How the U.S. Hispanic population is changing.* Pew Research Center. https://www.pewresearch.org/fact-tank/2017/09/18/how-the-u-s-hispanic-population-is-changing/

Flores, E., Cicchetti, D., & Rogosch, F. A. (2005). Predictors of resilience in maltreated and nonmaltreated Latino children. *Developmental Psychology, 41*(2), 338–351. https://doi.org/10.1037/0012-1649.41.2.338

Floríndez, L. I., Floríndez, D. C., Como, D. H., Secola, R., & Duker, L.I.S. (2020). Differing interpretations of health care encounters: A qualitative study of non-Latinx health care providers' perceptions of Latinx patient behaviors. *PLOS ONE, 15*(8), e0236706. https://doi.org/10.1371/journal.pone.0236706

Fluke, J., Harden, B. J., Jenkins, M., & Ruehrdanz, A. (2010). Research synthesis on child welfare: Disproportionality and disparities. *Disparities and disproportionality in child welfare: Analysis of the research, 1.* https://casala.org/wp-content/uploads/2015/12/Disparities-and-Disproportionality-in-Child-Welfare_An-Analysis-of-the-Research-December-2011-1.pdf#page=11

Fluke, J. D., Yuan, Y.-Y.T., Hedderson, J., & Curtis, P. A. (2003). Disproportionate representation of race and ethnicity in child maltreatment: Investigation and victimization. *Children and Youth Services Review, 25*(5–6), 359–373. https://doi.org/10.1016/S0190-7409(03)00026-4

Fonagy, P., Steele, M., Moran, G., Steele, H., & Higgitt, A. (1993). Measuring the ghost in the nursery: An empirical study of the relation between parents' mental representations of childhood experiences and their infants' security of attachment. *Journal of the American Psychoanalytic Association, 41*(4), 957–989. https://doi.org/10.1177/000306519304100403

Fong, R. (2004). *Culturally competent practice with immigrant and refugee children and families.* Guilford Press.

Fontes, L. (1993). Considering culture and oppression: Steps toward an ecology of sexual child abuse. *Journal of Feminist Family Therapy, 5*(1), 25–54. https://doi.org/10.1300/J086v05n01_03

Fontes, L. A. (2010). Considering culture in the clinical intake interview and report. In M.M. Leach & J.D. Aten (Eds.). *Cultural and the therapeutic process: A guide for mental health professionals* (pp. 37–64). Routledge.

Fontes, L. A., & McCloskey, K. A. (2011). Cultural issues in violence against women. In C.M. Renzetti, J. L. Edleson, & R. K. Bergen (Eds.). *Sourcebook on violence against women* (2nd Edition, pp. 151–168). SAGE.

Fortson, B. L., Klevens, J., Merrick, M. T., Gilbert, L. K., & Alexander, S. P. (2016). Preventing child abuse and neglect: A technical package for policy, norm, and programmatic activities. Atlanta, GA: National Center for Injury Prevention and Control, Centers for Disease Control and Prevention.

Foster, C. H. (2012). Race and child welfare policy: State-level variations in disproportionality. *Race and Social Problems, 4,* 93–101. https://doi.org /10.1007/s12552-012-9071-9

Fraizer-Anderson, P., Hood, S., & Hopson, R. K. (2012). Preliminary consideration of an African American culturally responsive evaluation system. In S. D. Lapan, M. T. Quartaroli, & F. J. Riemer (Eds.), *Qualitative research: An introduction to methods and designs* (pp. 347–372). Jossey-Bass.

Freire, P. (2014). *Pedagogy of the oppressed* (30th ed.). Bloomsbury Academic.

Freisthler, B., Bruce, E., & Needell, B. (2007). Understanding the geospatial relationship of neighborhood characteristics and rates of maltreatment for Black, Hispanic, and white children. *Social Work, 52*(1), 7–16. https://doi.org/10.1093/sw/52.1.

French, B. H., Lewis, J. A., Mosley, D. V., Adames, H. Y., Chavez-Dueñas, N. Y., Chen, G. A., & Neville, H. A. (2020). Toward a psychological framework of radical healing in communities of color. *The Counseling Psychologist, 48*(1), 14–46. https://doi.org/10.1177/0011000019843506

Frierson, H. T., Hood, S. Hughes, G. B., & Thomas, V. G. (2010). A guide to conducting culturally responsive evaluations. In J. Frechtling (Ed.), *The 2010 user-friendly handbook for project evaluation* (pp. 75–96). National Science Foundation.

Fuchsel, C.L.M., Murphy, S. B., & Dufresne, R. (2012). Domestic violence, culture, and relationship dynamics among immigrant Mexican women. *Affilia, 27*(3), 263–274. https://doi.org/10.1177/0886109912452403

Fuller, B., & García Coll, C. (2010). Learning from Latinos: Contexts, families, and child development in motion. *Developmental Psychology, 46*(3), 559–565. https://doi.org/10.1037/a0019412

Funk, C., & Martinez, J. H. (2014). *The shifting religious identity of Latinos in the United States.* Pew Research Center. https://www.pewforum.org/2014/05/07/the-shifting-religious-identity-of-latinos-in-the-united-states/

Gabbert, W. (2012). The longue durée of Colonial Violence in Latin America. *Historical Social Research, 37*(3), 254–275.

Gannotti, M. E., Kaplan, L. C., Handwerker, W. P., & Groce, N. E. (2004). Cultural influences on health care use: Differences in perceived unmet needs and expectations of providers by Latino and Euro-American parents of children with special health care needs. *Journal of Developmental and Behavioral Pediatrics, 25*(3), 156–165. https://doi.org/10.1097/00004703-200406000-00003

Garcia, A., Aisenberg, E., & Harachi, T. (2012). Pathways to service inequalities among Latinos in the child welfare system. *Children and Youth Services Review, 34*(5), 1060–1071. https://doi.org/10.1016/j.childyouth.2012.02.011

Garcia, A. R., Gupta, M., Greeson, J.K.P., Thompson, A., & DeNard C. (2017). Adverse childhood experiences among youth reported to child welfare: Results from the national survey of child & adolescent well-being. *Child Abuse & Neglect, 70*, 292–302. https://doi.org/10.1016/j.chiabu.2017.06.019

Garnett, B. R., Masyn, K. E., Austin, S. B., Miller, M., Williams, D. R., & Viswanath, K. (2014). The intersectionality of discrimination attributes and bullying among youth: An applied latent class analysis. *Journal of Youth and Adolescence, 43*, 1225–1239. https://doi.org/10.1007/s10964-013-0073-8

Garrett, T. M. (2020). COVID-19, wall building, and the effects on Migrant Protection Protocols by the Trump administration: The spectacle of the worsening human rights disaster on the Mexico-U.S. border. *Administrative Theory & Praxis, 42*(2), 240–248. https://doi.org/10.1080/10841806.2020.1750212

Gaxiola-Romero, J. C., & Frias Armenta, M. (2012). Factores protectores, estilos de crianza y maltrato infantil: Un modelo ecológico. *Psyecology, 3*(3), 259–270.

Gee, G. C., & Ford, C. L. (2011). Structural racism and health inequities: Old issues, new directions. *Du Bois Review: Social Science Research on Race, 8*(1), 115–132. https://doi.org/10.1017/S1742058X11000130

Gennetian, L., Guzman, L., Ramos-Olazagasti, M., & Wildsmith, E. (2019). *An economic portrait of low-income Hispanic families: Key findings from the first five years of studies from the National Research Center on Hispanic Children & Families.* Report 2019-03. National Research Center on

Hispanic Children & Families. https://www.hispanicresearchcenter.org /research-resources/an-economic-portrait-of-low-income-hispanic -families-key-findings-from-the-first-five-years-of-studies-from-the -national-research-center-on-hispanic-children-families

George, S., Duran, N., & Norris, K. (2014). A systematic review of barriers and facilitators to minority research participation among African Americans, Latinos, Asian Americans, and Pacific Islanders. *American Journal of Public Health, 104*(2), e16–e31. https://doi.org/10.2105/AJPH.2013.301706

Germán, M., Gonzales, N. A., Bonds McClain, D., Dumka, L., & Millsap, R. (2013). Maternal warmth moderates the link between harsh discipline and later externalizing behaviors for Mexican American adolescents, *Parenting, 13*(3), 169–177. https://doi.org/10.1080/15295192.2013.756353

Gershoff, E. T. (2002). Corporal punishment by parents and associated child behaviors and experiences: A meta-analytic and theoretical review. *Psychological Bulletin, 128*(4), 539–579. https://doi.org/10.1037/0033 -2909.128.4 .539

Gershoff, E. T. (2010). More harm than good: A summary of scientific research on the intended and unintended effects of corporal punishment on children. *Law and Contemporary Problems, 73*(2), 31–56. http://www .jstor.org/stable/25766386

Gershoff, E. T., Grogan-Kaylor, A., Lansford, J. E., Chang, L., Zelli, A., Deater-Deckard, K., & Dodge, K. A. (2010). Parent discipline practices in an international sample: Associations with child behaviors and moderation by perceived normativeness. *Child Development, 81*(2), 487–502. https://doi.org/10.1111/j.1467-8624.2009.01409.x

Gershoff, E. T., Lansford, J. E., Sexton, H. R., Davis-Kean, P., & Sameroff, A. J. (2012). Longitudinal links between spanking and children's externalizing behaviors in a national sample of White, Black, Hispanic, and Asian American families. *Child Development, 83*(3), 838–843. https://doi.org/10 .1111/j.1467-8624.2011.01732.x

Gilbert, R., Spatz Widom, C., Brown, K., Fergusson, D., Webb., E., & Janson, S. (2009). Burden and consequences of child maltreatment in high-income countries. *The Lancet, 373*(9657), 68–81. https://doi.org /10.1016/S0140-6736(08)61706-7

Gloria, A. M., & Castellanos, J. (2016). Latinas poderosas: Shaping mujerismo to manifest sacred spaces for healing and transformation. In T. Bryant-Davis & L. Comas-Díaz (Eds.), *Womanist and mujerista psychologies: Voices of fire, acts of courage* (pp. 93–119). American Psychological Association. https://doi.org/10.1037/14937-005

Gómez, E., & Kotliarenco, M. A. (2010). Resiliencia familiar: Un enfoque de investigación e intervención con familias multiproblematcias. *Revista de Psicología, 19*(2), 103–131. doi:10.5354/0719-0581.2010.17112

Gomez, J., Miranda, R., & Polanco, L. (2011). Acculturative stress, perceived discrimination, and vulnerability to suicide attempts among emerging adults. *Journal of Youth and Adolescence, 40*(11), 1465–1476. https:// doi.org/10.1007/s10964-011-9688-9

Gonzales, N. A., Coxe, S., Roosa, M. W., White, R.M.B., Knight, G. P., Zeiders, K. H., & Saenz, D. (2011). Economic hardship, neighborhood context, and parenting: Prospective effects on Mexican-American adolescent's mental health. *American Journal of Community Psychology,* *47*(1–2), 98–113. https://doi.org/10.1007%2Fs10464-010-9366-1

Gonzalez-Barrera, A., & Lopez, M. H. (2013, May 1). *A demographic portrait of Mexican-origin Hispanics in the United States.* Pew Research Center. https://www.pewresearch.org/hispanic/2013/05/01/a-demographic -portrait-of-mexican-origin-hispanics-in-the-united-states/

Gonzalez-Barrera, A., & Lopez, M. H. (2020, July 22). *Before COVID-19, many Latinos worried about their place in America and had experienced discrimination.* Pew Research Center. https://www.pewresearch.org/fact -tank/2020/07/22/before-covid-19-many-latinos-worried-about-their -place-in-america-and-had-experienced-discrimination/

Gonzalez, A., & MacMillan, H. L. (2008). Preventing child maltreatment: An evidence-based update. *Journal of Postgraduate Medicine, 54*(4), 280–286.

Gonzalez, F. R., Benuto, L. T., & Casas, J. B. (2020). Prevalence of interpersonal violence among Latinas: A systematic review. *Trauma, Violence, & Abuse, 21*(5), 977–990. https://doi.org/10.1177/1524838018806507

Goodman, L. A., Liang, B., Helms, J. E., Latta, R. E., Sparks, E., & Weintraub, S. R. (2004). Training counseling psychologists as social justice agents: Feminist and multicultural principals in action. *The Counseling Psychologist, 32*(6), 793–836. https://doi.org/10.1177/0011000004268802

Graff, G. (2014). The intergenerational trauma of slavery and its aftermath. *Journal of Psychohistory, 41*(3), 181–197.

Graham, L. M., Lanier, P., & Johnson-Montoyama, M. (2016). National profile of Latino/Latina children reported to the child welfare system for sexual abuse. *Children and Youth Services Review, 66,* 18–27. https:// doi.org/10.1016/j.childyouth.2016.04.008

Graham, L. M., Lanier, P., Finno-Velasquez, M., & Johnson-Motoyama, M. (2018). Substantiated reports of sexual abuse among Latinx children: Multilevel models of national data. *Journal of Family Violence, 33,* 481–490. https://doi.org/10.1007/s10896-018-9967-2

Gramlich, J. (2020, March 2). *How border apprehensions, ICE arrests and deportations have changed under Trump.* Pew Research Center. https:// www.pewresearch.org/fact-tank/2020/03/02/how-border-apprehensions -ice-arrests-and-deportations-have-changed-under-trump/

Grand, S. (2018). The Other within: White shame, Native American genocide. *Contemporary Psychoanalysis, 54*(1), 84–102. https://doi.org /10.1080/00107530.2017.1415106

Grand, S., & Salberg, J. (2021). Trans-generational transmission of trauma. In A. Hamburger, C. Hancheva, & V. D. Volkan (Eds.), *Social trauma—An interdisciplinary textbook* (pp. 209–215). Springer International Publishing. https://doi.org/10.1007/978-3-030-47817-9_22

Green, B. L., Ayoub, C., Dym Bartlett, J., Furrer, C., Chazan-Cohen, R., Buttitta, K., Von Ende, A., Koepp, A., & Regalbuto, E. (2020). Pathways to prevention: Early Head Start outcomes in the first three years lead to long-term reductions in child maltreatment. *Children and Youth Services Review, 118,* 105403. https://doi.org/10.1016/j.childyouth.2020.105403

Green, B. L., Ayoub, C., Dym Bartlett, J., Von Ende, A., Furrer, C., Chazan-Cohen, R., Vallotton, C., & Klevens, J. (2014). The effect of Early Head Start on child welfare system involvement: A first look at longitudinal child maltreatment outcomes. *Children and Youth Services Review, 42,* 127–135. https:/doi.org/10.1016/j.childyouth.2014.03.044

Griner, D., & Smith, T. B. (2006). Culturally adapted mental health intervention: A meta-analytic review. *Psychotherapy: Theory, Research, Practice, Training, 43*(4), 531–548. https://doi.org/10.1037/0033-3204.43.4.531

Grogan-Kaylor, A., & Otis, M. D. (2007). The predictors of parental use of corporal punishment *Family Relations, 56*(1), 80–91. https://doi.org/10.1111/j.1741-3729.2007.00441.x

Grogan-Kaylor, A., Ma, J., & Graham-Bermann, S. A. (2018). The case against physical punishment. *Current Opinion in Psychology, 19,* 22–27. https://doi.org/10.1016/j.copsyc.2017.03.022

Gubernskaya, Z., & Dreby, J. (2017). US immigration policy and the case for family unity. *Journal on Migration and Human Security, 5*(2), 417–430. https://doi.org/10.1177/233150241700500210

Guerrero, L., & Posthuma, R. A. (2014). Perceptions and behaviors of Hispanic workers: A review. *Journal of Managerial Psychology, 29*(6), 616–643. https://doi.org/10.1108/JMP-07-2012-0231

Guilamo-Ramos, V., Dittus, P., Jaccard, J., Johansson, M., Bouris, A., & Acosta, N. (2007). Parenting practices among Dominican and Puerto Rican mothers. *Social Work, 52*(1), 17–30. https://doi.org/10.1093/sw/52.1.17

Gulbas, L. E., & Zayas, L. H. (2017). Exploring the effects of U.S. immigration enforcement on the well-being of citizen children in Mexican immigrant families. *RSF: The Russell Sage Foundation Journal of the Social Sciences, 3*(4), 53–69. https://doi.org/10.7758/RSF.2017.3.4.04

Gutiérrez, R. A. (2019). *Mexican immigration to the United States.* Oxford Research Encyclopedia of American History. https://doi.org/10.1093/acrefore/9780199329175.013.146

Halgunseth, L. C., & Ispa, J. M. (2012). Mexican Parenting Questionnaire (MPQ). *Hispanic Journal of Behavioral Sciences, 34*(2), 232–250. https://doi.org/10.1177/0739986312437010

Hall, G.C.N., Ibaraki, A. Y., Huang, E. R., Marti, C. N., & Stice, E. (2016). A meta-analysis of cultural adaptations of psychological interventions. *Behavior Therapy, 47*(6), 993–1014. https://doi.org/10.1016/j.beth.2016.09.005

Hall, M. T., Huebner, R. A., Sears, J. S., Posze, L., Willauer, T., & Oliver, J. (2015). Sobriety Treatment and Recovery Teams in rural Appalachia: Implementation and outcomes. *Child Welfare, 94*(4), 119–138.

Hamby, S., Elm, J.H.L., Howell, K. H., & Merrick, M. T. (2021). Recognizing the cumulative burden of childhood adversities transforms science and practice for trauma and resilience. *American Psychologist, 76*(2), 230–242. https://doi.org/10.1037/amp0000763

Hamilton, E. R., & Hale, J. M. (2016). Changes in the transnational family structures of Mexican farm workers in the era of border militarization. *Demography, 53*(5), 1429–1451. https://doi.org/10.1007/s13524-016-0505-7

Hancock, T. U. (2005). Cultural competence in the assessment of poor Mexican families in the rural Southeastern United States. *Child Welfare, 84*(5), 689–711.

Hansen, H., Bourgois, P., & Drucker, E. (2014). Pathologizing poverty: New forms of diagnosis, disability, and structural stigma under welfare reform. *Social Science & Medicine, 103*, 76–83. https://doi.org/10.1016/j.socscimed.2013.06.033

Haralson, D. M., Hodgson, J. L., Brimhall, A. S., Baugh, E. J., & Knight, S. M. (2020). A comparison of primary care parenting programs for Latinx families. *Families, Systems, & Health, 38*(4), 428–438. https://doi.org/10.1037/fsh0000534

He, V. Y., Guthridge, S., Su, J. Y., Howard, D., Stothers, K., & Leach, A. (2020). The link between hearing impairment and child maltreatment among Aboriginal children in the Northern territory of Australia: Is there an opportunity for a public health approach in child protection? *BMC Public Health, 20*, 449. https://doi.org/10.1186/s12889-020-8456-8

Herman, J. L. (1992). *Trauma and recovery: The aftermath of violence—from domestic abuse to political terror.* Basic Books.

Hill, N. E., Bush, K. R., & Roosa, M. W. (2003) Parenting and family socialization strategies and children's mental health: Low-income Mexican-American and Euro-American mothers and children. *Child Development, 74*(1), 189–204. https://doi.org/10.1111/1467-8624.t01-1-00530

Hillstrom, K. A. (2009). *Are acculturation and parenting styles related to academic achievement among Latino students?* [Unpublished dissertation]. University of Southern California.

Hood, S., Hopson, R. K., & Kirkhart, K. E. (2015). Culturally responsive evaluation: Theory, practice, and future implications. In K. E. Newcomer, H. P. Hatry, & J. S. Wholey (Eds.). *Handbook of practical program evaluation* (pp. 281–317). Jossey-Bass.

hooks, b. (2015). The future of feminist activism and the quandary of gender. In J. H. Dragseth (Ed.), *Thinking woman: A philosophical approach to the quandary of gender* (pp. 158–178). Lutterworth Press.

Hopson, R. K. (2009). Reclaiming knowledge at the margins: Culturally responsive evaluation in the current evaluation moment. In K. E. Ryan, & J. B. Cousins (Eds.), *The SAGE international handbook of educational evaluation* (pp. 429–446). Sage Publishing. https://doi.org/10.4135/9781452226606.n24

Horowitz, J. M., Brown, A., & Cox, K. (2019, April 9). *Race in America 2019.* Pew Research Center. https://www.pewresearch.org/social-trends/2019/04/09/race-in-america-2019/

Hosoda, M., Nguyen, L. T., & Stone-Romero, E. F. (2012). The effect of Hispanic accents on employment decisions. *Journal of Managerial Psychology, 27*(4), 347–364. https://doi.org/10.1108/02683941211220162

Hovey, J. D. (2000). Psychosocial predictors of acculturative stress in Mexican immigrants. *The Journal of Psychology, 134*(5), 490–502. https://doi.org/10.1080/00223980009598231

Howard, J. A., & Renfrow, D. G. (2014). Intersectionality. In J. D. McLeod, E. J. Lawler, & M. Schwalbe (Eds.), *Handbook of the social psychology of inequality.* Springer, Dordrecht. https://doi.org/10.1007/978-94-017-9002-4_5

Huebner, R. A., Willauer, T., & Posze, L. (2012). The impact of Sobriety Treatment and Recovery Teams (START) on family outcomes. *Families in Society, 93*(3), 196–203. https://doi.org/10.1606/1044-3894.4223

Huey, S. J., Jr., & Polo, A. J. (2008). Evidence-based psychosocial treatments for ethnic minority youth. *Journal of Clinical Child & Adolescent Psychology, 37*(1), 262–301. https://doi.org/10.1080/15374410701820174

Hughes, R. C., Rycus, J. S., Saunders-Adams, S. M., Hughes, L. K., & Hughes, K. N. (2013). Issues in differential response. *Research on Social Work Practice, 23*(5), 493–520. https://doi.org/10.1177/1049731512466312

Hussey, J. M., Chang, J. J., & Kotch, J. B. (2006). Child Maltreatment in the United States: Prevalence, Risk Factors, and Adolescent Health Consequences. *Pediatrics, 118*(3), 933–942. https://doi.org/10.1542/peds.2005-2452

Infante, C., Idrovo, A. J., Sánchez-Domínguez, M. S., Vinhas, S., & González-Vázquez, T. (2012). Violence committed against migrants in transit: Experiences on the northern Mexican border. *Journal of Immigrant and Minority Health, 14*, 445–459. https://doi.org/10.1007/s10903-011-9489-y

Infurna, F. J., & Jayawickreme, E. (2019). Fixing the growth illusion: New directions for research in resilience and posttraumatic growth. *Current Directions in Psychological Science, 28*(2), 152–158. https://doi.org/10.1177/0963721419827017

Jang, S. T. (2019). Schooling experiences and educational outcomes of Latinx secondary school students living at the intersections of multiple social constructs. *Urban Education.* https://doi.org/10.1177/0042085919857793

Johnson-Motoyama, M., Dettlaff, A. J., & Finno, M. (2012). Parental nativity and the decision to substantiate: Findings from a study of Latino children in the second National Survey of Child and Adolescent Well-being (NSCAW II). *Children and Youth Services Review, 34*(11), 2229–2239. DOI:10.1016/j.childyouth.2012.07.017

Johnson-Motoyama, M., Moses, M., Conrad-Hiebner, A., & Mariscal, E.S. (2016). Development, CAPTA Part C referral and services among young children in the U.S. child welfare system: Implications for Latino children. *Child Maltreatment, 21*(3), 186–197. https://doi.org /10.1177/1077559516630831

Johnson-Motoyama, M., Putnam-Hornstein, E., Dettlaff, A. J., Zhao, K., Finno-Velasquez, M., & Needell, B. (2015). Disparities in reported and substantiated infant maltreatment by maternal Hispanic origin and nativity: A birth cohort study. *Maternal and Child Health Journal, 19*, 958–968. https://doi.org/10.1007/s10995-014-1594-9

Johnson, C., Sutton, E. S., & Thompson, D. (2005). Child welfare reform in Minnesota. *Protecting Children: A Professional Publication of American Humane, 20*(2–3), 55–61.

Johnson, M. A. (2007). The social ecology of acculturation: Implications for child welfare services to children of immigrants. *Children and Youth Services Review, 29*(11), 1426–1438. https://doi.org/10.1016/j.childyouth.2007.06.002

Jones, A. S. (2015). Implementation of differential response: A racial equity analysis. *Child Abuse & Neglect, 39*, 73–85. https://doi.org/10.1016 /j.chiabu.2014.04.013

Kaminski, J. W., Valle, L. A., Filene, J. H., & Boyle, C. L. (2008). A meta-analytic review of components associated with parent training program effectiveness. *Journal of Abnormal Child Psychology, 36*(4), 567–589. https://doi.org/10.1007/s10802-007-9201-9

Karaman, M. A., Cavazos Vela, J., Aguilar, A. A., Saldana, K., & Montenegro, M. C. (2019). Psychometric properties of U.S.-Spanish versions of the grit and resilience scales with a Latinx population. *International Journal of the Advancement of Counseling, 41*, 125–136. https://doi.org /10.1007/s10447-018-9350-2

Kelly-Irving, M., & Delpierre, C. (2019). A critique of the adverse childhood experiences framework in epidemiology and public health: Uses and misuses. *Social Policy and Society, 18*(3), 445–456. https://doi.org/10.1017 /S1474746419000101

Kepple, N. J. (2017). The complex nature of parental substance use: Examining past year and prior use behaviors as correlates of child maltreatment frequency. *Substance Use & Misuse, 52*(6), 811–821. https://doi.org/10.1080 /10826084.2016.1253747

Kerrigan, M. R., & Johnson, A. T. (2019). Qualitative approaches to policy research in education: Contesting the evidence-based, neoliberal regime. *American Behavioral Scientist, 63*(3), 287–295. https://doi.org/10.1177 /0002764218819693

Khaleque, A., & Rohner, R. P. (2012). Pancultural associations between perceived parental acceptance and psychological adjustment of children and adults: A meta-analytic review of worldwide research. *Journal of Cross-Cultural Psychology, 43*(5), 784–800. https://doi.org/10.1177 /0022022111406120

Kiehne, E. (2016). Latino critical perspective in social work. *Social Work,* *61*(2), 119–126. https://doi.org/10.1093/sw/swwoo1

Kim, H., Wildeman, C., Jonson-Reid, M., & Drake, B. (2017). Lifetime prevalence of investigating child maltreatment among US children. *American Journal of Public Health, 107,* 274–280. https://doi.org/10.2105 /AJPH.2016.303545

Kim, S. Y., Chen, S., Hou, Y., Zeiders, K. H., & Calzada, E. J. (2019). Parental socialization profiles in Mexican-origin families: Considering cultural socialization and general parenting practices. *Cultural Diversity and Ethnic Minority Psychology, 25*(3), 439–450. https://doi.org/10.1037 /cdp0000234

Kim, S. Y., Zhang, M., Chen, S., Song, J., Lopez, B. G., Rodriguez, E. M., Calzada, E. J., Hou, Y., Yan, J., & Shen, Y. (2020). Bilingual language broker profiles and academic competence in Mexican-origin adolescents. *Developmental Psychology, 56*(8), 1582–1595. https://doi.org/10.1037 /dev0001010

Kimber, M., Henriksen, C. A., Davidov, D. M., Goldstein, A. L., Pitre, N. Y., Tonmyr, L., & Afifi, T. O. (2015). The association between immigrant generational status, child maltreatment history and intimate partner violence (IPV): Evidence from a nationally representative survey. *Social Psychiatry & Psychiatric Epidemiology, 50,* 1135–1144. https://doi.org /10.1007/s00127-014-1002-1

Kirmayer, L. J., Gone, J. P., & Moses, J. (2014). Rethinking historical trauma. *Transcultural Psychiatry, 51*(3), 299–319. https://doi.org/10.1177 /1363461514536358

Klein, S., & Merritt, D. H. (2014). Neighborhood racial & ethnic diversity as a predictor of child welfare system involvement. *Children and Youth Services Review, 41,* 95–105. https://doi.org/10.1016/j.childyouth.2014.03.009

Kliethermes, M., Schacht, M., & Drewry, K. (2014). Complex trauma. *Child and Adolescent Psychiatric Clinics of North America, 23*(2), 339–361. https://doi.org/10.1016/j.chc.2013.12.009

Koerner, S. S., Shirai, Y., & Pedroza, R. (2013). Role of religious/spiritual beliefs and practices among Latino family caregivers of Mexican descent. *Journal of Latina/o Psychology, 1*(2), 95–111. https://doi.org/10.1037 /a0032438

Kreuter, M. W., Lukwago, S. N., Bucholtz, D. C., Clark, E. M., & Sanders-Thompson, V. (2003). Achieving cultural appropriateness in health promotion programs: Targeted and tailored approaches. *Health Education & Behavior, 30*(2), 133–146. https://doi.org/10.1177 /1090198102251021

Krieg, A. (2009). The experience of collective trauma in Australian Indigenous communities. *Australasian Psychiatry, 17*(1_suppl), S28–S32. https://doi.org/10.1080/10398560902948621

Krogstad, J. M., & Gonzalez-Barrera, A. (2015, March 24). *A majority of English-speaking Hispanics in the U.S. are bilingual.* Pew Research

Center. https://www.pewresearch.org/fact-tank/2015/03/24/a-majority
-of-english-speaking-hispanics-in-the-u-s-are-bilingual/

Krug, E. G., Dahlberg, L. L., Mercy, J. A., Zwi, A. B., & Lozano, R.
(2002). *World report on violence and health.* World Health Organization. http://apps.who.int/iris/bitstream/handle/10665/42495
/9241545615_eng.pdf;jsessionid=6BC4487431B7D23655475342896414
BA?sequence=1

Kumpfer, K. L., Alvarado, R., Smith, P., & Bellamy, N. (2002). Cultural
sensitivity and adaptation in family-based prevention interventions.
Prevention Science, 3, 241–246. https://doi.org/10.1023/A:101990
2902119

Kwak, K. (2003). Adolescents and their parents: A review of intergenerational family relations for immigrant and non-immigrant families.
Human Development, 46(2–3), 115–136. https://doi.org/10.1159
/000068581

LaBrenz, C. A., Findley, E., Graaf, G., Baiden, P., Kim, J., Choi, M. J., &
Chakravarty, S. (2021). Racial/ethnic disproportionality in reunification
across U.S. child welfare systems. *Child Abuse & Neglect, 114,* 104894.
https://doi.org/10.1016/j.chiabu.2020.104894

LaBrenz, C. A., Panisch, L. S., Lawson, J., Borcyk, A. L., Gerlach, B.,
Tennant, P. S., Nulu, S., & Faulkner, M. (2020). Adverse childhood
experiences and outcomes among at-risk Spanish-speaking Latino
families. *Journal of Child and Family Studies, 29*(5), 1221–1235. https://
doi.org/10.1007/s10826-019-01589-0.

Ladson-Billings, G. (1994). *The dreamkeepers: Successful teachers of African
American children.* Wiley Publishers.

LaLiberte, T., Crudo, T., & Skallet, H.O. (2015). *CW360: A comprehensive
look at prevalent child welfare issues.* Center for Advanced Studies in
Child Welfare, School of Social Work, University of Minnesota.

Lancaster, E., & Lumb, J. (1999). Bridging the gap: Feminist theory and
practice reality in work with the perpetrators of child sexual abuse. *Child
and Family Social Work, 4*(2), 119–129. https://doi.org/10.1046/j.1365-220
6.1999.00120.x

Lansford, J. E., Chang, L., Dodge, K. A., Malone, P. S., Oburu, P.,
Palmérus, K., Bacchini, D., Pastorelli, C., Bombi, A. S., Zelli, A.,
Tapanya, S., Chaudhary, N., Deater-Deckard, K., Manke, B., & Quinn, N.
(2005). Physical discipline and children's adjustment: cultural normativeness as a moderator. *Child Development, 76*(6), 1234–1246. https://doi
.org/10.1111/j.1467-8624.2005.00847.x

Lansford, J. E., Godwin, J., Uribe Tirado, L. M., Zelli, A., Al-Hassan, S. M.,
Bacchini, D., Bombi, A. S., Bornstein, M. H., Chang, L., Deater-
Deckard, K., Di Giunta, L., Dodge, K. A., Malone, P. S., Oburu, P.,
Pastorelli, C., Skinner, A. T., Sorbring, E., Tapanya, S., & Peña Alampay, L.
(2015). Individual, family, and culture level contributions to child
physical abuse and neglect: A longitudinal study in nine countries.

Development and psychopathology, 27(4pt2), 1417–1428. https://doi.org /10.1017/S095457941500084X

Lara, M., Gamboa, C., Kahramanian, M. I., Morales, L. S., & Hayes Bautista, D. E. (2005). Acculturation and Latino health in the United States: A review of the literature and its sociopolitical context. *Annual Review of Public Health, 26*(1), 367–397. https://doi.org/10.1146/annurev .publhealth.26.021304.144615

Larkin, H., & Park, J. (2012). Adverse childhood experiences (ACEs), service use, and service helpfulness among people experiencing homelessness. *Families in Society, 93*(2), 85–93. https://doi.org/10.1606/1044-3894 .4192

Larkin, H., Beckos, B. A., & Shields, J. J. (2012). Mobilizing resilience and recovery in response to adverse childhood experiences (ACE): A Restorative Integral Support (RIS) case study. *Journal of Prevention & Intervention in the Community, 40*(4), 335–346. https://doi.org /10.1080/10852352.2012.707466

Larzelere, R. E., Ferrer, E., Kuhn, B. R., & Danelia, K. (2010). Differences in causal estimates from longitudinal analyses of residualized versus simple gain scores: Contrasting controls for selection and regression artifacts. *International Journal of Behavioral Development, 34*(2), 180–189. https://doi.org/10.1177/0165025409351386

Larzelere, R. E., Kuhn, B. R. (2005). Comparing child outcomes of physical punishment and alternative disciplinary tactics: A meta-analysis. *Clinical Child & Family Psychology Review, 8*, 1–37. https://doi.org/10.1007 /s10567-005-2340-z

Latz, I., Lusk, M., & Heyman, J. (2019). Provider perceptions of the effects of current U.S. immigration enforcement policies on service utilization in a border community. *Social Development Issues, 41*(1), 49–63. https://www .proquest.com/openview/f563107e74eff94a6c0d97f451b4cf60/1?pq -origsite=gscholar&cbl=2035675

Laub, D., & Hamburger, A. (Eds.). (2017). *Psychoanalysis and Holocaust testimony: Unwanted memories of social trauma (1st ed.).* Routledge/ Taylor & Francis Group. https://doi.org/10.4324/9781315717456

Lawrence, C., Zuckerman, M., Smith, B. D., & Liu, J. (2012). Building cultural competence in the child welfare workforce: A mixed-methods analysis. *Journal of Public Child Welfare, 6*(2), 225–241. https://doi.org /10.1080/15548732.2012.667747

Lázaro, S., & López, F. (2010). Continuidad de los efectos del maltrato durante la infancia en adolescentes acogidos en centros de protección. *Infancia y Aprendizaje: Journal for the Study of Education and Development, 33*(2), 255–268. https://doi.org/10.1174/021037010791114599

Leake, R., Holt, K., Potter, C., & Ortega, D. M. (2010). Using simulation training to improve culturally responsive child welfare practice. *Journal of Public Child Welfare, 4*(3), 325–346. https://doi.org/10.1080 /15548732.2010.496080

Lee, E. S. (1966). A theory of migration. *Demography, 3*(1), 47–57. https://doi.org/10.2307/2060063

Lee, S. J., & Altschul, I. (2015). Spanking of young children: Do immigrant and U.S.-born Hispanic parents differ? *Journal of Interpersonal Violence, 30*(3), 475–498. https://doi.org/10.1177/0886260514535098

Lee, S. J., Altschul, I., & Gershoff, E. T. (2013). Does warmth moderate longitudinal associations between maternal spanking and child aggression in early childhood? *Developmental Psychology, 49*(11), 2017–2028. https://doi.org/10.1037/a0031630

Lee, S. J., Altschul, I., Shair, S. R., & Taylor, C. A. (2011). Hispanic fathers and risk for maltreatment in father-involved families of young children. *Journal of the Society for Social Work and Research, 2*(2), 125–142. https://doi.org/10.5243/jsswr.2011.7

Lee, S. J., Grogan-Kaylor, A., & Berger, L. (2014). Parental spanking of 1-year-old children and subsequent Child Protective Services involvement. *Child Abuse & Neglect, 38*(5), 875–883. https://doi.org/10.1016/j.chiabu.2014.01.018

Legano, L., Desch, L. W., Messner, S. A., Idzerda, S., & Flaherty, E. G. (2021). Maltreatment of children with disabilities. *Pediatrics, 147*(5), e2021050920. https://doi.org/10.1542/peds.2021-050920

Leslie, L. K., Landsverk, J., Ezzet-Lofstro, R., Tschann, J. M., Slymen, D. J., & Garland, A. F. (2000). Children in foster care: Factors influencing outpatient mental health service use. *Child Abuse & Neglect, 24*(4), 465–476. https://doi.org/10.1016/S0145-2134(00)00116-2

Li, F., Godinet, M. T., & Arnsberger, P. (2011). Protective factors among families with children at risk of maltreatment: Follow up to early school years. *Children and Youth Service Review, 33*(1), 139–148. https://doi.org/10.1016/j.childyouth.2010.08.026

Libby, A. M., Orton, H. D., Barth, R. P., Webb, M. B., Burns, B. J., Wood, P., & Spicer, P. (2006). Alcohol, drug, and mental health specialty treatment services and race/ethnicity: A national study of children and families involved with child welfare. *American Journal of Public Health, 96*(4), 628–631. https://doi.org/10.2105/AJPH.2004.059436

Logan, B. J. (2018, March 22). *Foster care prevention: Testimony before the Senate Committee on Health and Human Services.* Texas Public Policy Foundation. https://files.texaspolicy.com/uploads/2018/08/16104444/2018-04-Testimony-FosterCarePrevention-CFC-Logan.pdf

Loman, L. A., & Siegel, G. L. (2005). Alternative response in Minnesota: Findings of the program evaluation. *Protecting Children, 20*(2–3), 78–92.

Lopez, G., & Gonzalez-Barrerra, A. (2016, March 1). *Afro-Latino: A deeply rooted identity among U.S. Hispanics.* Pew Research Center. https://www.pewresearch.org/fact-tank/2016/03/01/afro-latino-a-deeply-rooted-identity-among-u-s-hispanics/

Lopez, M. H., Gonzalez-Barrera, A., & Krogstad, J. M. (2018, October 25). *More Latinos have serious concerns about their place in America under*

Trump. Pew Research Center. https://www.pewresearch.org/hispanic
/2018/10/25/more-latinos-have-serious-concerns-about-their-place-in
-america-under-trump/

Lorenzo-Blanco, E. I., Meca, A., Unger, J. B., Romero, A., Szapocznik, J.,
Piña-Watson, B., Cano, M. Á., Zamboanga, B. L., Baezconde-Garbanati, L.,
Des Rosiers, S. E., Soto, D. W., Villamar, J. A., Lizzi, K. M., Pattarroyo, M., &
Schwartz, S. J. (2017). Longitudinal effects of Latino parent cultural
stress, depressive symptoms, and family functioning on youth emotional
well-being and health risk behaviors. *Family Process, 56*(4), 981–996.
https://doi.org/10.1111/famp.12258

Lothridge, J., McCroskey, J., Pecora, P. J., Chambers, R., & Fatemi, M.
(2012). Strategies for improving child welfare services for families of
color: First findings of a community-based initiative in Los Angeles.
Children and Youth Services Review, 34(1), 281–288. https://doi.org
/10.1016/j.childyouth.2011.10.025

Lovato-Hermann, K., Dellor, E., Tam, C. C., Curry, S., & Freisthler, B.
(2017). Racial disparities in service referrals for families in the child
welfare system. *Journal of Public Child Welfare, 11*(2), 133–149. https://
doi.org/10.1080/15548732.2016.1251372

Maccoby, E. E., & Martin, J. A. (1983). Socialization in the context of the
family: Parent-child interaction. In P. H. Mussen & E. M. Hetherington
(Eds.), *Handbook of child psychology: Socialization, personality, and social
development* (4th ed., pp. 1–101). Wiley.

MacLeod, J., & Nelson, G. (2000). Programs for the promotion of family
wellness and the prevention of child maltreatment: A meta-analytic
review. *Child Abuse & Neglect, 24*(9), 1127–1149. https://doi.org/10.1016
/s0145-2134(00)00178-2

Maguire-Jack, K., & Font, S. A. (2017). Community and individual risk
factors for physical child abuse and child neglect: Variations by poverty
status. *Child Maltreatment, 22*(3), 215–226. https://doi.org/10.1177
/1077559517711806

Maguire-Jack, K., Lanier, P., & Lombardi, B. (2020). Investigating racial
differences in clusters of adverse childhood experiences. *American
Journal of Orthopsychiatry, 90*(1), 106–114. https://doi.org/10.1037
/ort0000405

Maguire-Jack, K., Lanier, P., Johnson-Motoyama, M., Welch, H., &
Dineen, M. (2015). Geographic variation in racial disparities in child
maltreatment: The influence of county poverty and population density.
Child Abuse & Neglect, 47, 1–13. https://doi.org/10.1016/j.chiabu.2015
.05.020

Maker, A. H., Shah, P. V., & Agha, Z. (2005). Child physical abuse:
Prevalence, characteristics, predictors, and beliefs about parent-child
violence in South Asian, Middle Eastern, East Asian, and Latina women
in the United States. *Journal of Interpersonal Violence, 20*(11), 1406–1428.
https://doi.org/10.1177/0886260505278713

Malkoff, A. C., Grace, M., Kapke, T. L., & Gerdes, A. C. (2019). Family functioning in Latinx families of children with ADHD: The role of parental gender and acculturation. *Journal of Child and Family Studies, 29*, 1108–1122. https://doi.org/10.1007/s10826-019-01673-5

Mallon, G. P. (2020). From the editor: The impact of trauma-informed care and cultural humility in child welfare systems. *Child Welfare, 98*(4), V+. https://link.gale.com/apps/doc/A656271039/HRCA?u=anon~80539972 &sid=googleScholar&xid=aabc68a9

Manongdo, J. A., & Ramírez García, J. I. (2011). Maternal parenting and mental health of Mexican American youth: A bidirectional and prospective approach. *Journal of Family Psychology, 25*(2), 261–270. https://doi.org/10.1037/a0023004

Mariscal, E. S. (2020). Resilience following exposure to intimate partner violence and other violence: A comparison of Latino and non-Latino youth. *Children and Youth Services Review, 113*, 104975. https://doi.org /10.1016/j.childyouth.2020.104975

Martinez, C. R., Jr., & Eddy, J. M. (2005). Effects of culturally adapted parent management training on Latino youth behavioral health outcomes. *Journal of Consulting and Clinical Psychology, 73*(5), 841–851. https://doi.org/10.1037/0022-006X.73.5.841

Martínez, E. C. (2014). Latino Catholicism and indigenous heritage as a subfield of Latino studies: A critical evaluation of new approaches. *Cultural Encounters, Conflicts, and Resolutions, 1*(2). https:// engagedscholarship.csuohio.edu/cecr/vol1/iss2/3

Mather, M. (2016, September 28). *Trends and challenges facing America's Latino children*. Population Reference Bureau. https://www.prb.org /trends-and-challenges-facing-americas-latino-children/

Mazzucato, V., & Schans, D. (2011). Transnational families and the well-being of children: Conceptual and methodological challenges. *Journal of Marriage and Family, 73*(4), 704–712. https://doi.org/10.1111 /j.1741-3737.2011.00840.x

McCue Horwitz, S., Hurlburt, M. S., Goldhaber-Fiebert, J. D., Heneghan, A. M., Zhang, J., Rolls-Reutz, J., Fisher, E., Landsverk, J., & Stein, R.E.K. (2012). Mental health service use by children investigated by child welfare agencies. *Pediatrics, 130*(5), 861–869. https://doi.org /10.1542/peds.2012-1330

McLoyd, V. C., & Smith, J. (2002). Physical discipline and behavior problems in African American, European American, and Hispanic children: Emotional support as a moderator. *Journal of Marriage and Family, 64*(1), 40–53. https://doi.org/10.1111/j.1741-3737.2002.00040.x

McMillin, S. E., Bultas, M. W., Zander, T., Wilmott, J., Underwood, S., Broom, M. A., & Zand, D. H. (2016). The role of maternal knowledge of child development in predicting risk for child maltreatment. *Clinical Pediatrics, 55*(4), 374–376. https://doi.org/10.1177 /0009922815586054

McPhatter, A. R. (1999). Cultural competence in child welfare: What is it? How do we achieve it? What happens without it? In S. Jackson & S. Brissett-Chapman (Eds.), *Serving African American Children* (pp. 251–256). Child Welfare League of America, Inc.

Mejia, A., Leijten, P., Lachman, J. M., & Parra-Cardona, J. R. (2016). Different strokes for different folks? Contrasting approaches to cultural adaptation of parenting interventions. *Prevention Science, 18*, 630–639. https://doi.org/10.1007/s11121-016-0671-2

Meléndez Guevara, A. M., Lindstrom Johnson, S., Elam, K., Hilley, C., Mcintire, C., & Morris, K. (2021). Culturally responsive trauma-informed services: A multilevel perspective from practitioners serving Latinx children and families. *Community Mental Health Journal, 57*, 325–329. https://doi.org/10.1007/S10597-020-00651-2

Mendoza, M. M., Dmitrieva, J., Perreira, K. M., Hurwich-Reiss, E., & Watamura, S. E. (2017). The effects of economic and sociocultural stressors on the well-being of children and Latino immigrants living in poverty. *Cultural Diversity and Ethnic Minority Psychology, 23*(1), 15–26. https://doi.org/10.1037/cdp0000111

Merianos, A. L., King, K. A., Vidourek, R. A., & Nabors, L. A. (2015). Recent alcohol use and binge drinking based on authoritative parenting among Hispanic youth nationwide. *Journal of Child and Family Studies, 24*(7), 1966–1976. https://doi.org/10.1007/s10826 -014-9996-2

Merritt, D. H. (2021). Lived experiences of racism among child welfare-involved parents. *Race and Social Problems, 13*(1), 63–72. https://doi.org /10.1007/s12552-021-09316-5

Mersky, J. P., & Janczewski, C. E. (2018). Racial and ethnic differences in the prevalence of adverse childhood experiences: Findings from a low-income sample of U.S. women. *Child Abuse & Neglect, 76*, 480–487. https://doi.org/10.1016/j.chiabu.2017.12.012

Millett, L. S. (2016). The healthy immigrant paradox and child maltreatment: A systematic review. *Journal of Immigrant and Minority Health, 18*(5), 1199–1215. https://doi.org/10.1007/s10903-016-0373-7

Mindell, R., Vidal de Haymes, M., & Francisco, D. (2003). A culturally responsive practice model for urban Indian child welfare services. *Child Welfare, 82*(2), 201–217.

Miranda, A. O., Bilot, J. M., Peluso, P. R., Berman, K., & Van Meek, L. G. (2006). Latino families: The relevance of the connection among acculturation, family dynamics, and health for family counseling research and practice. *The Family Journal, 14*(3), 268–273. https://doi.org /10.1177/1066480706287805

Miranda, A. O., Estrada, D., & Firpo-Jimenez, M. (2000). Differences in family cohesion, adaptability, and environment among Latino families in dissimilar stages of acculturation. *The Family Journal, 8*(4), 341–350. https://doi.org/10.1177/1066480700084003

Mistry, R. S., Benner, A. D., Biesanz, J. C., Clark, S. L., & Howes, C. (2010). Family and social risk, and parental investments during the early childhood years as predictors of low-income children's school readiness outcomes. *Early Childhood Quarterly, 25*(4), 432–449. https://doi.org /10.1016/j.ecresq.2010.01.002

Mitchell, M. M., Armstrong, G., & Armstrong, T. (2020). Disproportionate school disciplinary responses: An exploration of prisonization and minority threat hypothesis among Black, Hispanic, and Native American students. *Criminal Justice Policy Review, 31*(1), 80–102. https:// doi.org/10.1177/0887403418813672

Mogro-Wilson, C. (2011). Resilience in vulnerable and at-risk Latino families. *Infants & Young Children, 24*(3), 267–279. https://doi.org /10.1097/IYC.0b013e31822006b2

Molina, K. M., Estrella, M. L., Durazo-Arvizu, R., Malcarne, V. L., Llabre, M. M., Isasi, C. R., Ornelas, I. J., Perreira, K. M., Penedo, F. J., Brondolo, E., Gallo, L., & Daviglus, M. L. (2019). Perceived discrimination and physical health-related quality of life: The Hispanic Community Health Study/Study of Latinos (HCHS/SOL) Sociocultural Ancillary Study. *Social Science & Medicine, 222*, 91–100. https://doi.org /10.1016/j.socscimed.2018.12.038

Molnar, B. E., Beatriz, E. D., & Beardslee, W. R. (2016). Community-level approaches to child maltreatment prevention. *Trauma, Violence, & Abuse, 17*(4), 387–397. https://doi.org/10.1177/1524838016658879

Monico, C., Rotabi, K. S., & Lee, J. (2019). Forced child-family separations in the Southwestern U.S. border under the "Zero-Tolerance" policy: Preventing human rights violations and child abduction into adoption (Part 1). *Journal of Human Rights and Social Work, 4*, 164–179. https:// doi.org/10.1007/s41134-019-0089-4

Moon, S. S., Kang, S-Y., & An, S. (2009). Predictors of immigrant children's school achievement: A comparative study. *Journal of Research in Childhood Education, 23*(3), 278–289. https://doi.org/10.1080/02568540909594661

Morelato, G. (2011). Resilience en maltrato infantil: Aportes para la comprensión de factores desde un modelo ecológico. *Revista de Psicología, 29*(2), 205–224.

Moreno, A., Navarro, C., Molleda, J. C., & Fuentes-Lara, M. C. (2019). Measurement and predictors of resilience among Latin American public relations professionals: An application of the Connor-Davidson Resilience Scale (CD-RISC). *Journal of Communication Management, 23*(4), 393–411. https://doi.org/10.1108/JCOM-01-2019-004

Morgan, J., Robinson, D., & Aldridge, J. (2002). Parenting stress and externalizing child behaviour. *Child & Family Social Work, 7*(3), 219–225. https://doi.org/10.1046/j.1365-2206.2002.00242.x

Mosher, D. K., Hook, J. N., Captari, L. E., Davis, D. E., DeBlaere, C., & Owen, J. (2017). Cultural humility: A therapeutic framework for engaging diverse clients. *Practice Innovations, 2*(4), 221–233. https:// doi.org/10.1037/pri0000055

Motel, S., & Patten, E. (2012, June). *The 10 largest Hispanic origin groups: Characteristics, rankings, top counties.* Pew Research Center. https://www .pewresearch.org/hispanic/2012/06/27/the-10-largest-hispanic-origin -groups-characteristics-rankings-top-counties/

Muñoz, S. M., Vigil, D., Jach, E., & Rodriguez-Gutierrez, M. (2018). Unpacking resilience and trauma: Examining the "Trump effect" in higher education for undocumented Latinx college students. *Association of Mexican American Educators Journal, 12*(3), 33–52. https://doi.org /10.24974/amae.12.3.405

Music, G. (2016). *Nurturing natures: Attachment and children's emotional, sociocultural and brain development.* Routledge.

Myers, R., Chou, C. P., Sussman, S., Baezconde-Garbanati, L., Pachon, H., & Valente, T. W. (2009). Acculturation and substance use: Social influence as a mediator among Hispanic alternative high school youth. *Journal of Health and Social Behavior, 50*(2), 164–179. https://doi.org/10.1177 /002214650905000204

Nadan, Y., Spilsbury, J. C., & Korbin, J. E. (2015). Culture and context in understanding child maltreatment: Contributions of intersectionality and neighborhood-based research. *Child Abuse & Neglect, 41,* 40–48. https://doi.org/10.1016/j.chiabu.2014.10.021

Nair, N., Taylor, Z. E., Evich, C. D., & Jones, B. L. (2020). Relations of positive parenting, effortful control, and resilience in rural Midwestern Latinx early adolescents. *Children and Youth Services Review, 113.* https://doi.org/10.1016/j.childyouth.2020.105003

Namy, S., Carlson, C., O'Hara, K., Nakuti, J., Bukuluki, P., Lwanyaage, J., Namakula, S., Nanyunja, B., Wainberg, M. L., Naker, D., & Michau, L. (2017). Towards a feminist understanding of the intersecting violence against women and children in the family. *Social Science & Medicine, 184,* 40–48. https://doi.org/10.1016/j.socscimed.2017.04.042

National Academies of Sciences, Engineering, and Medicine. (2015*). The integration of immigrants into American society.* The National Academies Press. https://doi.org/10.17226/21746

National Association of Social Workers (2015). Standards and indicators for cultural competence. https://www.socialworkers.org/LinkClick.aspx ?fileticket=7dVckZAYUmk%3D&portalid=0

National Child and Traumatic Stress Network (2008). *Child trauma toolkit for educators.* https://www.nctsn.org/sites/default/files/resources//child _trauma_toolkit_educators.pdf

National Research Center on Hispanic Children and Families (2017). *La familia: Latino families strong and stable, despite limited resources.* https://www.hispanicresearchcenter.org/?nrc-news=la-familia-latino -families-strong-and-stable-despite-limited-resources

Nellis, A. (2016). *The color of justice: Racial and ethnic disparity in state prisons.* The Sentencing Project. https://www.sentencingproject.org /publications/color-of-justice-racial-and-ethnic-disparity-in-state -prisons/

Noe-Bustamante, L., & Flores, A. (2019, September 16). *Facts on Latinos in the U.S.* Pew Research Center. https://www.pewresearch.org/hispanic/fact-sheet/latinos-in-the-u-s-fact-sheet/

Nomaguchi, K., & House, A. N. (2013). Racial-ethnic disparities in maternal parenting stress: The role of structural disadvantages and parenting values. *Journal of Health and Social Behavior, 54*(3), 386–404. https://doi.org/10.1177/0022146513498511

Núñez, A. M. (2014). Employing multilevel intersectionality in educational research: Latino identities, contexts, and college access. *Educational Researcher, 43*(2), 85–92. https://doi.org/10.3102/0013189X14522320

Nybell, L. M., & Gray, S. S. (2004). Race, place, space: Meanings of cultural competence in three child welfare agencies. *Social Work, 49*(1), 17–26. https://doi.org/10.1093/sw/49.1.17

O'Gara, J., Calzada, E. J., & Kim, S. Y. (2019). The father's role in risk and resilience among Mexican-American adolescents. *American Journal of Orthopsychiatry, 90*(1), 70–77. https://doi.org/10.1037/ort0000394

O'Gara, J., Calzada, E. J., LaBrenz, C., & Barajas, R. G. (2020). Examining the longitudinal effect of spanking on young Latinx child behavior problems. *Journal of Child and Family Studies, 29*, 3080–3090. https://doi.org/10.1007/s10826-020-01818-x

Ortega, R. M., & Faller, K. C. (2011). Training child welfare workers from an intersectional cultural humility perspective: A paradigm shift. *Child Welfare, 90*(5), 27–49.

Oscea Hawkins, A., Kmett Danielson, C., de Arellano, M. A., Hanson, R. F., Ruggiero, K. J., Smith, D. W., Saunders, B. E., & Kilpatrick, D. G. (2010). Ethnic/racial differences in the prevalence of injurious spanking and other child physical abuse in a national survey of adolescents. *Child Maltreatment, 15*(3), 242–249. https://doi.org/10.1177/1077559510367938

Osterling, K. L., D'Andrade, A., & Austin, M. J. (2008). Understanding and addressing racial/ethnic disproportionality in the front end of the child welfare system. *Journal of Evidence-Based Social Work, 5*(1–2), 9–30. https://doi.org/10.1300/J394v05n01_02

Oxhandler, H. K. & Parrish, D. E. (2017). Integrating clients' religion/spirituality in clinical practice: A comparison among social workers, psychologists, counselors, marriage and family therapists, and nurses. *Journal of Clinical Psychology, 74*(4), 680–694. https://doi.org/10.1002/jclp.22539

Padilla, A. M., & Perez, W. (2003). Acculturation, social identity, and social cognition: A new perspective. *Hispanic Journal of Behavioral Sciences, 25*(1), 35–55. https://doi.org/10.1177/0739986303251694

Palomar Lever, J., & Gomez Valdez, N. E. (2010). Desarrollo de una escala de medición de la resiliencia con mexicanos (RESI-M). *Interdisciplinaria, 27*(1), 7–22.

Palusci, V. J. (2011). Risk factors and services for child maltreatment among infants and young children. *Children and Youth Services Review, 33*(8), 1374–1382. https://doi.org/10.1016/j.childyouth.2011.04.025

Paradies, Y., Ben, J., Denson, N., Elias, A., Priest, N., Pieterse, A., Gupta, A., Kelaher, M., & Gee, G. (2015). Racism as a determinant of health: A systematic review and meta-analysis. *PloS One, 10*(9), e0138511. https://doi.org/10.1371/journal.pone.0138511

Parke, R. D., Coltrane, S., Duffy, S., Buriel, R., Dennis, J., Powers, J., French, S., & Widaman, K. F. (2004). Economic stress, parenting, and child adjustment in Mexican American and European American families. *Child Development, 75*(6), 1632–56. https://doi.org/10.1111/j.1467–8624.2004.00807.x. PMID: 15566370

Parra Cardona, J., Holtrop, K., Córdova, D., Jr, Escobar-Chew, A. R., Horsford, S., Tams, L., Villarruel, F. A., Villalobos, G., Dates, B., Anthony, J. C., & Fitzgerald, H. E. (2009). "Queremos aprender": Latino immigrants' call to integrate cultural adaptation with best practice knowledge in a parenting intervention. *Family Process, 48*(2), 211–231. https://doi.org/10.1111/j.1545-5300.2009.01278.x

Passel, J. S., & Suro, R. (2005). *Rise, peak and decline: Trends in U.S. immigration 1992–2004.* Pew Hispanic Center.

Patterson, G. R. (1982). *Coercive family process.* Castalia.

Peer, J. W., & Hillman, S. B. (2014). Stress and resilience for parents of children with intellectual and developmental disabilities: A review of key factors and recommendations for practitioners. *Journal of Policy Practice in Intellectual Disabilities, 11*(2), 92–98. https://doi.org/10.1111/jppi.12072

Perez-Brena, N. J., Cookston, J. T., Fabricius, W. V., & Saenz, D. (2012). Patterns of father self-evaluations among Mexican and European American men and links to adolescent adjustment. *Fathering: A Journal of Theory, Research, and Practice about Men as Fathers, 10*(2), 213–235. https://doi.org/10.3149/fth.1002.213

Perreira, K. M., Chapman, M., & Stein, G. L. (2006). Becoming an American parent: Overcoming challenges and finding strengths in a new immigrant Latino community. *Journal of Family Issues, 27,* 1383–1414.

Perry, B. D. (2001). The neuroarcheology of childhood maltreatment. In K. Franey, R. Geffner, & R. Falconer, *The cost of maltreatment: Who pays? We all do* (pp. 15–37). Family Violence and Sexual Assault Institute.

Perry, B. D., Pollard, R. A., Blakley, T. L., Baker, W. L., & Vigilante, D. (1995). Childhood trauma, the neurobiology of adaptation and "use-dependent" development of the brain: How "states" become "traits." *Infant Mental Health Journal, 16*(4), 271–291.

Pew Research Center. (2015, December 17). *Parenting in America: Outlook, worries, aspirations are strongly linked to financial situation.* file:///Users/ec29546/Downloads/2015-12-17_parenting-in-america_FINAL.pdf

Pfannenstiel, J. C., & Seltzer, D. A. (1989). New Parents as Teachers: Evaluation of an early parent education program. *Early Childhood Quarterly, 4*(1), 1–18. https://doi.org/10.1016/S0885-2006(89)90025-2

Physicians for Human Rights (2021, January). Praying for hand soap and masks: Health and human rights violations in U.S. immigration detention during the COVID-19 pandemic. https://phr.org/our-work/resources/praying-for-hand-soap-and-masks/

Pierce, R. L., & Pierce, L. H. (1996). Moving toward cultural competence in the child welfare system. *Children and Youth Services Review, 18*(8), 713–731. https://doi.org/10.1016/S0190-7409(96)00032-1

Pinquart, M., & Kauser, R. (2018). Do the associations of parenting styles with behavior problems and academic achievement vary by culture? Results from a meta-analysis. *Cultural Diversity & Ethnic Minority Psychology, 24*(1), 75–100. https://doi.org/10.1037/cdp0000149

Piquero, A. R. (2008). Disproportionate minority contact. *The Future of Children, 18*(2), 59–79.

Polinsky, M. L., Pion-Berlin, L., Long, T., & Wolf, A. M. (2011). Parents Anonymous outcome evaluation: Promising findings for child maltreatment reduction. *Journal of Juvenile Justice, 1*(1), 33–47.

Polinsky, M. L., Pion-Berlin, L., Williams, S., & Wolf, A. M. (2010). Preventing child abuse and neglect: A national evaluation of Parents Anonymous® groups. *Child Welfare, 89*(6), 43–62.

Pong, S., Hao, L., & Gardner, E. (2005). The roles of parenting styles and social capital in the school performance of immigrant Asian and Hispanic adolescents. *Social Science Quarterly, 86*, 928–950. https://doi.org/10.1111/j.0038-4941.2005.00364.x

Popple, P., & Vecchiolla, F. (2007). *Child Welfare Social Work: An Introduction*. Pearson.

Portes, P. R., & Zady, M. F. (2002). Self-esteem in the adaptation of Spanish-speaking adolescents: The role of immigration, family conflict, and depression. *Hispanic Journal of Behavioral Sciences, 24*(3), 296–318. https://doi.org/10.1177/0739986302024003003

Priest, N., Paradies, Y., Trenerry, B., Truong, M., Karlsen, S., & Kelly, Y. (2013). A systematic review of studies examining the relationship between reported racism and health and wellbeing for children and young. *Social Science and Medicine, 95*, 115–127. https://doi.org/10.1016/j.socscimed.2012.11.031

Prilleltensky, I., & Gonick, L. (1996). Polities change, oppression remains: On the psychology and politics of oppression. *Political Psychology, 17*(1), 127–148. https://doi.org/10.2307/3791946

Przeworski, A., & Piedra, A. (2020). The role of the family for sexual minority Latinx individuals: A systematic review and recommendations for clinical practice. *Journal of GLBT Family Studies, 16*(2), 211–240. https://doi.org/10.1080/1550428X.2020.1724109

Putnam, F. (2003). Ten-year research update review: Child sexual abuse. *Journal of the American Academy of Child & Adolescent Psychiatry, 42*, 269–278. https://doi.org/10.1097/00004583-200303000-00006

Putnam-Hornstein, E., Needell, B., King, B., & Johnson-Motoyama, M. (2013). Racial and ethnic disparities: A population-based examination of risk factors for involvement with child protective services. *Child Abuse & Neglect, 37*(1), 33–46. https://doi.org/10.1016/j.chiabu.2012.08.005

Putnam-Hornstein, E., Webster, D., Needell, B., & Magruder, J. (2011). A public health approach to child maltreatment surveillance: Evidence from a data linkage project in the United States. *Child Abuse Review, 20*(4), 256–273. https://doi.org/10.1002/car.1191

Quesada, J., Hart, L. K., & Bourgois, P. (2011). Structural vulnerability and health: Latino migrant laborers in the United States. *Medical Anthropology, 30*(4), 339–362. https://doi.org/10.1080/01459740.2011.576725

Quiocho, A.M.L., & Daoud, A. M. (2006). Dispelling myths about Latino parent participation in schools. *The Educational Forum, 70*(3), 255–267. https://doi.org/10.1080/00131720608984901

Ramirez, A., Aguilar, R., Merck, A., Sukumaran, P., & Gamse, C. (2019). *The state of Latino housing, transportation, and green space: A research review.* Salud America & Robert Wood Johnson Foundation.

Ramirez, J., & Hosch, H. M. (1991). *The influence of acculturation on family functioning among Hispanic Americans in a bicultural community.* ERIC Clearinghouse.

Raymond, K. S., & Griffith, D. P. (2008). Impact of intensive family preservation services on disproportionality of out-of-home placement of children of color in one state's child welfare system. *Child Welfare, 87*(5), 87–105.

Reece, R. (2019). Color crit: Critical race theory and the history and future of colorism in the United States. *Journal of Black Studies, 00*, 1–23. https://doi.org/10.1177/0021934718803735

Regalado, M., Sareen, H., Inkelas, M., Wissow, L. S., & Halfon, N. (2004). Parents' discipline of young children: Results from the National Survey of Early Childhood Health. *Pediatrics, 113*(6 Suppl), 1952–1958. PMID: 15173466.

Renfroe, S. (2020). Building a life despite it all: Structural oppression and resilience of undocumented Latina migrants in Central Florida. *The Journal for Undergraduate Ethnography, 10*(1), 35–52.

Resick, P. A., Bovin, M. J., Calloway, A. L., Dick, A. M., King, M. W., Mitchell, K. S., Suvak, M. K., Wells, S. Y., Stirman, S. W., & Wolf, E. J. (2012). A critical evaluation of the complex PTSD literature: Implications for DSM-5. *Journal of Traumatic Stress, 25*(3), 241–251. https://doi.org/10.1002/jts.21699

Rivaux, S. L., James, J., Wittenstrom, K., Baumann, D., Sheets, J., Henry, J., & Jeffries, V. (2008). The intersection of race, poverty and risk: Understanding the decision to provide services to clients and to remove children. *Child Welfare, 87*(2), 151–68.

Rivera, H. P. (2002). Developing collaborations between child welfare agencies and Latino communities. *Child Welfare, 81*(2), 371–384.

Roberts, S. O., & Rizzo, M. T. (2021). The psychology of American racism. *American Psychologist, 76*(3), 475–487. https://doi.org/10.1037/amp0000642

Rodil, K. (2019). U.S. intervention and corrective justice require open borders. *Georgetown Immigration Law Journal, 33*(2), 327–349.

Rodriguez, C., & Henderson, R. (2010). Who spares the rod? Religious orientation, social conformity, and child abuse potential. *Child Abuse & Neglect, 34*, 84–94. https://doi.org/10.1016/j.chiabu.2009.07.002

Rodriguez, C. M., & Richardson, M. J. (2007). Stress and anger as contextual factors and pre-existing cognitive schemas: Predicting parental child maltreatment risk. *Child Maltreatment, 12*, 325–337.

Rodriguez, N., Myers, H. F., Mira, C. B., Flores, T., & Garcia-Hernandez, L. (2002). Development of the Multidimensional Acculturative Stress Inventory for adults of Mexican origin. *Psychological Assessment, 4*, 451–461. https://doi.org/10.1037/1040-3590.14.4.451

Rodríguez, S. A., Perez-Brena, N. J., Updegraff, K. A., & Umaña-Taylor, A. J. (2014). Emotional closeness in Mexican-origin adolescents' relationships with mothers, fathers, and same-sex friends. *Journal of Youth and Adolescence, 43*(12), 1953–1968. https://doi.org/10.1007/s10964-013-0004-8

Rogers, J. (2012). Anti-oppressive social work research: Reflections on power in the creation of knowledge. Social Work Education: *The International Journal, 31*(7), 866–879. https://doi.org/10.1080/02615479.2011.602965

Rogerson, S. (2012). Unintended and unavoidable: The failure to protect rule and its consequences for undocumented parents and their children. *Family Court Review: An Interdisciplinary Journal, 50*(4), 580–593. https://doi.org/10.1111/j.1744-1617.2012.01477.x

Romero, A. J., & Ruiz, M. (2007). Does familism lead to increased parental monitoring?: Protective factors for coping with risky behavior. *Journal of Child & Family Studies, 16*, 143–154. https://doi.org/10.1007/s10826-006-9074-5

Rosanbalm, K. D., Dodge, K. A., Murphy, R., O'Donnell, K., Christopoulos, C., Gibbs, S. W., Appleyard, K., & Daro, D. (2010). Evaluation of a collaborative community-based child maltreatment prevention initiative. *Protecting Children, 25*(4), 8–23.

Rosenblum, M. R., & Soto, A.G.R. (2015). *An analysis of unauthorized immigrants in the United States by country and region of birth*. Migration Policy Institute. https://www.migrationpolicy.org/sites/default/files/publications/Unauth-COB-Report-FINALWEB.pdf

Ross, L. (2010). Notes from the field: Learning cultural humility through critical incidents and central challenges in community-based participatory research. *Journal of Community Practice, 18*(2–3), 315–335. https://doi.org/10.1080/10705422.2010.490161

Roth, B. J., Crea, T. M., Jani, J., Underwood, D., Hasson III, R. G., Evans, K., Zuch, M., Hornung, E. (2018). Detached and afraid: U.S. immigration policy and the practice of forcibly separating parents and young children at the border. *Child Welfare, 96*(5), 29–49.

Rothenberg, W., Lansford, J., Bornstein, M., Chang, L., Deater-Deckard, K., Giunta, L. D., Dodge, K., Malone, P., Oburu, P., Pastorelli, C., Skinner, A. T., Sorbring, E., Steinberg, L., Tapanya, S., Tirado, L. M., Yotanyamanee-wong, S., Alampay, L., Al-Hassan, S. M., & Bacchini, D. (2020). Effects of parental warmth and behavioral control on adolescent externalizing and internalizing trajectories across cultures. *Journal of Research on Adolescence, 30*(4), 835–885. https://doi.org/10.1111/jora.12566

Roygardner, D., Hughes, K. N., & Palusci, V. J. (2020). Leveraging family and community strengths to reduce child maltreatment. *The ANNALS of the American Academy of Political and Social Science, 692*(1), 119–139. https://doi.org/10.1177/0002716220978402

Sabogal, F., Marín, G., Otero-Sabogal, R., Marín, B. V., & Perez-Stable, E. J. (1987). Hispanic familism and acculturation: What changes and what doesn't? *Hispanic Journal of Behavioral Sciences, 9*(4), 397–412. https://doi.org/10.1177/07399863870094003

Salas-Wright, C. P., Vaughn, M. G., Clark, T. T., Terzis, L. D., & Cordova, D. (2015). Substance use disorders among first- and second-generation immigrant adults in the United States: Evidence of an immigrant paradox. *Journal of Studies on Alcohol and Drugs, 75*(6), 958–967. https://doi.org/10.15288/jsad.2014.75.958

Salinas, C., Jr., & Lozano, A. (2019). Mapping and recontextualizing the evolution of the term Latinx: An environmental scanning in higher education. *Journal of Latinos and Education, 18*(4), 302–315. https://doi.org/10.1080/15348431.2017.1390464

Sanders-Phillips, K. (2009). Racial discrimination: A continuum of violence exposure for children of color. *Clinical Child and Family Psychological Review, 12*, 174–195. https://doi.org/10.1007/s10567-009-0053-4

Sanders-Phillips, K., & Kliewer, W. (2020). Violence and racial discrimination in South African youth: Profiles of a continuum of exposure. *Journal of Child and Family Studies, 29*, 1336–1349. https://doi.org/10.1007/s10826-019-01559-6

Santander, R. S., Zubarew, G. T., Satnelices, C. L., Argollo, M. P., Cerda, L. J., & Bórquez, P. M. (2008). Family influence as a protective factor against risk behaviors in Chilean adolescents. *Medical Journal of Chile Revista Médica de Chile, 136*(3), 317–324.

Santisteban, D. A., Coatsworth, J. D., Briones, E., Kurtines, W., & Szapocznik, J. (2012). Beyond acculturation: An investigation of the relationship of familism and parenting to behavior problems in Hispanic youth. *Family Process, 51*(4), 470–82. https://doi.org/10.1111/j.1545-5300.2012.01414.x

Scannapieco, M., & Connell-Carrick, K. (2005). Focus on the first years: Correlates of substantiation of child maltreatment for families with children o to 4. *Children and Youth Services Review, 27*, 1307–1323.

Scannapieco, M., & Connell-Carrick, K. (2005). *Understanding child maltreatment: An ecological and developmental perspective*. Oxford University Press.

Schene, P., (2001). Meeting each family's needs: Using differential response in reports of child abuse and neglect. *Best practice, next practice: National Child Welfare Resource Center for Family-Centered Practice*, 1–14.

Schraufnagel, T., Wagner, A., Miranda, J., & Roy-Byrne, P. (2006). Treating minority patients with depression and anxiety: What does the evidence tell us? *General Hospital Psychiatry, 28*, 27–36.

Scott, J., Faulkner, M., Cardoso, J. B., & Burstain, J. (2014). Kinship care and undocumented Latino children in the foster care system: Navigating the child welfare-immigrant crossroads. *Child Welfare, 93*, 53–69.

Sege, R. D., Siegel, B. S., & Council on Child Abuse and Neglect; Committee on Psychosocial Aspects of Child and Family Health. (2018). Effective discipline to raise healthy children. Pediatrics, 142, 3112.

Seldak, A. J., Mettenburg, J., Basena, M., Petta, I., McPherson, K., Greene, A., & Li, S. (2010). *Fourth National Incidence Study of Child Abuse and Neglect: Report to Congress*. U.S. Department of Health and Human Services, Administration for Children and Families, Washington, DC.

Semanchin Jones, A. (2014). Implementation of differential response: A racial equity analysis. *Child Abuse & Neglect 39*, 73–85. https://doi.org/10.1016/j.chiabu.2014.04.013

Sentell, T., Shumway, M., & Snowden, L. (2007). Access to mental health treatment by English language proficiency and race/ethnicity. *Journal of General Internal Medicine, 22* (Suppl 2), 289–293. https://doi.org/10.1007/s11606-007-0345-7

Serrano-Villar, M., Calzada, E. J., & Huang, K. Y. (2017). The role of social support in the parenting practices of Latina mothers. *Child Psychiatry and Human Development, 48*, 597–609. https://doi.org/10.1007/s10578-016-0685-9

Shahjahan, R. A. (2011). Decolonizing the evidence-based education and policy movement: Revealing the colonial vestiges in educational policy, research, and neoliberal reform. *Journal of Education Policy, 26*(2), 181–206. https://doi.org/10.1080/02680939.2010.508176

Shetgiri, R., Kataoka, S. H., Ryan, G. W., Miller Askew, L., Chung, P. J., & Schuster, M. A. (2009). Risk and resilience in Latinos: A community-based participatory research study. *American Journal of Preventive Medicine, 37*(6), S217–S224. https://doi.org/10.1016/j.amepre.2009.08.001

Shields, J., & Abu Alrob, Z. (2020). *COVID-19, migration, and the Canadian immigration system: Dimensions, impact and resilience*. York University.

Shorey, R. C., Stuart, G. L., McNulty, J. K., & Moore, T. M. (2013). Acute alcohol use temporally increases the odds of male perpetrated dating violence: A 90-day diary analysis. *Addictive Behaviors, 39*(1), 365–368. https://doi.org/10.1016/j.addbeh.2013.10.025

Silveira, F., Shafer, K., Dufur, M. J., & Roberson, M. (2020). Ethnicity and parental discipline practices: A cross-national comparison. *Journal of Marriage and Family, 83*(3), 644–666. https://doi.org/10.1111/jomf.12715

Slopen, N., Chen, Y., Guida, J. L., Albert, M. A., & Williams, D. R. (2017). Positive childhood experiences and ideal cardiovascular health in midlife: Associations and mediators. *Preventive Medicine, 97,* 72–79.

Smith, A. L., Cross, D., Winkler, J. Jovanovic, T., & Bekh, B. (2014). Emotional dysregulation and negative affect mediate the relationship between maternal history of child maltreatment and maternal child abuse potential. *Journal of Family Violence, 29,* 483–494. https://doi.org/10.1007/s10896-014-9606-5

Smith, B. W., Dalen, J., Wiggins, K., Tooley, E., Christopher, P., & Bernard, J. (2008). The brief resilience scale: Assessing the ability to bounce back. *International Journal of Behavioral Medicine, 15*(3), 194–200.

Smith, E. A. (2020). U.S. involvement in the Northern Triangle and its effects on immigration. *University of Michigan Undergraduate Research Journal,* 14, 25–32. https://doi.org/10.3998/umurj.16481002.0014.008

Smokowski, P. R., & Bacallao, M. L. (2007). Acculturation, internalizing mental health symptoms, and self-esteem: Cultural experiences of Latino adolescents in North Carolina. *Child Psychiatry and Human Development, 37*(3), 273–292. https://doi.org/10.1007/s10578-006-0035-4

Smokowski, P. R., Rose, R., & Bacallao, M. L. (2008). Acculturation and Latino family processes: How cultural involvement, biculturalism, and acculturation gaps influence family dynamics. *Family Relations, 57*(3), 295–308. https://doi.org/10.1111/j.1741-3729.2008.00501.x

Sonn, C. C., & Fisher, A. T. (1998). Sense of community: Community resilient responses to oppression and change. *Journal of Community Psychology, 26*(5), 457–472. https://doi.org/10.1002/(SICI)1520-6629(199809)26:5<457::AID-JCOP5>3.0.CO;2O

Soto, A., Smith, T. B., Griner, D., Domenech Rodriguez, M., & Bernal, G. (2018). Cultural adaptations and therapist multicultural competence: Two meta-analytic reviews. *Journal of Clinical Psychology, 74*(11), 1907–1923. https://doi.org/10.1002/jclp.22679

Sotomayor-Peterson, M., Figueredo, A. J., Christensen, D. H., & Taylor, A. R. (2012). Couples' cultural values, shared parenting, and family emotional climate within Mexican American families. *Family Process, 51*(2), 218–233. https://doi.org/10.1111/j.1545-5300.2012.01396.x

Squires, G. D. (2007). Demobilization of the individualistic bias: Housing market discrimination as a contributor to labor market and economic inequality. *The Annals of the American Academy of Political and Social Science, 609,* 200–214.

St. John, R. (2011). *America in the world, line in the sand: A history of the Western U.S.-Mexico border.* Princeton University Press.

Stacciarini, J.M.R., Smith, R. F., Wiens, B., Perez, A., Locke, B., & LaFlam, M. (2015). I didn't ask to come to this country . . . I was a child: The mental health implications of growing up undocumented. *Journal of Immigrant and Minority Health, 17*, 1225–1230. https://doi.org/10.1007/s10903-014-0063-2

Stacks, A. M., Oshio, T., Gerard, J., & Roe, J. (2009). The moderating effect of parental warmth on the association between spanking and child aggression: A longitudinal approach. *Infant and Child Development, 18*(2), 178–194. https://doi.org/10.1002/icd.596

Stein, G. L., Cupito, A. M., Mendez, J. L., Prandoni, J., Huq, N., & Westerberg, D. (2014). Familism through a developmental lens. *Journal of Latina/o Psychology, 2*(4), 224–250. https://doi.org/10.1037/lat0000025

Stith, S. M., Liu, T., Davies, L. C., Boykin, E. L., Alder, M. C., Harris, J. M., Som, A., McPherson, M., & Dees, J.E.M.E.G. (2009). Risk factors in child maltreatment: A meta-analytic review of the literature. *Aggression and Violent Behavior, 14*(1), 13–29. https://doi.org/10.1016/j.avb.2006.03.006

Stoltenborgh, M., Bakermans-Kranenburg, M. J., & van IJzendoorn, M. H. (2013). The neglect of child neglect: A meta-analytic review of the prevalence of neglect. *Social Psychiatry and Psychiatric Epidemiology, 48*(3), 345–355. https://doi.org/10.1007/s00127-012-0549-y

Stoltenborgh, M., Bakermans-Kranenburg, M. J., van IJzendoorn, M. H., & Alink, L.R.A. (2013). Cultural–geographical differences in the occurrence of child physical abuse? A meta-analysis of global prevalence. *International Journal of Psychology, 48*, 81–94. https://doi.org/10.1080/00207594.2012.697165

Sturge-Apple, M. L., Toth, S. L., Suor, J. H., & Adams, T. R. (2019). Parental maltreatment. In M.H. Bornstein (Ed.), *Handbook of parenting: Social conditions and applied parenting* (3rd ed., Vol. 4, pp. 556–589). Routledge. https://doi.org/10.4324/9780429398995

Suárez-Orozco, C., Motti-Stefanidi, F., Marks, A., & Katsiaficas, D. (2018). An integrative risk and resilience model for understanding the adaptation of immigrant-origin children and youth. *American Psychologist, 73*(6), 781–796. https://doi.org/10.1037/amp0000265

Suârez-Orozco, C., Todorova, I.L.G., & Louie, J. (2002). Making up for lost time: the experience of separation and reunification among immigrant families. *Family Process, 41*(4), 625–643. https://doi.org/10.1111/j.1545-5300.2002.00625.x

Substance Abuse and Mental Health Services Administration. (2014). SAMHSA's concept of trauma and guidance for a trauma-informed approach (p. 27) [HHS Publication No. (SMA) 14-4884]. https://ncsacw.samhsa.gov/userfiles/files/SAMHSA_Trauma.pdf

Suleiman, L. P. (2003). *Creating a Latino child welfare agenda: A strategic framework for change.* Committee for Hispanic Children and Families. https://www.chcfinc.org/wp-content/uploads/2014/04/8.-CHCF-Creating-a-Latino-Child-Welfare-Agenda-A-Strategic-Framework-for-Change-July-15-2003.pdf

Taft, C. T., O'Farrell, T. J., Doron-LaMarca, S., Panuzio, J., Suvak, M. K., & Gagnon, D. R. (2010). Longitudinal risk factors for intimate partner violence among men in treatment for alcohol use disorders. *Journal of Consulting and Clinical Psychology, 78*(6), 924–935. https://doi.org /10.1037/a0021093

Taillieu, T. L., Afifi, T. O., Mota, N., Keyes, K. M., & Sareen, J. (2014). Age, sex, and racial differences in harsh physical punishment: results from a nationally representative United States sample. *Child Abuse & Neglect, 38*(12), 1885–1894. https://doi.org/10.1016/j.chiabu.2014.10.020

Taylor, B., & Behnke, A. O. (2005). Fathering across the border: Latino fathers in Mexico and the U.S. *Fathering: A Journal of Theory, Research, and Practice About Men As Fathers, 3*(2), 99–120. https://doi.org /10.3200/CTCH.53.2.57-61

Taylor, C. A., Guterman, N. B., Lee, S. J., & Rathouz, P. R. (2009). Intimate partner violence, maternal stress, nativity, and risk for maternal maltreatment of young children. *American Journal of Public Health, 99*, 175–183. https://doi.org/10.2105/AJPH.2007.126722

Tedeschi, R. G., & Calhoun, L. G. (1996). The posttraumatic growth inventory: Measuring the positive legacy of trauma. *Journal of Traumatic Stress, 9*(3), 455–471. https://doi.org/10.1007/BF02103658

Terrazas-Carrillo, E., & Sabina, C. (2019). Dating violence attitudes among Latino college students: An examination of gender, machismo, and marianismo. *Violence and Victims, 34*(1), 194–210. https://doi.org /10.1891/0886-6708.VV-D-17-00172

Terrazas, J., Alero Muruthi, B., Thompson Cañas, R. E., Jackson, J. B., & Bermudez, J. M. (2020). Liminal legality among mixed-status Latinx families: Considerations for critically engaged clinical practice. *Contemporary Family Therapy, 42*, 360–368. https://doi.org/10.1007 /s10591-020-09545-7

Tervalon, M., & Murray-Garcia, J. (1998). Cultural humility versus cultural competence: A critical distinction in defining physician training outcomes in multicultural education. *Journal of Healthcare for the Poor and Underserved, 9*(2), 117–125. https://doi.org/10.1353/hpu.2010.0233

Texas Department of Family and Protective Services (n.d.). CPS family preservation (FPR): Children served. https://www.dfps.state.tx.us /About_DFPS/Data_Book/Child_Protective_Services/Family _Preservation/Children_Served.asp

Thompson, R. A. (1995). *Preventing child maltreatment through social support: A critical analysis*. Sage Publications, Inc.

Thornberry, T. P., Henry, K. L., Smith, C. A., Ireland, T. O., Greenman, S. J., & Lee, R. D. (2013). Breaking the cycle of maltreatment: The role of safe, stable, and nurturing relationships. *Journal of Adolescent Health, 53*(4), S25–S31. https://doi.org/10.1016/j.jadoheath.2013.04.019

Thyer, B. A. (2008). The quest for evidence-based practice?: We are all positivists! *Research on Social Work Practice, 18*(4), 339–345. https:// doi.org/10.1177/1049731507313998

Tinkler, A. S., & Tinkler, B. (2016). Enhancing cultural humility through critical service-learning in teacher preparation. *Multicultural Perspectives, 18*(4), 191–201. https://doi.org/10.1080/15210960.2016 .1222282

Torres, K., & Mathur, R. (2018, March 9). *Fact sheet: Family first prevention services act.* https://www.campaignforchildren.org/resources/fact-sheet /fact-sheet-family-first-prevention-services-act/

Torres, L. (2010). Predicting levels of Latino depression: Acculturation, acculturative stress, and coping. *Cultural Diversity and Ethnic Minority Psychology, 16,* 256–263. https://doi.org/10.1037/a0017357

TRAC Reports, Inc. (2021, March). *Details on MPP (Remain in Mexico) deportation proceedings.* trac.syr.edu/phptools/immigration/mpp/

Tsao, C. M., Hsing, H. C., Wang, H. H., & Ming Guo, S. H. (2019). The factors related to maternal-fetal attachment: Examining the effect of mindfulness, stress and symptoms during pregnancy. *Archives Nursing Practice and Care, 5*(1), 1–7. https://doi.org/10.17352/2581 -4265.000035

Tse, L. (1995). Language brokering among Latino adolescents: Prevalence, attitudes, and school performance. *Hispanic Journal of Behavioral Sciences, 17*(2), 180–193. https://doi.org/10.1177/07399863950172003

Ulibarri, M. D., Ulloa, E. C., & Camacho, L. (2009). Prevalence of sexually abusive experiences in childhood and adolescence among a community sample of Latinas: A descriptive study. *Journal of Child Sexual Abuse, 18,* 405–421. https://doi.org /10.1080/10538710903051088

Ullman, S. E., & Filipas, H. H. (2005). Ethnicity and child sexual abuse experiences of female college students. *Journal of Child Sexual Abuse, 14,* 67–89. https://doi.org/10.1300/J070v14n03_04 United Nations High Commissioner for Refugees (HNHCR). (2019). Global trends: Forced displacement in 2018. Geneva. https://www.unhcr.org /5d08d7ee7.pdf

Updegraff, K. A., Delgado, M. Y. & Wheeler, L. A. (2009). Exploring mothers' and fathers' relationships with sons versus daughters: Links to adolescent adjustment in Mexican immigrant families. *Sex Roles, 60,* 559–574. https://doi.org/10.1007/s11199-008-9527-y

U.S. Congress Joint Economic Committee. (2015). *The economic state of the Latino community in America, October 2015.* https://www.jec.senate.gov /public/_cache/files/2d162187-e1cc-4629-a39e-7f0853194280/jec-hispanic -report-final.pdf

U.S. Department of Health & Human Services. (2019). *Child Maltreatment 2017.* Administration for Children and Families, Administration on Children, Youth and Families, Children's Bureau. https://www.acf.hhs .gov/cb/research-data-technology/ statistics-research/child-maltreatment

U.S. Department of Health & Human Services. (2019). *Head Start programs.* Office of Head Start.

U.S. Department of Health & Human Services. (2020, June). *The AFCARS Report: Preliminary FY 2019 estimates as of June 23, 2020, No. 27.*

Administration for Children and Families, Administration on Children, Youth and Families, Children's Bureau. https://www.acf.hhs.gov/sites /default/files/documents/cb/afcarsreport27.pdf

U.S. Department of Health and Human Services. (2021). *Child maltreatment 2019*. https://www.acf.hhs.gov/sites/default/files/documents/cb /cm2019_4.pdf

U.S. Department of Housing and Urban Development. (2013). *Housing discrimination against racial and ethnic minorities 2012: Executive summary*. https://www.huduser.gov/portal/Publications/pdf/HUD-514 _HDS2012_execsumm.pdf

U.S. Department of Justice (2021, January 13). *DOJ OIG releases report on the Department of Justice's planning and implementation of its Zero Tolerance Policy and its coordination with the Departments of Homeland Security and Health and Human Services*. https://oig.justice.gov/news/doj-oig -releases-report-department-justices-planning-and-implementation-its -zero-tolerance

Uzogara, E. E. (2019). Gendered racism biases: Associations of phenotypes with discrimination and internalized oppression among Latinx American women and men. *Race and Social Problems, 11,* 80–92. https://doi.org /10.1007/s12552-018-9255-z

Valdez, C. R., Ramirez Stege, A., Martinez, E., D'Costa, S., & Chavez, T. (2018). A community-responsive adaptation to reach and engage Latino families affected by maternal depression. *Family Process, 57*(2), 539–556. https://doi.org/10.1111/famp.12310

Valdez, Z., & Golash-Boza, T. (2017). Towards an intersectionality of race and ethnicity. *Ethnic and Racial Studies, 40*(13), 2256–2261. https://doi .org/10.1080/01419870.2017.1344277

Van der Kolk, B. (2015). *The body keeps the score: Brain, mind, and body in the healing of trauma*. Penguin Publishing Group.

Van Krieken, R., (1986). Social theory and child welfare. *Theory and Society, 15,* 401–429. https://doi.org/10.1007/BF00172234

Vega, L.A.A. (2021). Central American asylum seekers in Southern Mexico: Fluid (im)mobility in protracted migration trajectories. *Journal of Immigrant & Refugee Studies, 19*(4), 349–363. https://doi.org/10.1080 /15562948.2020.1804033

Vesely, C. K., Letiecq, B. L., & Goodman, R. D. (2017). Immigrant family resilience in context: Using a community-based approach to build a new conceptual model. *Journal of Family Theory & Review, 9*(1), 93–110. https://doi.org/10.1111/jftr.12177

Viruell-Fuentes, E. A., Miranda, P. Y., & Abdulrahim, S. (2012). More than culture: Structural racism, intersectionality theory, and immigrant health. *Social Science & Medicine, 75,* 2099–2106. https://doi.org /10.1016/j.socscimed.2011.12.037

Wade, R., Shea, J. A., Rubin, D., & Wood, J. (2014). Adverse childhood experiences of low-income urban youth. *Pediatrics, 134*(1), e13–e20. https://doi.org/10.1542/peds.2013-2475

Walker, N. E., Brooks, C. M., & Wrightsman, L. S. (1999). *Children's rights in the United States: In search of a national policy.* Sage Publications.

Walsh, F. (2015). *Strengthening family resilience* (3rd ed.) Guilford Press.

Walsh, W. A., & Mattingly, M. J., (2012). *Understanding child abuse in rural and urban America: Risk factors and maltreatment substantiation.* The Carsey School of Public Policy at the Scholars' Repository. https://scholars.unh.edu/carsey/170

Wamser-Nanney, R., & Vandenberg, B. R. (2013). Empirical support for the definition of a complex trauma event in children and adolescents: Complex trauma event in children. *Journal of Traumatic Stress, 26*(6), 671–678. https://doi.org/10.1002/jts.21857

Warner, L. A., Alegría, M., & Canino, G. (2012). Childhood maltreatment among Hispanic women in the United States: An examination of subgroup differences and impact on psychiatric disorder. *Child Maltreatment, 17,* 119–131. https://doi.org/10.1177/1077559512444593

Washington State Department of Children, Youth, and Families (n.d.). *ECEAP & Head Start.* https://www.dcyf.wa.gov/services/earlylearning-childcare/eceap-Head Start

Weissman, M. M., Feder, A., Pilowsky, D. J., Olfson, M., Fuentes, M., Blanco, C., Lantigua, R., Gameroff, M. J., & Shea, S. (2004). Depressed mothers coming to primary care: Maternal reports of problems with their children. *Journal of Affective Disorders, 78,* 93–100. https://doi.org/10.1016/S0165-0327(02)00301-4

Wells, K. (2009). Substance abuse and child maltreatment. *Pediatric Clinics of North America, 56,* 345–362.

White, K., & Willis, E. (2002). Positivism resurgent: The epistemological foundations of evidence-based medicine. *Health Sociology Review, 11*(1–2), 5–15. https://doi.org/10.5172/hesr.2002.11.1-2.5

White, R.M.B., Liu, Y., Gonzales, N. A., Knight, G. P., & Tein, J. Y. (2016). Neighborhood qualification of the association between parenting and problem behavior trajectories among Mexican-Origin father-adolescent dyads. *Journal of Research on Adolescence, 26*(4), 927–946. https://doi.org/10.1111/jora.12245

White, R.M.B., Liu, Y., Nair, R. L., & Tein, J.-Y. (2015). Longitudinal and integrative tests of family stress model effects on Mexican origin adolescents. *Developmental Psychology, 51,* 649–662. https://doi.org/10.1037/a0038993

White, R.M.B., Roosa, M. W., & Zeiders, K. H. (2012). Neighborhood and family intersections: Prospective implications for Mexican American adolescents' mental health. *Journal of Family Psychology, 26*(5), 793–804. https://doi.org/10.1037/a0029426

White, R.M.B., Roosa, M. W., Weaver, S. R., & Nair, R. L. (2009). Cultural and contextual influences on parenting in Mexican American families. *Journal of Marriage and Family, 71,* 61–79. https://doi.org/10.1111/j.1741-3737.2008.00580.x

White, R.M.B., Zeiders, K. H., Gonzales, N. A., Tein, J., & Roosa, M. W. (2013). Cultural values, U.S. neighborhood danger, and Mexican American parents' parenting. *Journal of Family Psychology, 27,* 265–275. https://doi.org/10.1037/a0032888

Whittaker, J. K., & Tracy, E. M. (2017). Family preservation services and education for social work practice; Stimulus and response. In C. Booth, E. M. Tracy, J. Kinney, & J. K. Whittaker (Eds.), *Reaching high-risk families* (pp. 29–41). Routledge.

Williams, M. T., Metzger, I. W., Leins, C., & DeLapp, C. (2018). Assessing racial trauma within a DSM–5 framework: The UConn racial/ethnic stress & trauma survey. *Practice Innovations, 3*(4), 242–260.

Windham, A. M., Rosenberg, L., Fuddy, L., McFarlane, E., Sia, C., Duggan, A. K. (2004). Risk of mother-reported child abuse in the first 3 years of life. *Child Abuse and Neglect, 28,* 645–667.

Yancu, C. N., & Farmer, D. F. (2017). Product or process: Cultural competence or cultural humility? *Palliative Medicine and Hospice Care, 3*(1), e1–e4. https://doi.org/10.17140/PMHCOJ-3-e005

Yasui, M., & Dishion, T. J. (2007). The ethnic context of child and adolescent problem behavior: Implications for child and family interventions. *Clinical Child and Family Psychology Review, 10*(2), 137–179. https://doi.org/10.1007/s10567-007-0021-9

York University (2021). *The praxis of migrant transformative resilience: Understanding how collective action among immigrant communities impacts on resilience and system change.* bmrc-irmu.info.yorku.ca/the-praxis-of-migrant-transformative-resilience-understanding-how-collective-action-among-immigrant-communities-impacts-on-resilience-and-system-change-2/

Zambrana, R. (2011). *Latinos in American society.* Cornell University Press.

Zayas, L. H., & Gulbas, L. E. (2017). Processes of belonging for citizen-children of undocumented Mexican immigrants. *Journal of Child & Family Studies, 26,* 2463–2474. https://doi.org/10.1007/s10826-017-0755-z

Zeiders, K. H., Umaña-Taylor, A. J., Martinez-Fuentes, S., Updegraff, K. A., Douglass Bayless, S., & Jahromi, L. B. (2021). Latina/o youths' discrimination experiences in the U.S. Southwest: Estimates from three studies. *Applied Developmental Science, 25*(1), 51–61. https://doi.org /10.1080/1088691.2018.1527695

Zhai, F., Waldfogel, J., & Brooks-Gunn, J. (2011). Estimating the effects of Head Start on parenting and child maltreatment. *Children and Youth Services Review, 35*(7), 1119–1129. https://doi.org/10.1016/j.childyouth .2011.03.008

Index

About the Authors

ESTHER J. CALZADA is the associate dean for equity and inclusion and the Norma and Clay Leben Professor in Child and Family Behavioral Health at the University of Texas at Austin. She is a clinical child psychologist whose research focuses on parenting and early child development in Latinx families.

MONICA FAULKNER is research associate professor at the University of Texas at Austin and the director of the Texas Institute for Child and Family Wellbeing. She is a licensed master-level social worker in Texas. Her research focuses on building programs and strategies to improve child welfare programs.

CATHERINE A. LABRENZ is assistant professor at the University of Texas at Arlington School of Social Work and a licensed master-level social worker in Texas. Her research focuses on building resilience to break cycles of child maltreatment. She has worked with families involved in child welfare in Santiago, Chile.

MILTON A. FUENTES is professor of psychology at Montclair State University in New Jersey and a licensed psychologist in New Jersey and New York. His scholarship focuses on equity, diversity, and inclusion. He has authored several peer-reviewed articles, book chapters, and books in this area.

THE PREVENTING CHILD MALTREATMENT COLLECTION

PREVENTING CHILD MALTREATMENT IN THE U.S.: MULTICULTURAL CONSIDERATIONS	PREVENTING CHILD MALTREATMENT IN THE U.S.: THE LATINX COMMUNITY PERSPECTIVE	PREVENTING CHILD MALTREATMENT IN THE U.S.: AMERICAN INDIAN AND ALASKA NATIVE PERSPECTIVES	PREVENTING CHILD MALTREATMENT IN THE U.S.: THE BLACK COMMUNITY PERSPECTIVE
Milton A. Fuentes, Rachel R. Singer, and Renee L. DeBoard-Lucas	Esther J. Calzada, Monica Faulkner, Catherine LaBrenz, and Milton A. Fuentes	Royleen J. Ross, Julii M. Green, and Milton A. Fuentes	Melissa Phillips, Shavonne J. Moore-Lobban, and Milton A. Fuentes
9781978822573 Paper	9781978822887 Paper	9781978821101 Paper	9781978820630 Paper
9781978822580 Cloth	9781978822894 Cloth	9781978821118 Cloth	9781978820647 Cloth

The Preventing Child Maltreatment collection is a four-book miniseries within the Violence Against Women and Children series at Rutgers University Press. This collection, curated by Milton A. Fuentes from Montclair State University, is devoted to advancing an understanding of the dynamics of child maltreatment across ethnically diverse populations. Starting with *Preventing Child Maltreatment in the U.S.: Multicultural Considerations*, which provides a general examination of child maltreatment through the interaction of feminist, multicultural, and social justice lenses, the rest of the series takes a closer look at Native American/Alaska Native, Black, and Latinx communities in order to provide insight for social workers who may encounter those populations within their scope of treatment. Policymakers, practitioners, graduate students, and social workers of all kinds will find this collection of great interest.

R RUTGERS UNIVERSITY PRESS
rutgersuniversitypress.org